Cocoon Entwined

4

Yuriko Hara

Contents

Chapter 23

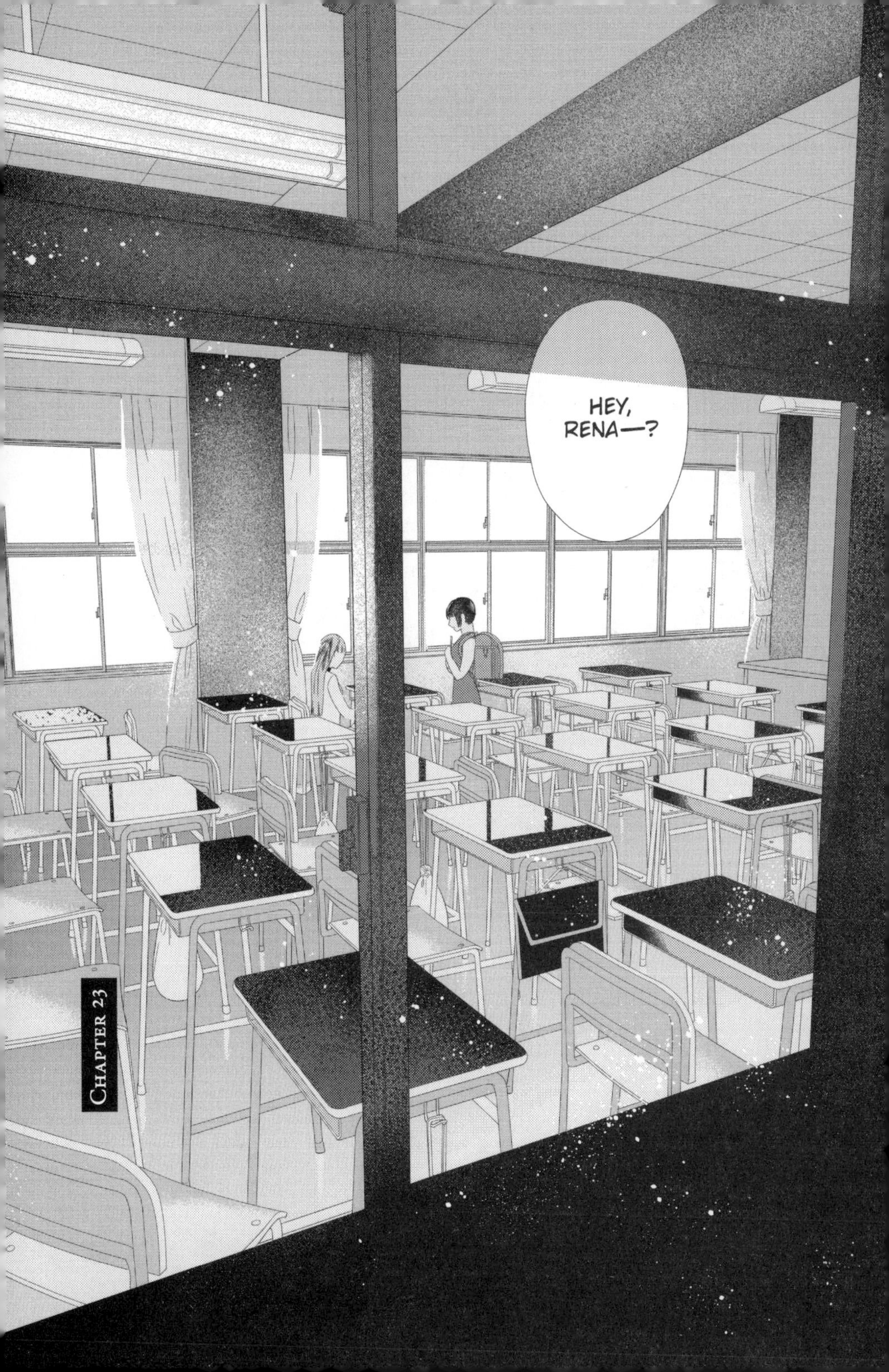
HEY, RENA—?

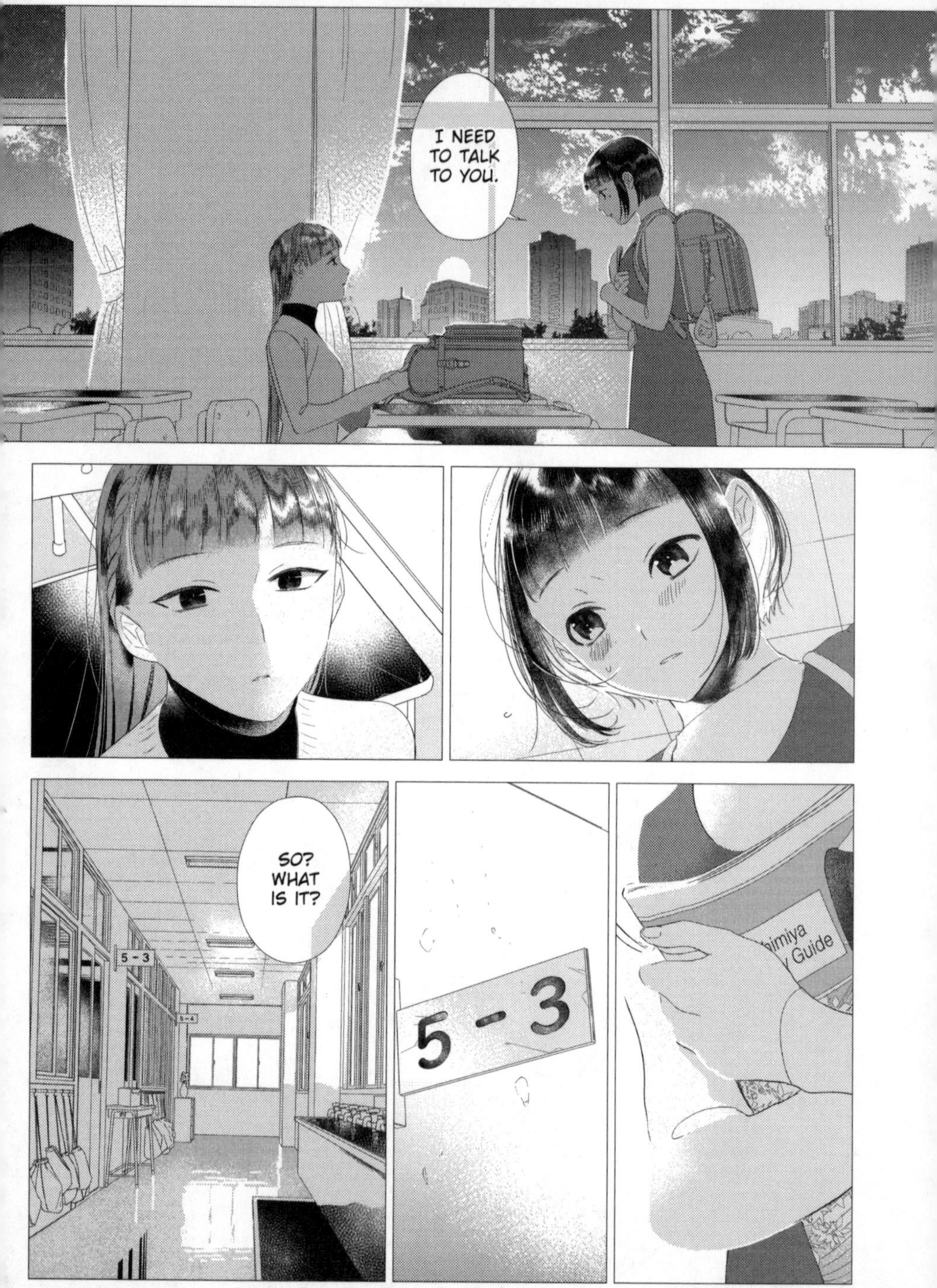
I NEED TO TALK TO YOU.
5 - 3
SO? WHAT IS IT?

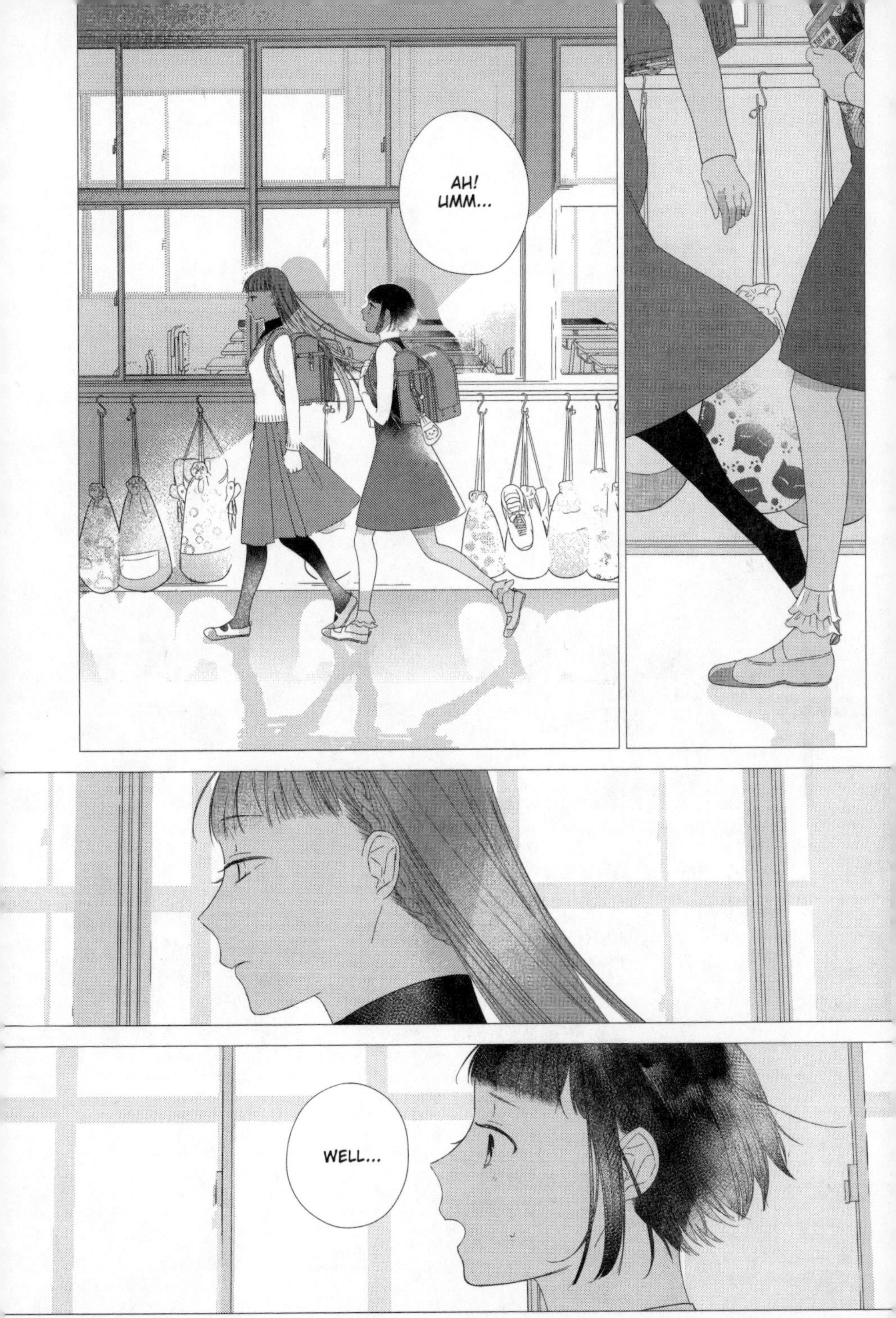
AH! UMM...
WELL...

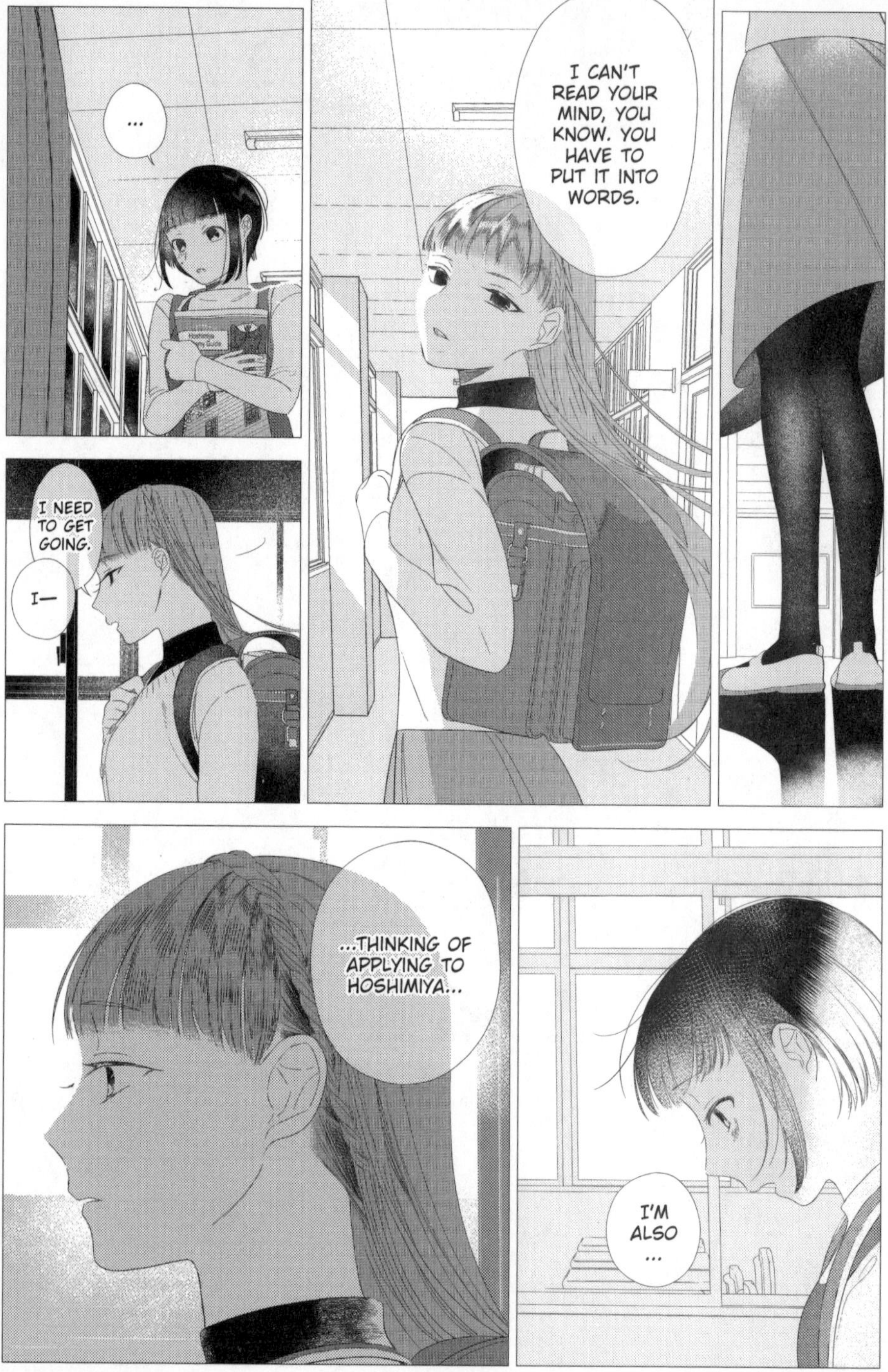
I CAN'T READ YOUR MIND, YOU KNOW. YOU HAVE TO PUT IT INTO WORDS.
...
I NEED TO GET GOING.
I—
I'M ALSO ...
...THINKING OF APPLYING TO HOSHIMIYA...

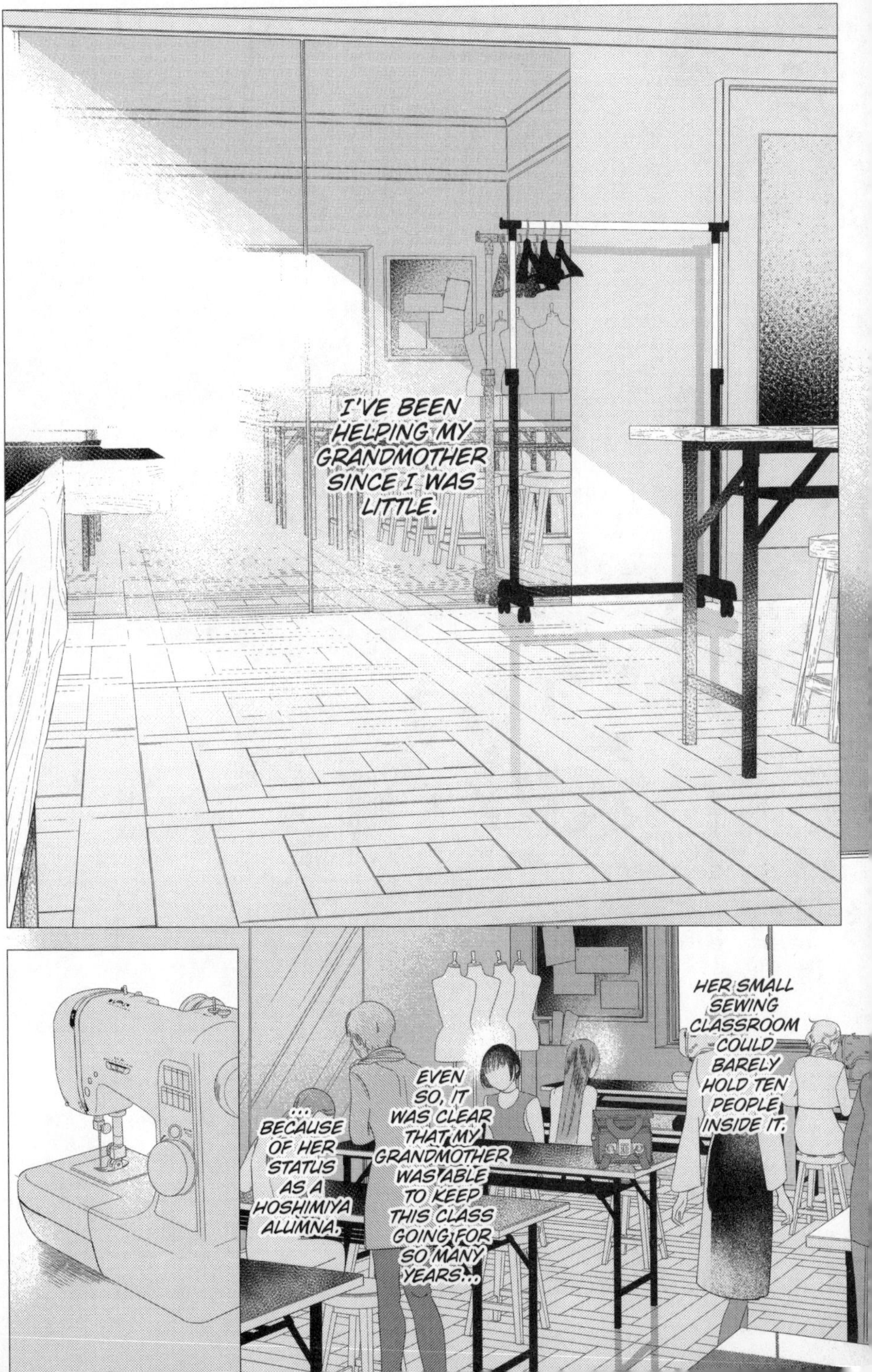
I'VE BEEN HELPING MY GRANDMOTHER SINCE I WAS LITTLE.
HER SMALL SEWING CLASSROOM COULD BARELY HOLD TEN PEOPLE INSIDE IT.
EVEN SO, IT WAS CLEAR THAT MY GRANDMOTHER WAS ABLE TO KEEP THIS CLASS GOING FOR SO MANY YEARS...
...BECAUSE OF HER STATUS AS A HOSHIMIYA ALUMNA.

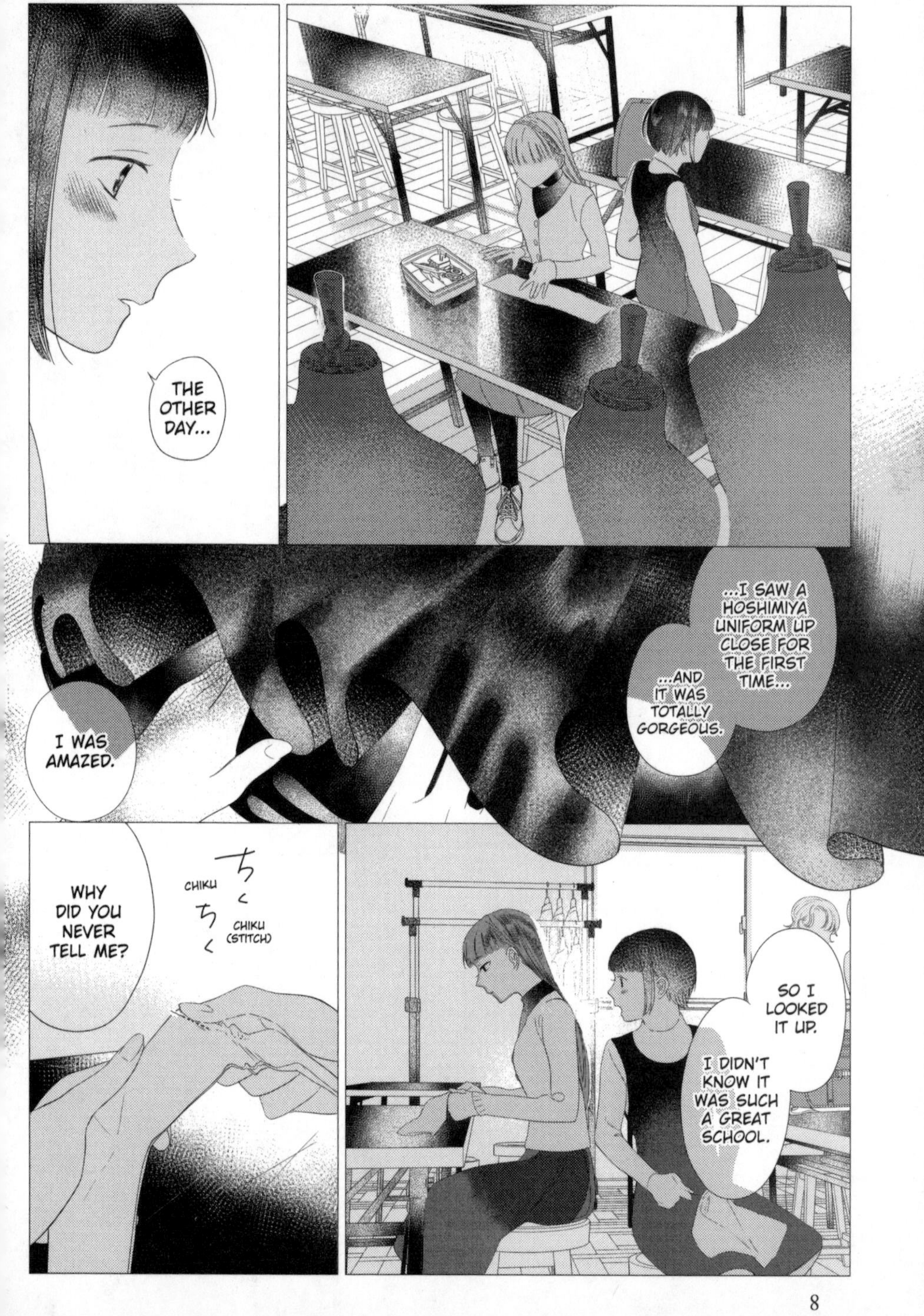
THE OTHER DAY...
...I SAW A HOSHIMIYA UNIFORM UP CLOSE FOR THE FIRST TIME...
...AND IT WAS TOTALLY GORGEOUS.
I WAS AMAZED.
SO I LOOKED IT UP.
I DIDN'T KNOW IT WAS SUCH A GREAT SCHOOL.
ちく ちく
CHIKU CHIKU (STITCH)
WHY DID YOU NEVER TELL ME?

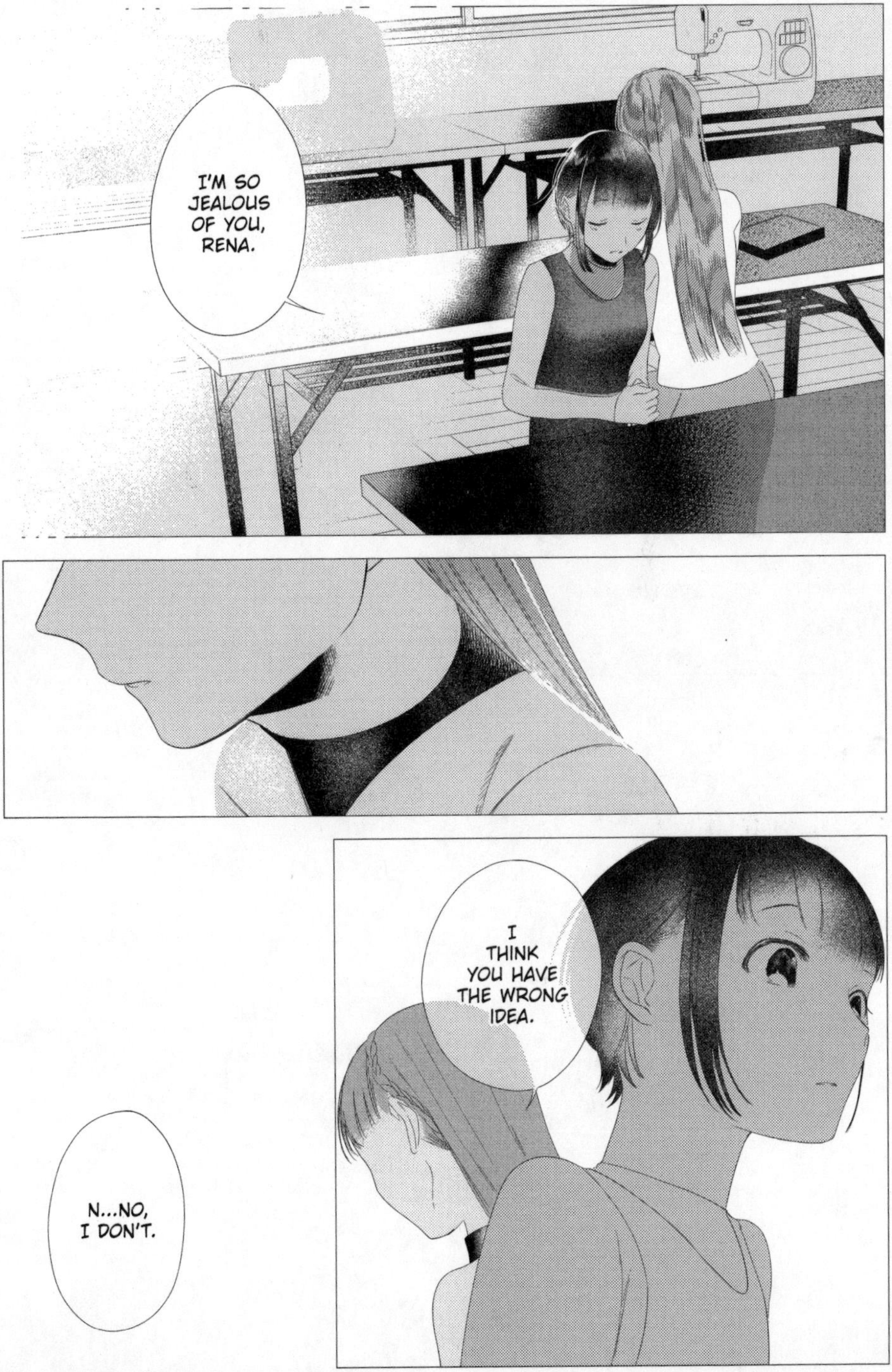
I'M SO JEALOUS OF YOU, RENA.
I THINK YOU HAVE THE WRONG IDEA.
N...NO, I DON'T.

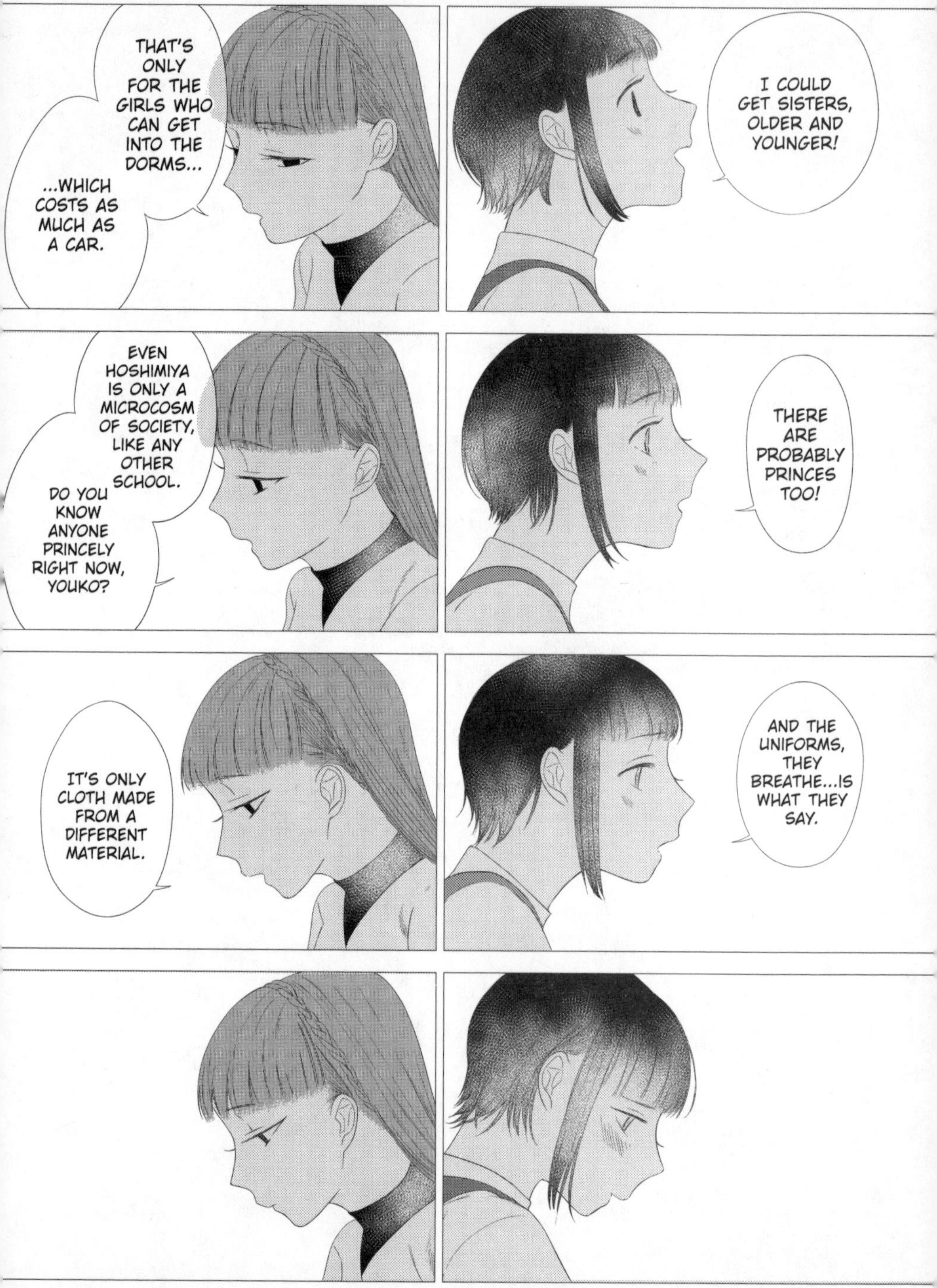
I COULD GET SISTERS, OLDER AND YOUNGER!
THAT'S ONLY FOR THE GIRLS WHO CAN GET INTO THE DORMS...
...WHICH COSTS AS MUCH AS A CAR.
THERE ARE PROBABLY PRINCES TOO!
EVEN HOSHIMIYA IS ONLY A MICROCOSM OF SOCIETY, LIKE ANY OTHER SCHOOL.
DO YOU KNOW ANYONE PRINCELY RIGHT NOW, YOUKO?
AND THE UNIFORMS, THEY BREATHE...IS WHAT THEY SAY.
IT'S ONLY CLOTH MADE FROM A DIFFERENT MATERIAL.

YOUKO.
YOU DON'T CHOOSE SCHOOLS LIKE HOSHIMIYA JUST BECAUSE YOU LIKE THEM.
IF YOU ENROLL JUST BECAUSE OF THAT, YOU'D ONLY WIND UP...
...SICK OF THE GAP BETWEEN YOUR EXPECTATIONS AND REALITY.
ESPECIALLY AT HOSHIMIYA.
LET GO OF THAT "LOVE" FIRST, AND WE'LL TALK.
THEN...

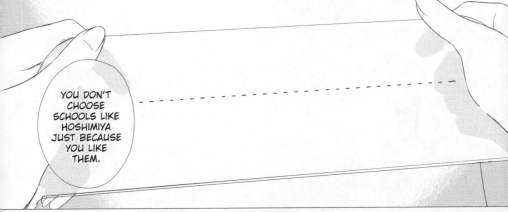

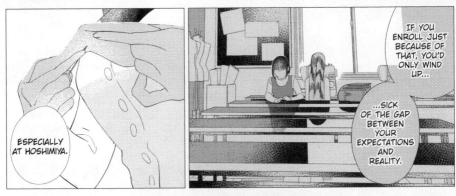

ARE
YOU...

...
WORKING
SO HARD
FOR
SOMETHING
YOU HATE?

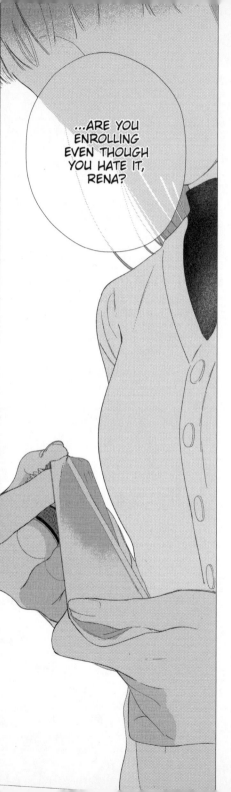

...ARE YOU
ENROLLING
EVEN THOUGH
YOU HATE IT,
RENA?

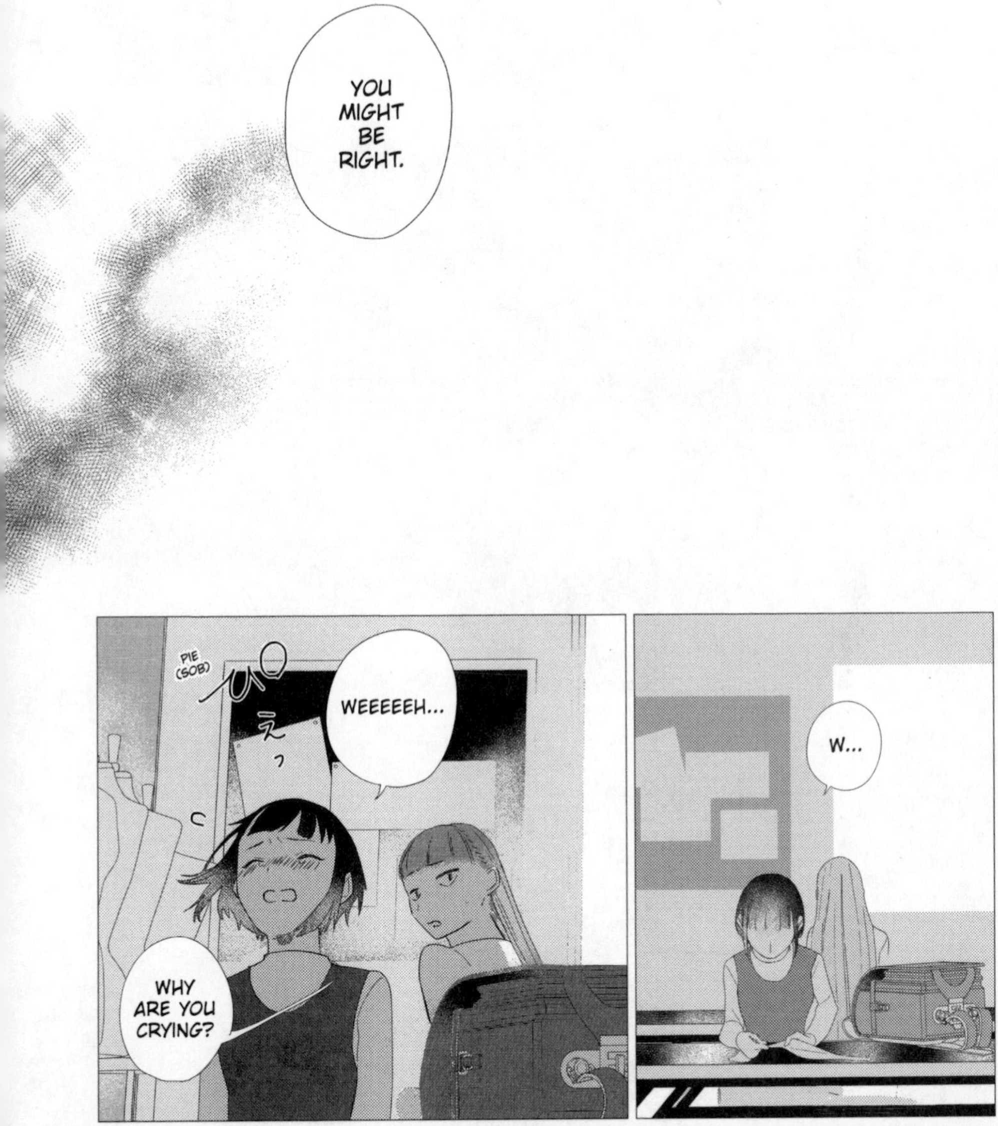
YOU MIGHT BE RIGHT.
W...
WEEEEEH...
PIE (SOB)
WHY ARE YOU CRYING?

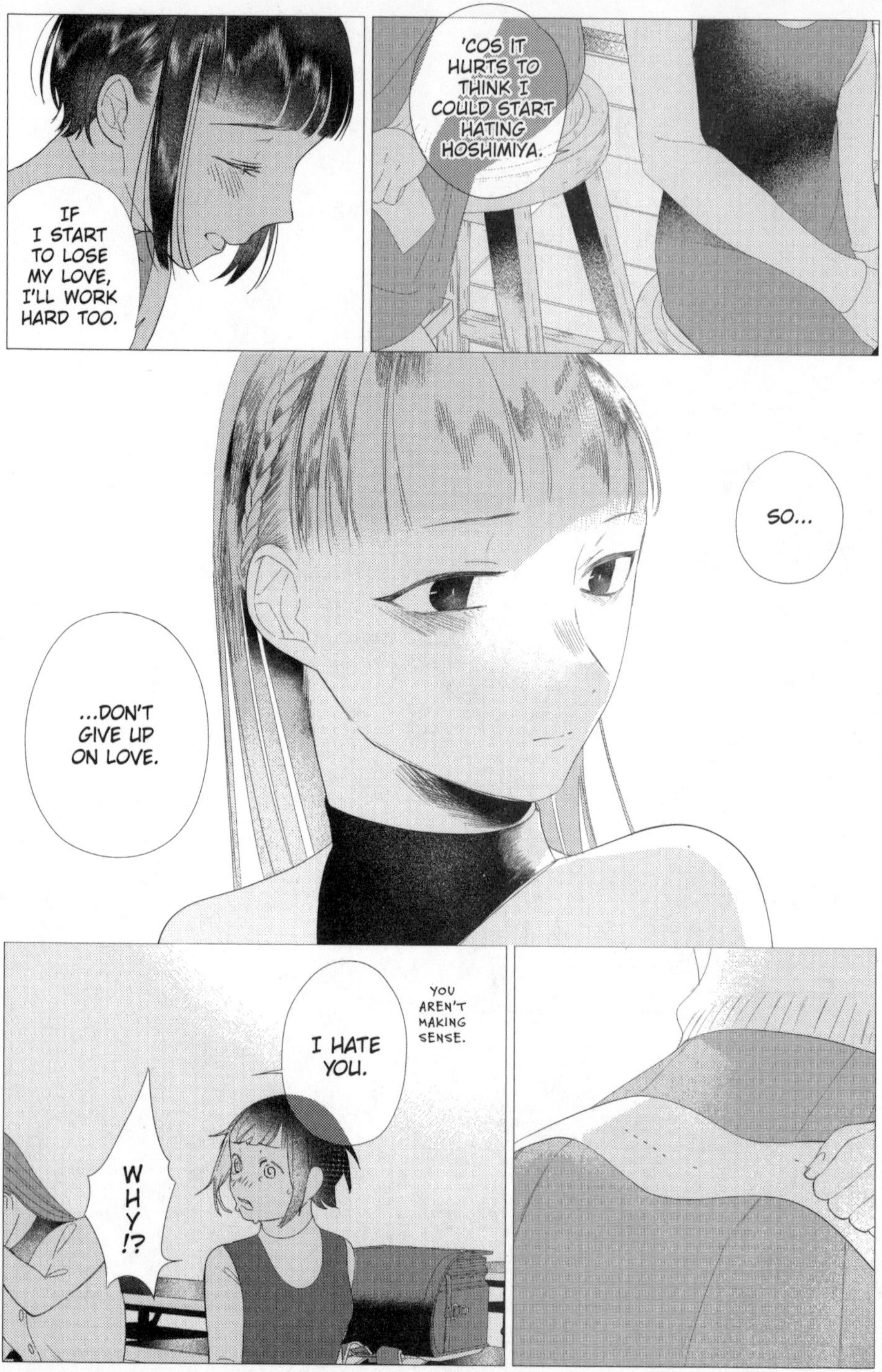
'COS IT HURTS TO THINK I COULD START HATING HOSHIMIYA.
IF I START TO LOSE MY LOVE, I'LL WORK HARD TOO.
SO...
...DON'T GIVE UP ON LOVE.
I HATE YOU.
YOU AREN'T MAKING SENSE.
WHY!?

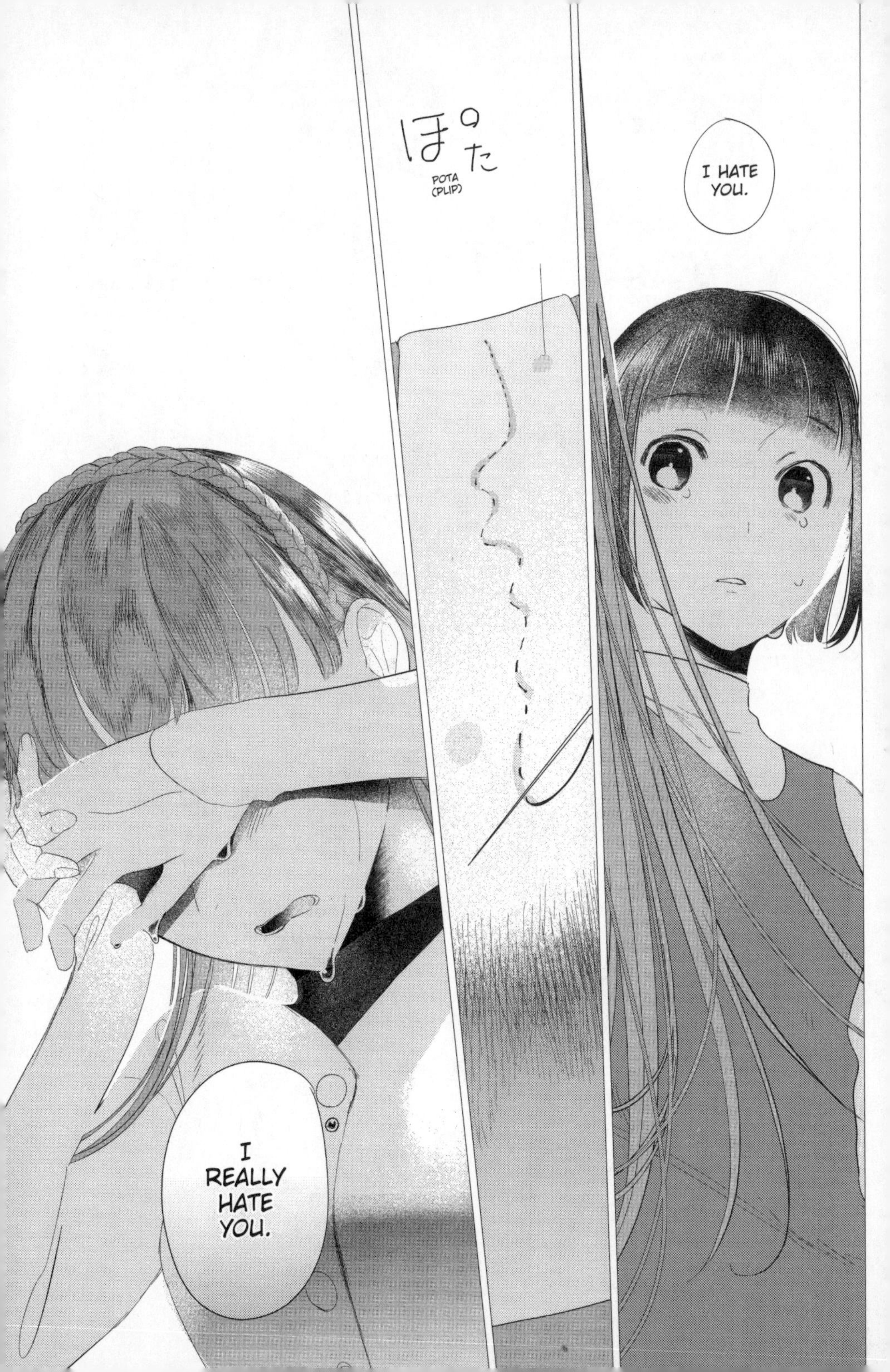
I HATE YOU.
ぽた
POTA (PLIP)
I REALLY HATE YOU.

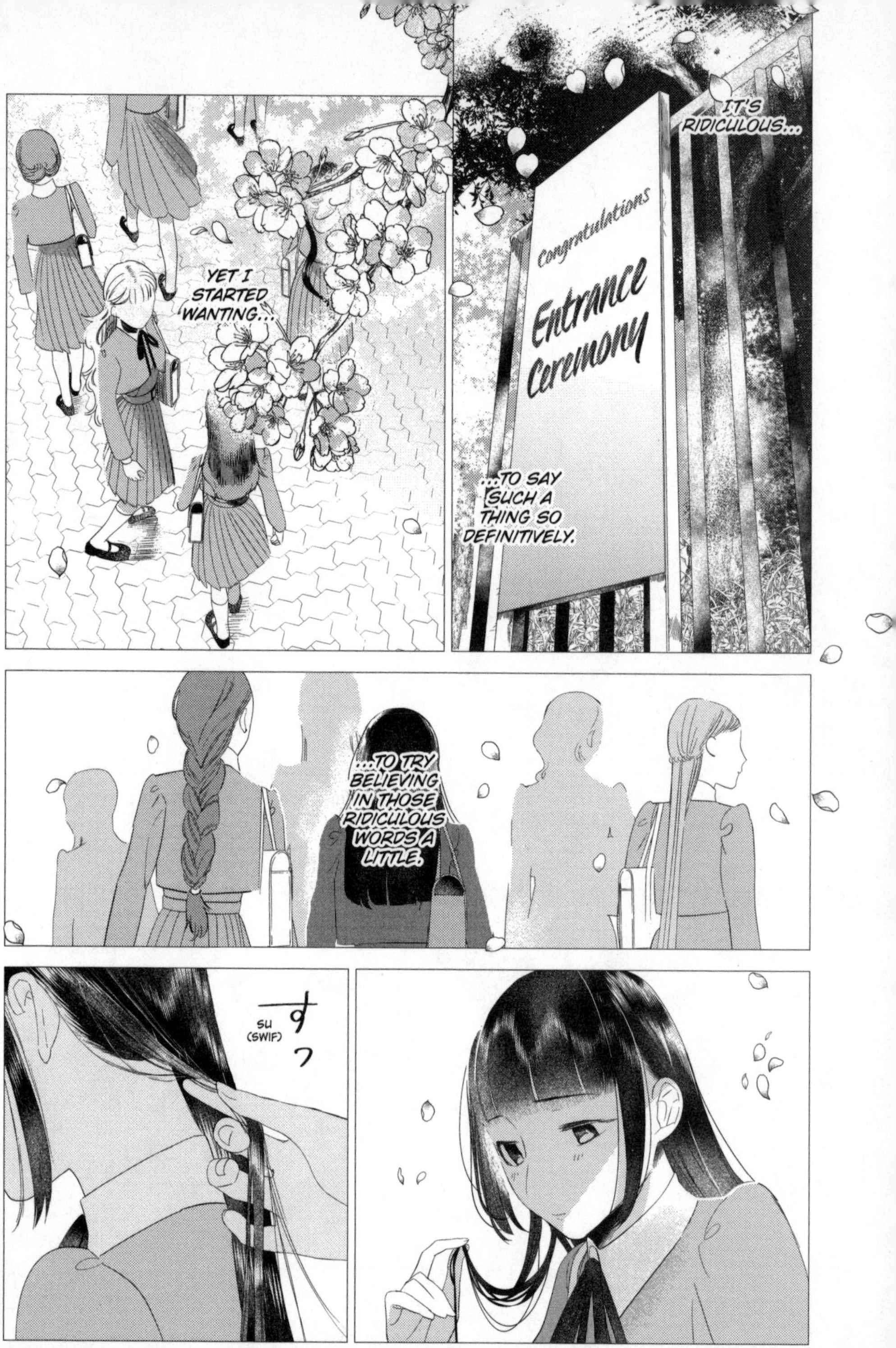
IT'S RIDICULOUS...
Congratulations
Entrance Ceremony
...TO SAY SUCH A THING SO DEFINITIVELY.
YET I STARTED WANTING...
...TO TRY BELIEVING IN THOSE RIDICULOUS WORDS A LITTLE.
すっ
SU (SWIF)

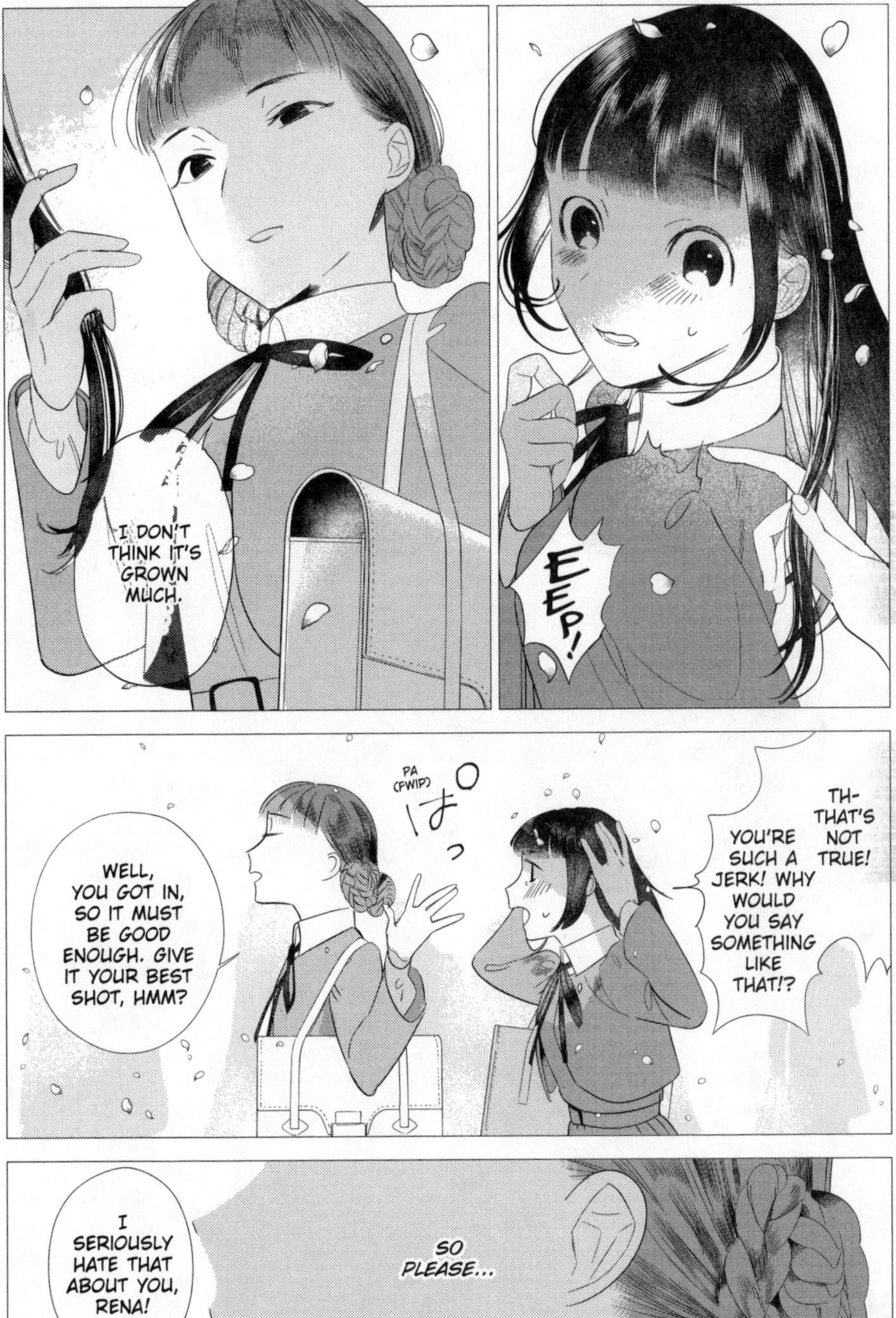
EEP!
I DON'T THINK IT'S GROWN MUCH.
TH-THAT'S NOT TRUE!
YOU'RE SUCH A JERK! WHY WOULD YOU SAY SOMETHING LIKE THAT!?
ぱっ
PA (FWIP)
WELL, YOU GOT IN, SO IT MUST BE GOOD ENOUGH. GIVE IT YOUR BEST SHOT, HMM?
SO PLEASE...
I SERIOUSLY HATE THAT ABOUT YOU, RENA!

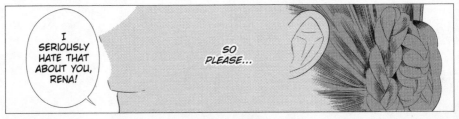

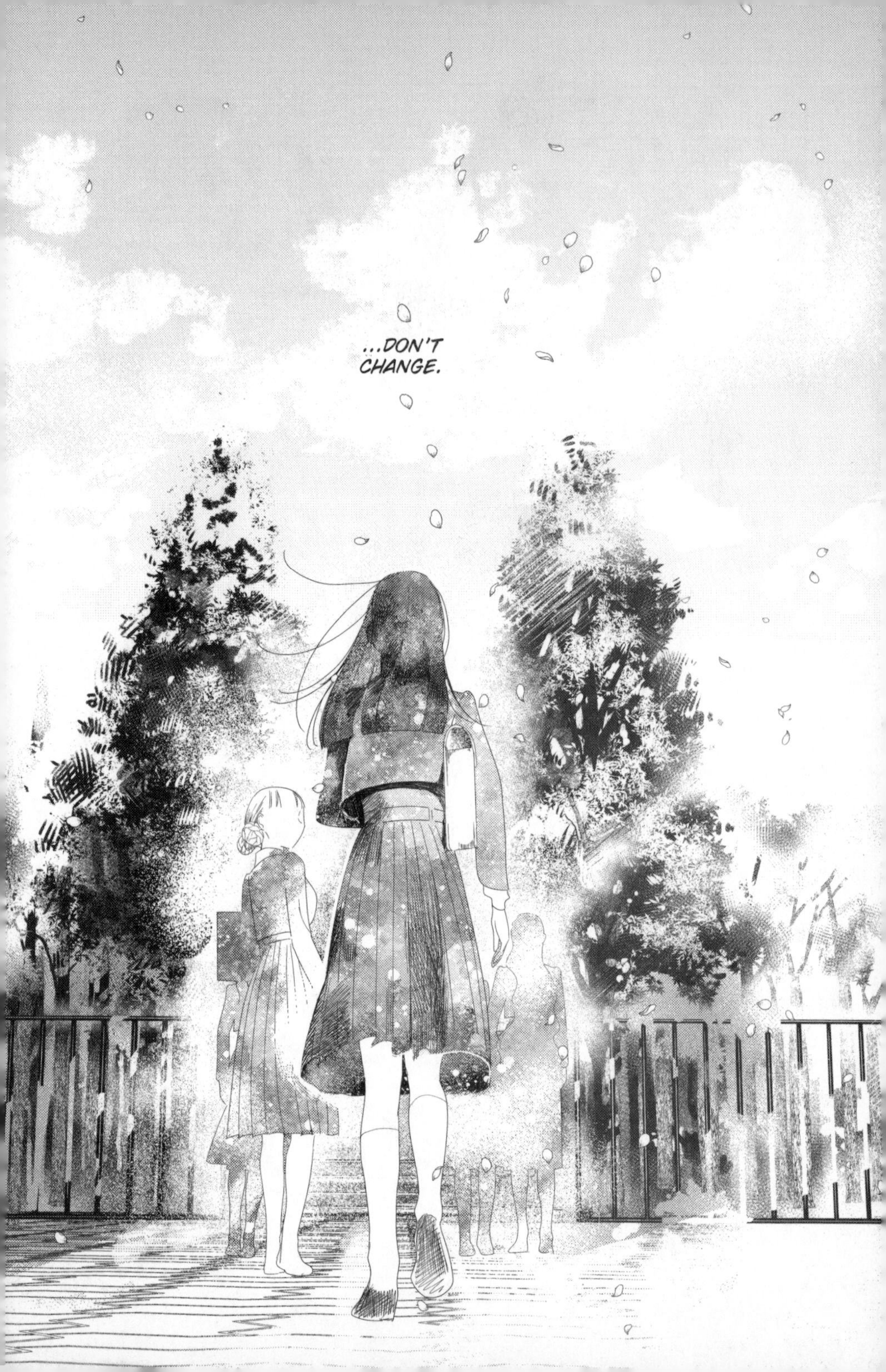
...DON'T CHANGE.

Cocoon
Entwined

"I failed to become a prince..."

One day, a girl disappears from Hoshimiya Girls' Academy, where the traditional uniforms are made of hair. With her disappearance, "school prince" Hana Saeki loses the object of her love.

Meanwhile, Youko Yokozawa—who has accepted her own love for Hana—shines as her feelings turn into a source of strength.

What will become of the pair as they get hurt and hurt each other...?

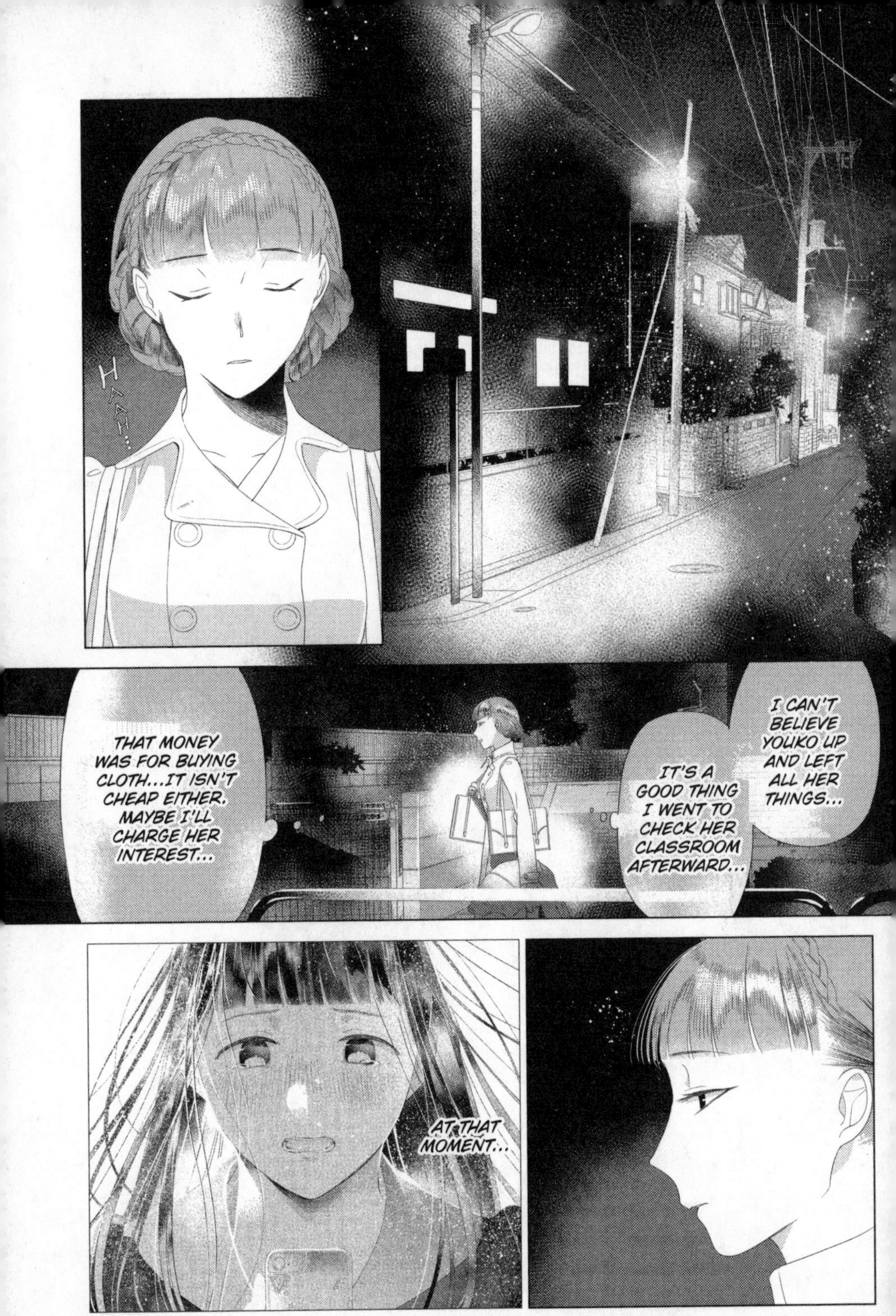
HAAAH...
I CAN'T BELIEVE YOUKO UP AND LEFT ALL HER THINGS...
IT'S A GOOD THING I WENT TO CHECK HER CLASSROOM AFTERWARD...
THAT MONEY WAS FOR BUYING CLOTH...IT ISN'T CHEAP EITHER. MAYBE I'LL CHARGE HER INTEREST...
AT THAT MOMENT...

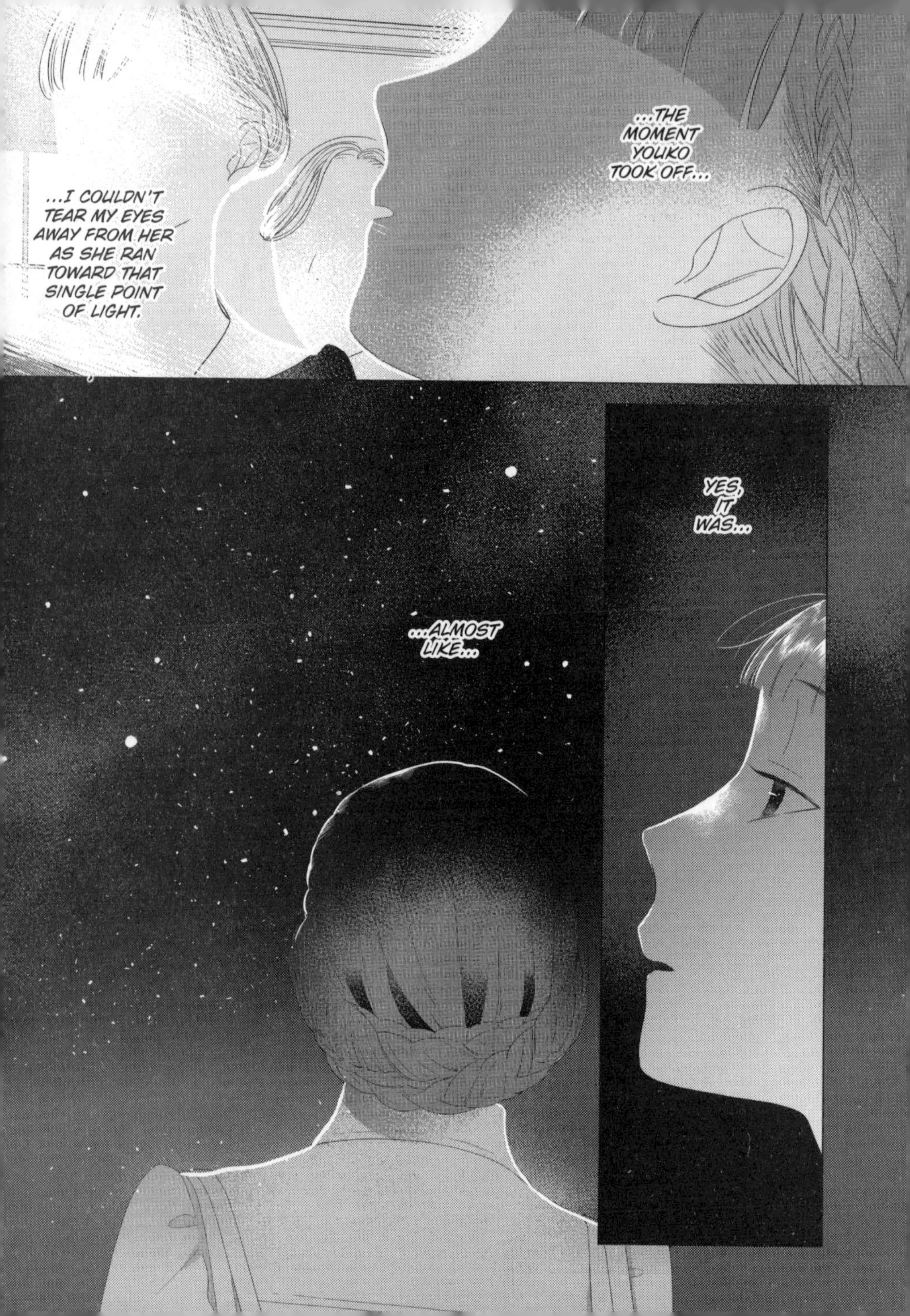
...THE MOMENT YOUKO TOOK OFF...
...I COULDN'T TEAR MY EYES AWAY FROM HER AS SHE RAN TOWARD THAT SINGLE POINT OF LIGHT.
YES, IT WAS...
...ALMOST LIKE...

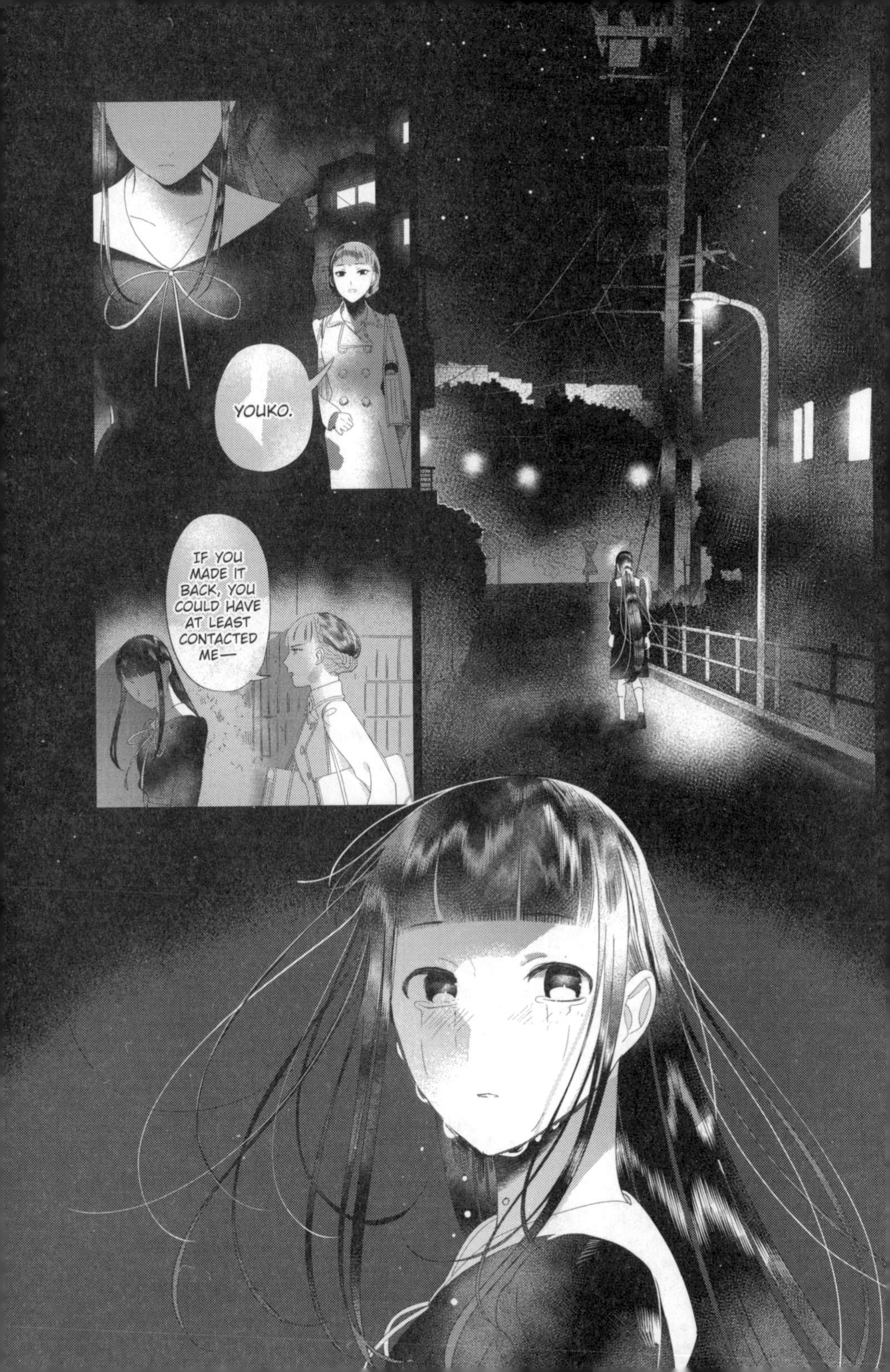
YOUKO.
IF YOU MADE IT BACK, YOU COULD HAVE AT LEAST CONTACTED ME—

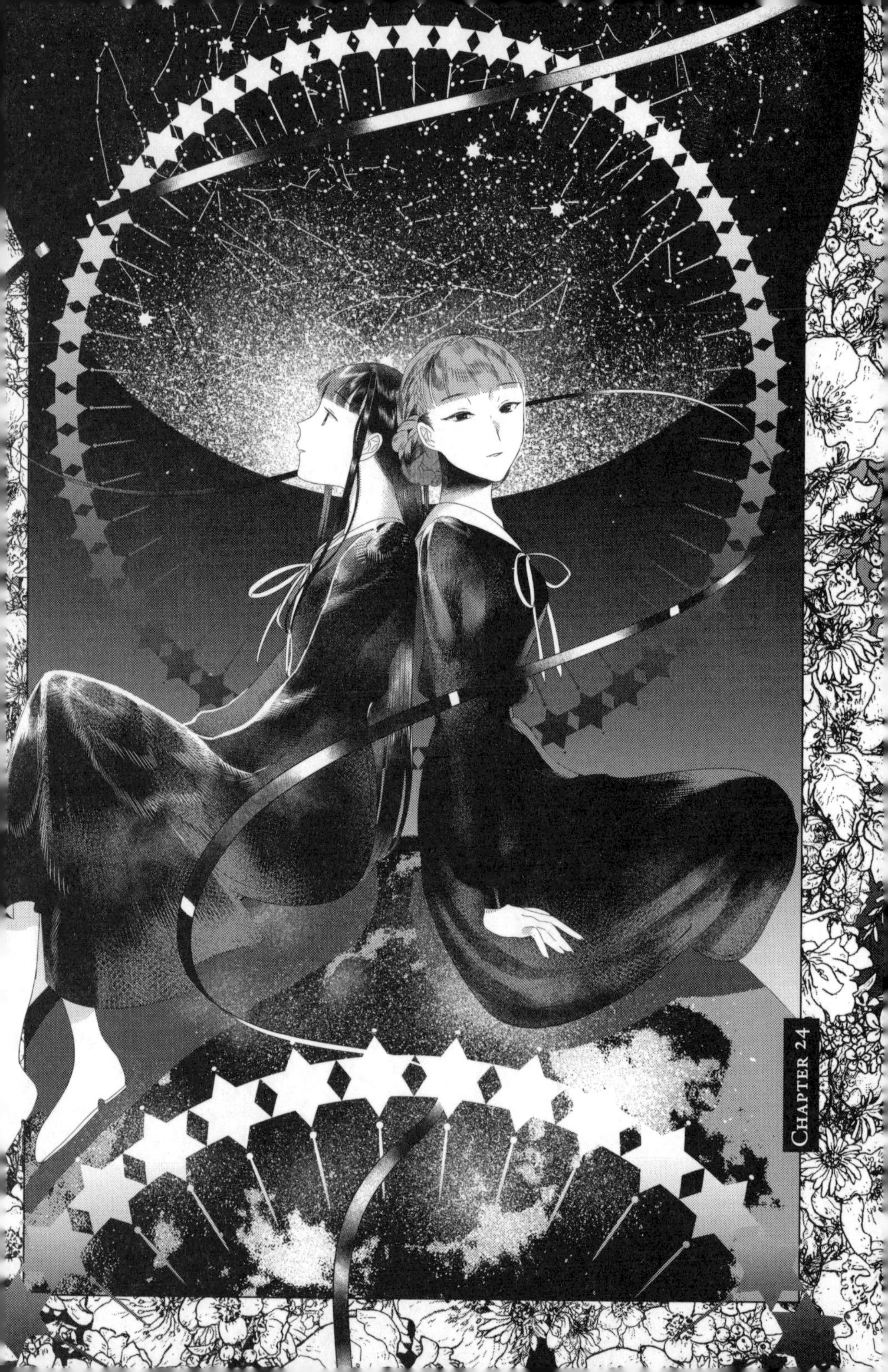
Chapter 24

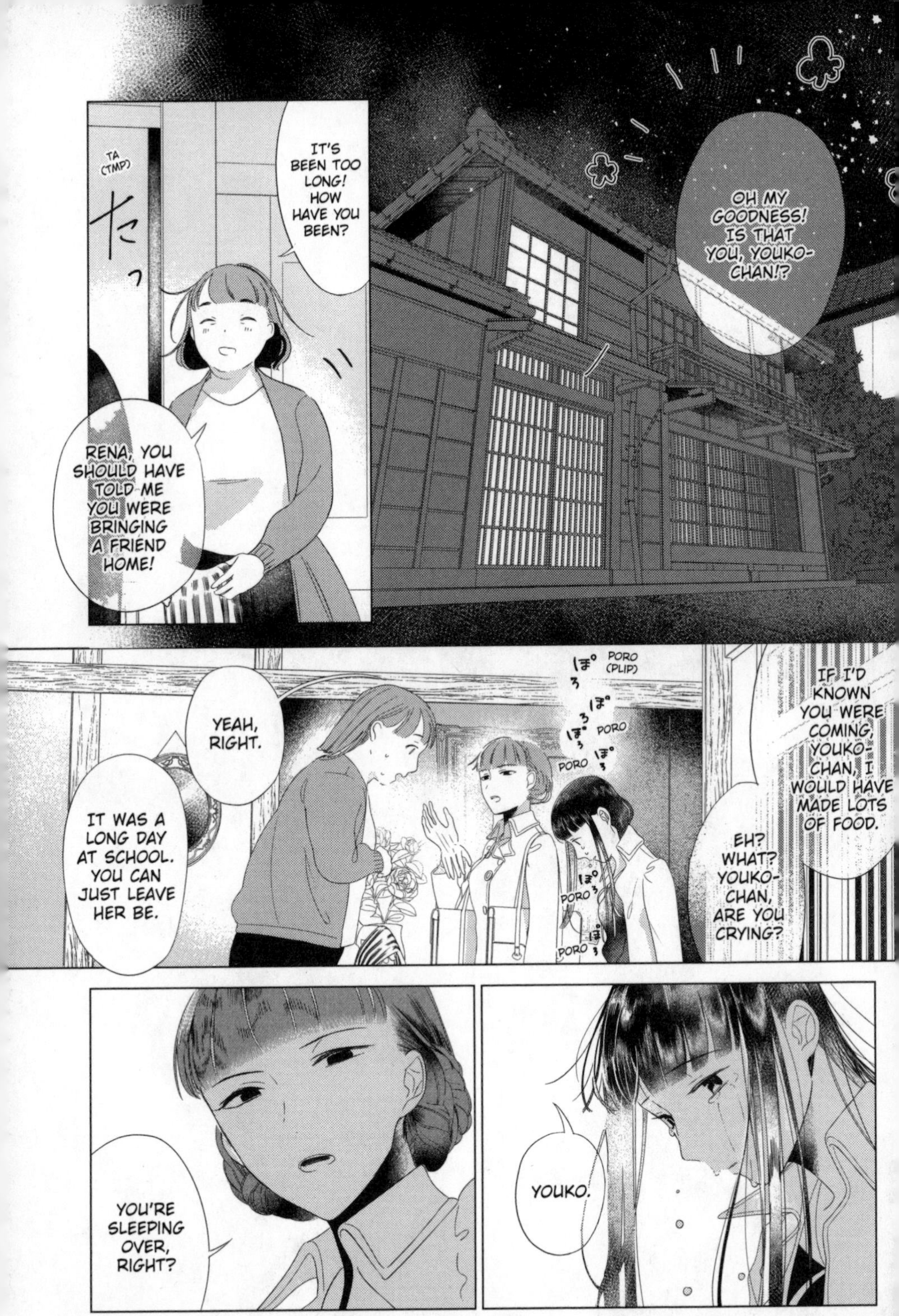
OH MY GOODNESS! IS THAT YOU, YOUKO-CHAN!?
TA (TMP)
IT'S BEEN TOO LONG! HOW HAVE YOU BEEN?
RENA, YOU SHOULD HAVE TOLD ME YOU WERE BRINGING A FRIEND HOME!
IF I'D KNOWN YOU WERE COMING, YOUKO-CHAN, I WOULD HAVE MADE LOTS OF FOOD.
EH? WHAT? YOUKO-CHAN, ARE YOU CRYING?
PORO (PLIP)
PORO
PORO
PORO
PORO
YEAH, RIGHT.
IT WAS A LONG DAY AT SCHOOL. YOU CAN JUST LEAVE HER BE.
YOUKO.
YOU'RE SLEEPING OVER, RIGHT?

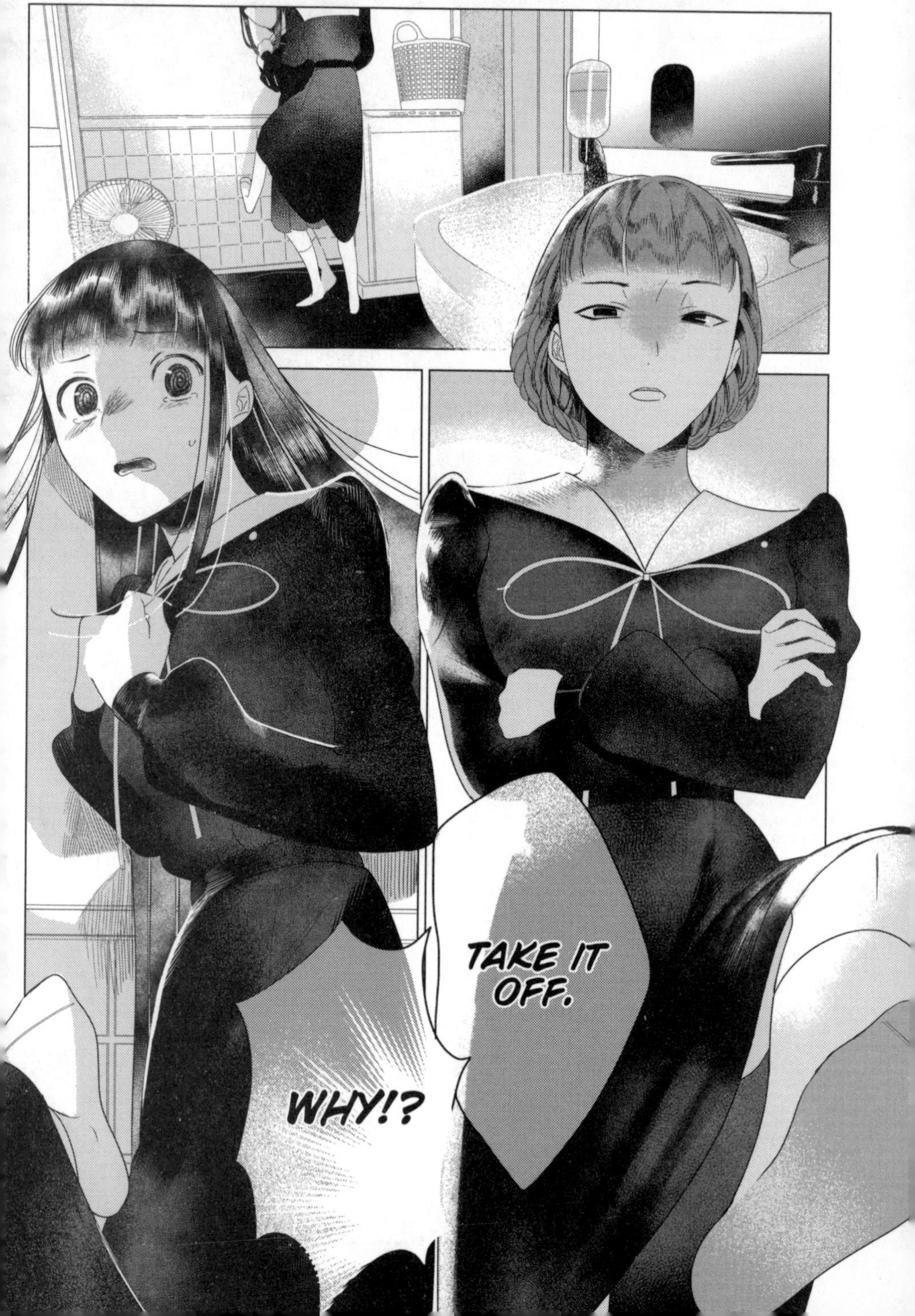
TAKE IT OFF.
WHY!?

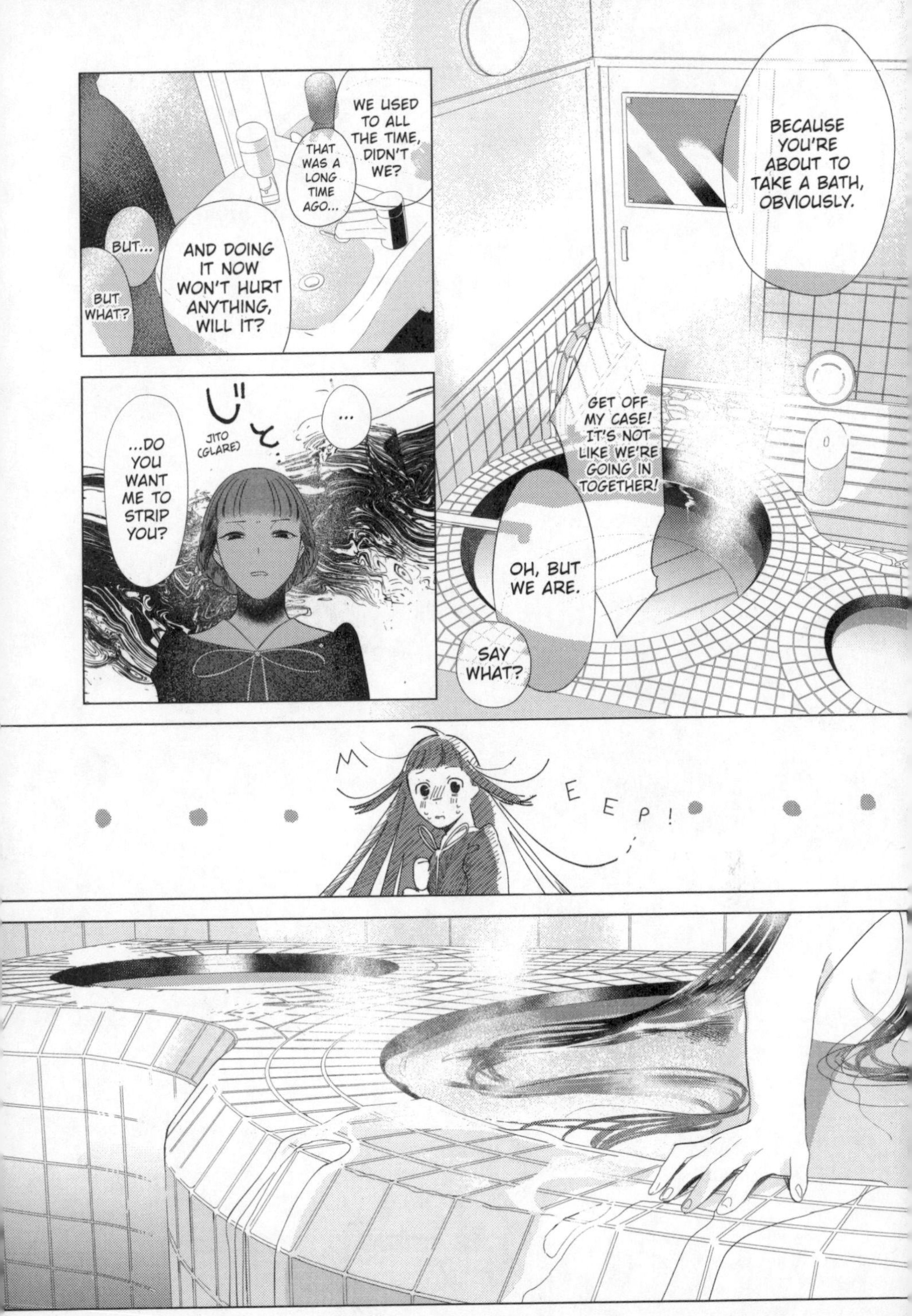
BECAUSE YOU'RE ABOUT TO TAKE A BATH, OBVIOUSLY.
GET OFF MY CASE! IT'S NOT LIKE WE'RE GOING IN TOGETHER!
OH, BUT WE ARE.
SAY WHAT?
WE USED TO ALL THE TIME, DIDN'T WE?
THAT WAS A LONG TIME AGO...
AND DOING IT NOW WON'T HURT ANYTHING, WILL IT?
BUT...
BUT WHAT?
...
じと
JITO (GLARE)
...DO YOU WANT ME TO STRIP YOU?
MEEP!

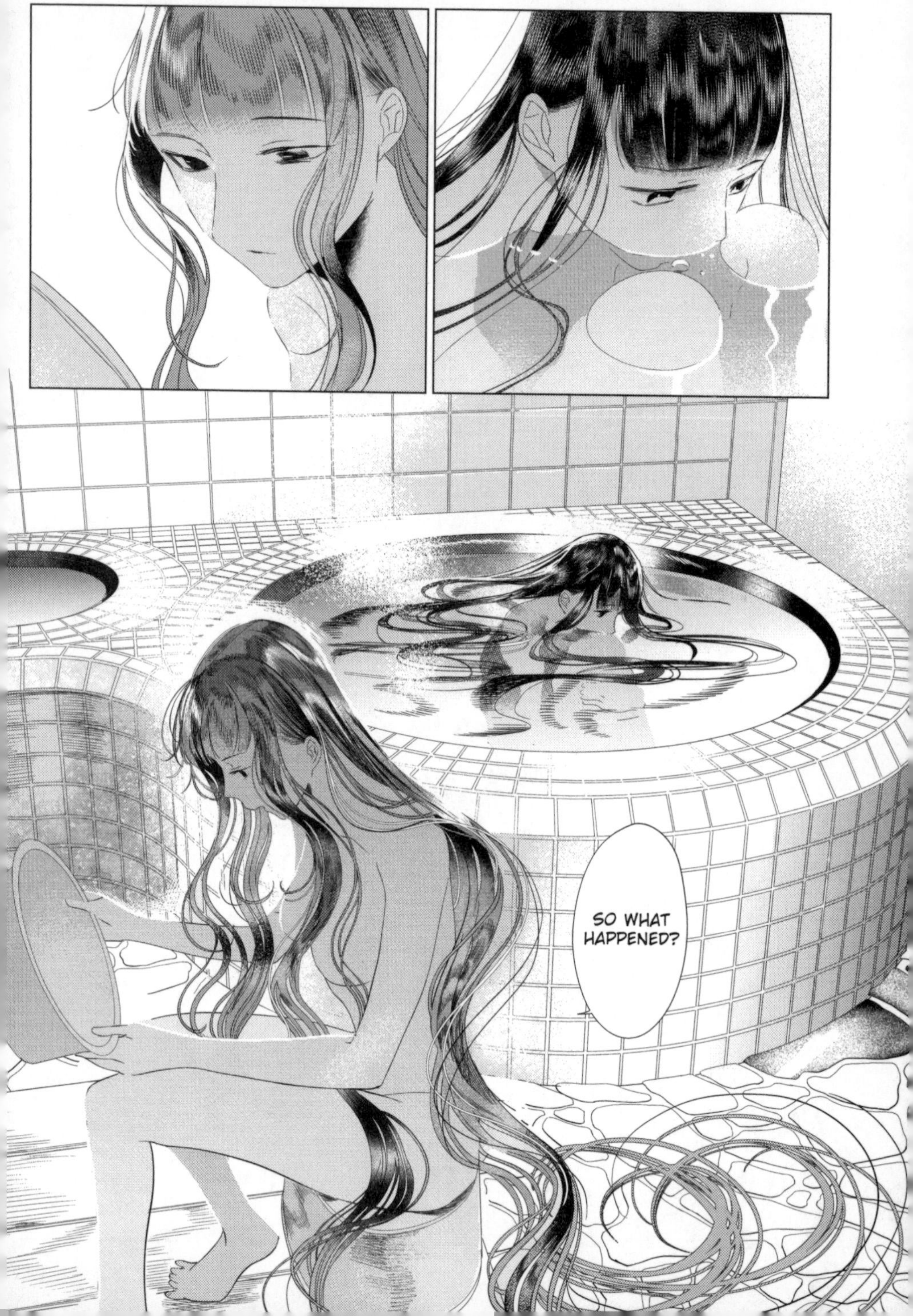
SO WHAT HAPPENED?

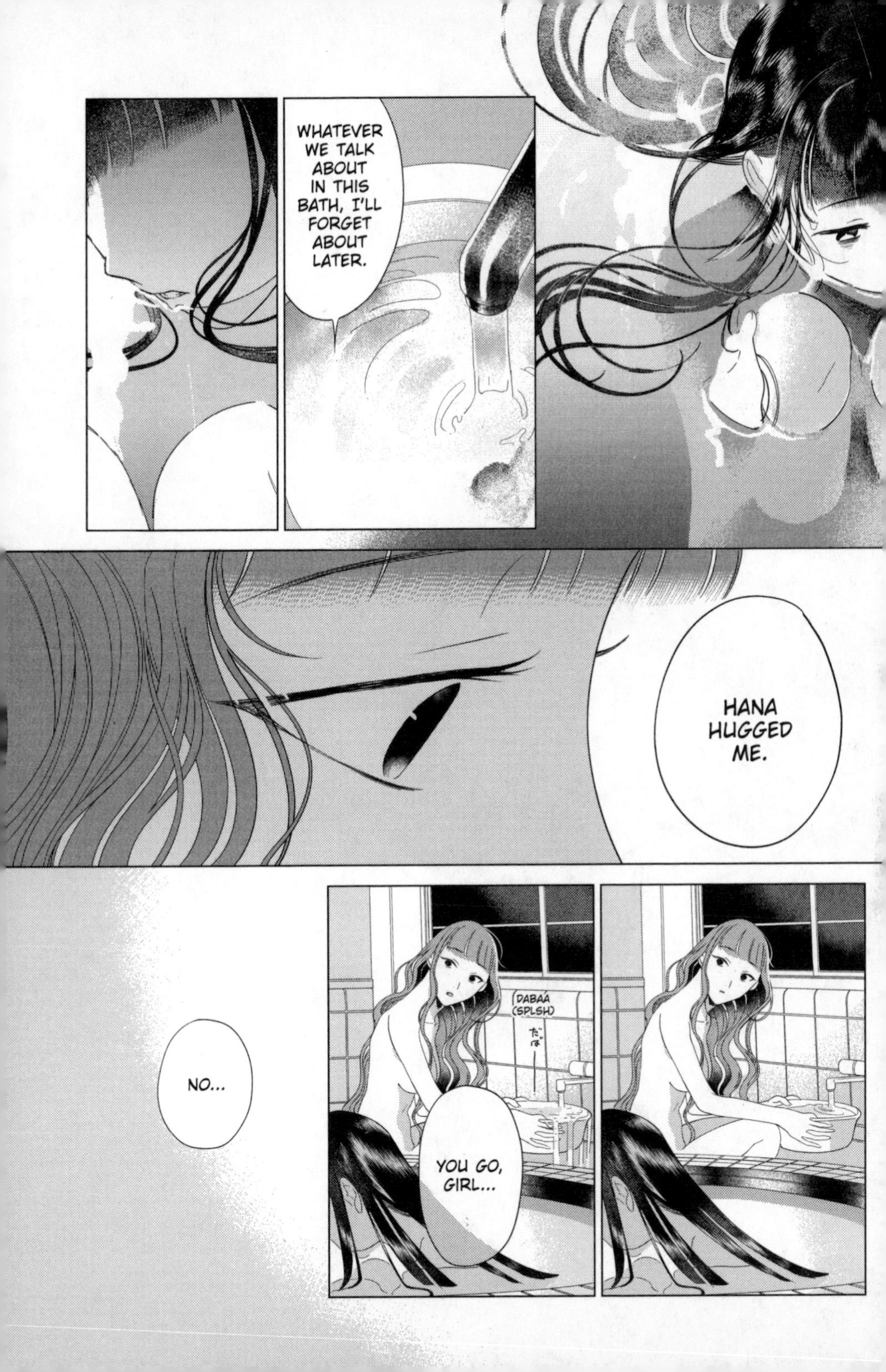
WHATEVER WE TALK ABOUT IN THIS BATH, I'LL FORGET ABOUT LATER.
HANA HUGGED ME.
DABAA (SPLSH)
YOU GO, GIRL...
NO...

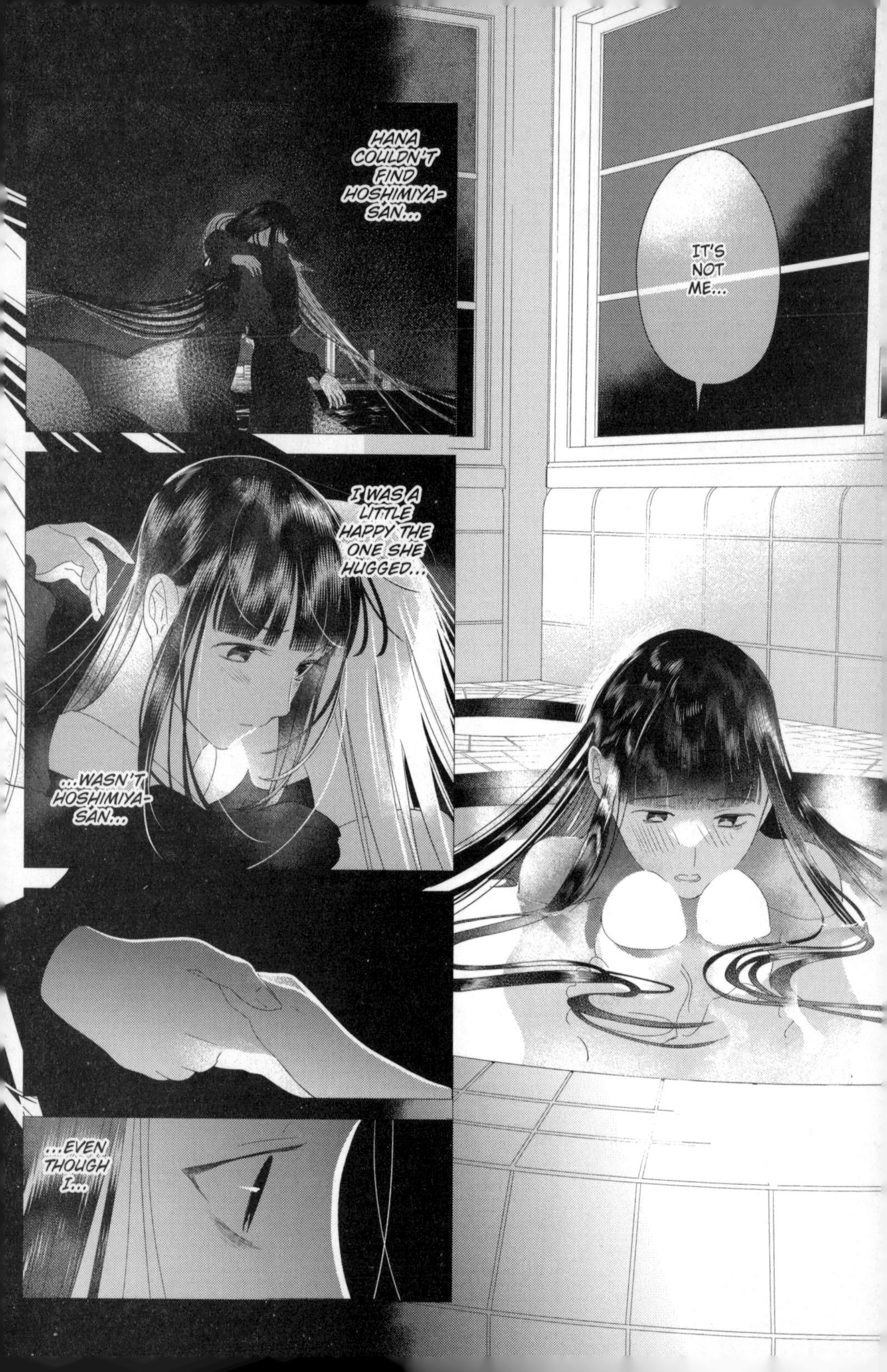
IT'S NOT ME...
HANA COULDN'T FIND HOSHIMIYA-SAN...
I WAS A LITTLE HAPPY THE ONE SHE HUGGED...
...WASN'T HOSHIMIYA-SAN...
...EVEN THOUGH I...

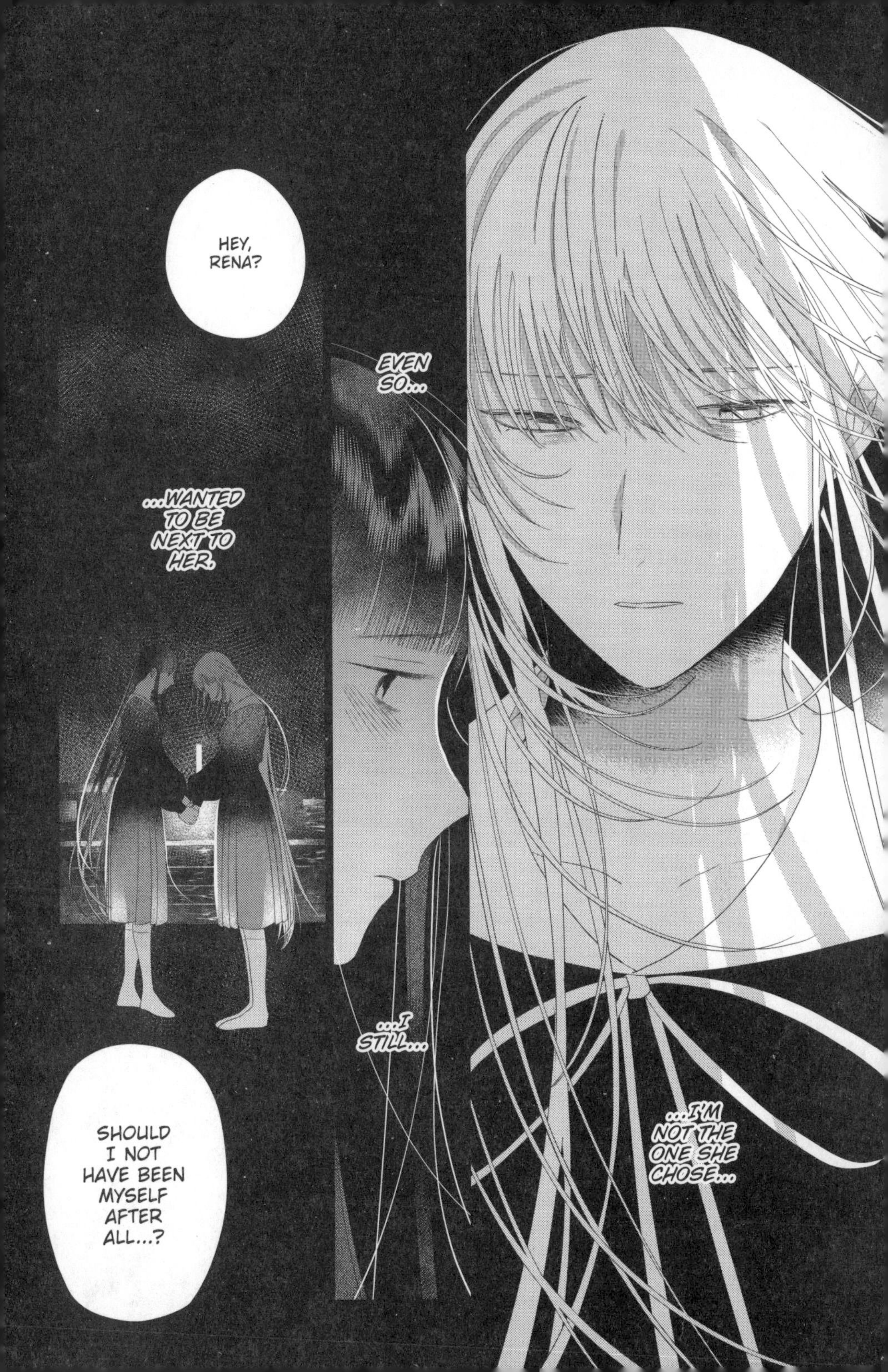
...I'M NOT THE ONE SHE CHOSE...
EVEN SO...
...I STILL...
HEY, RENA?
...WANTED TO BE NEXT TO HER.
SHOULD I NOT HAVE BEEN MYSELF AFTER ALL...?

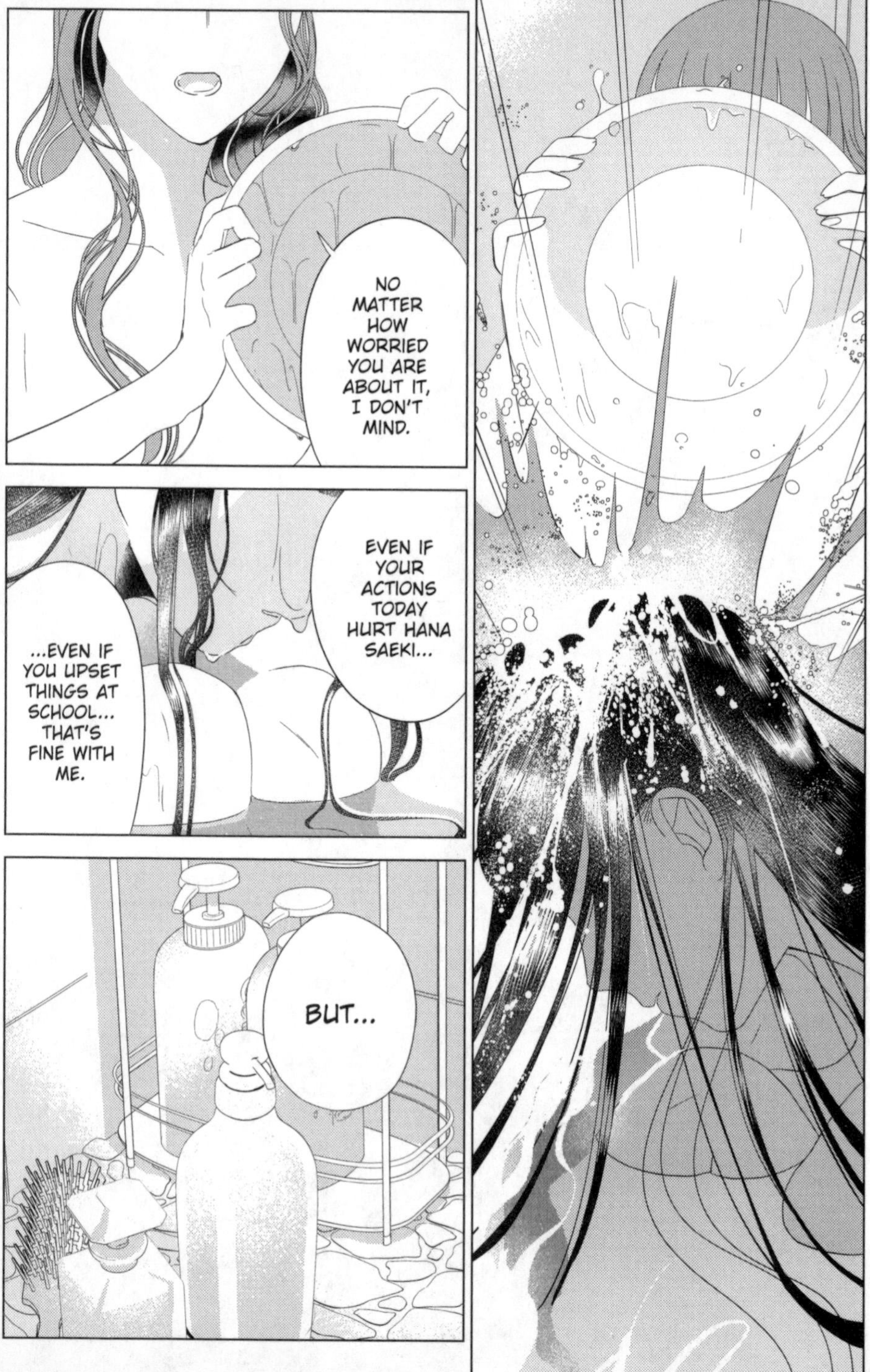
NO MATTER HOW WORRIED YOU ARE ABOUT IT, I DON'T MIND.
EVEN IF YOUR ACTIONS TODAY HURT HANA SAEKI...
...EVEN IF YOU UPSET THINGS AT SCHOOL... THAT'S FINE WITH ME.
BUT...

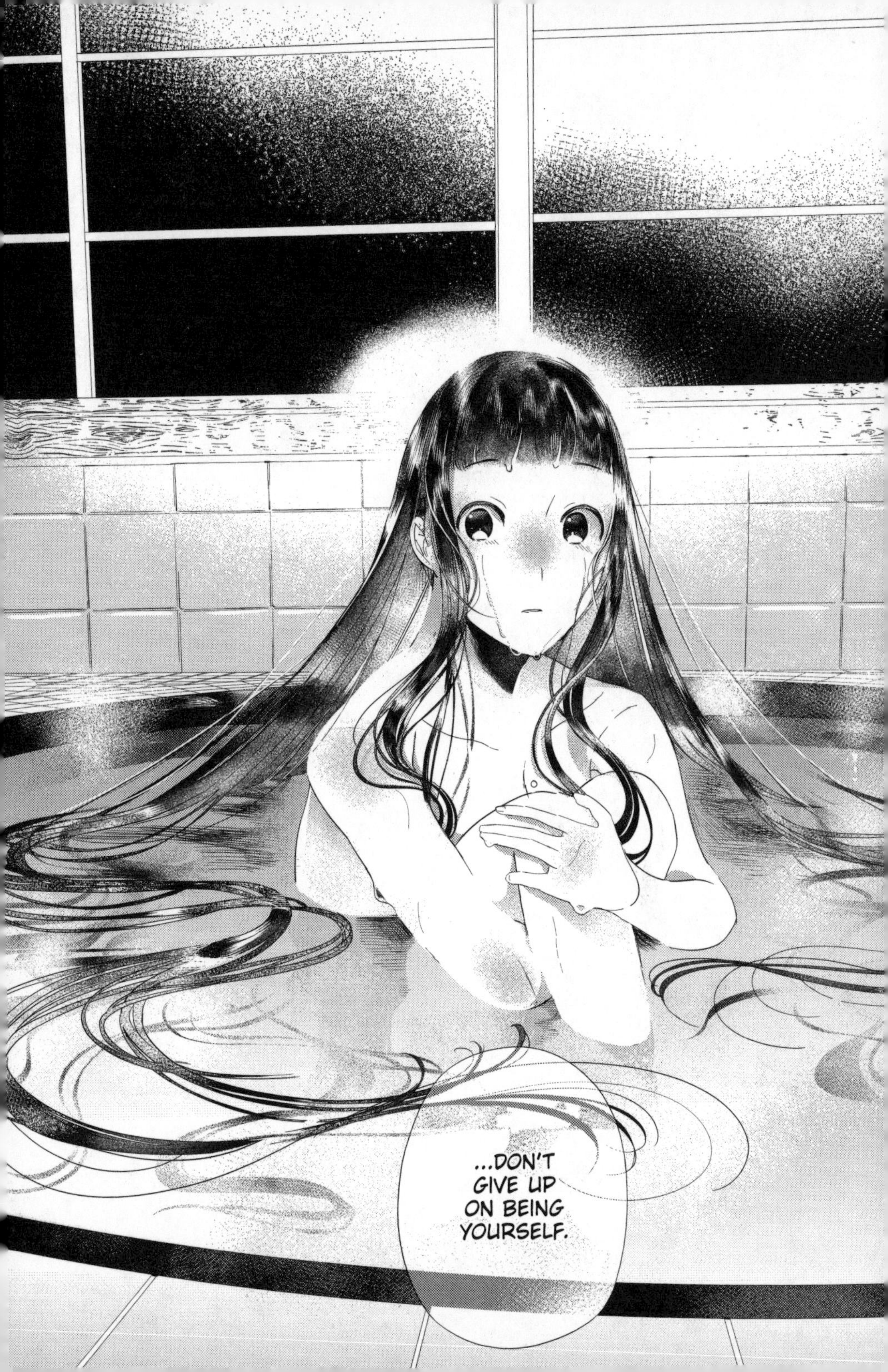
...DON'T GIVE UP ON BEING YOURSELF.

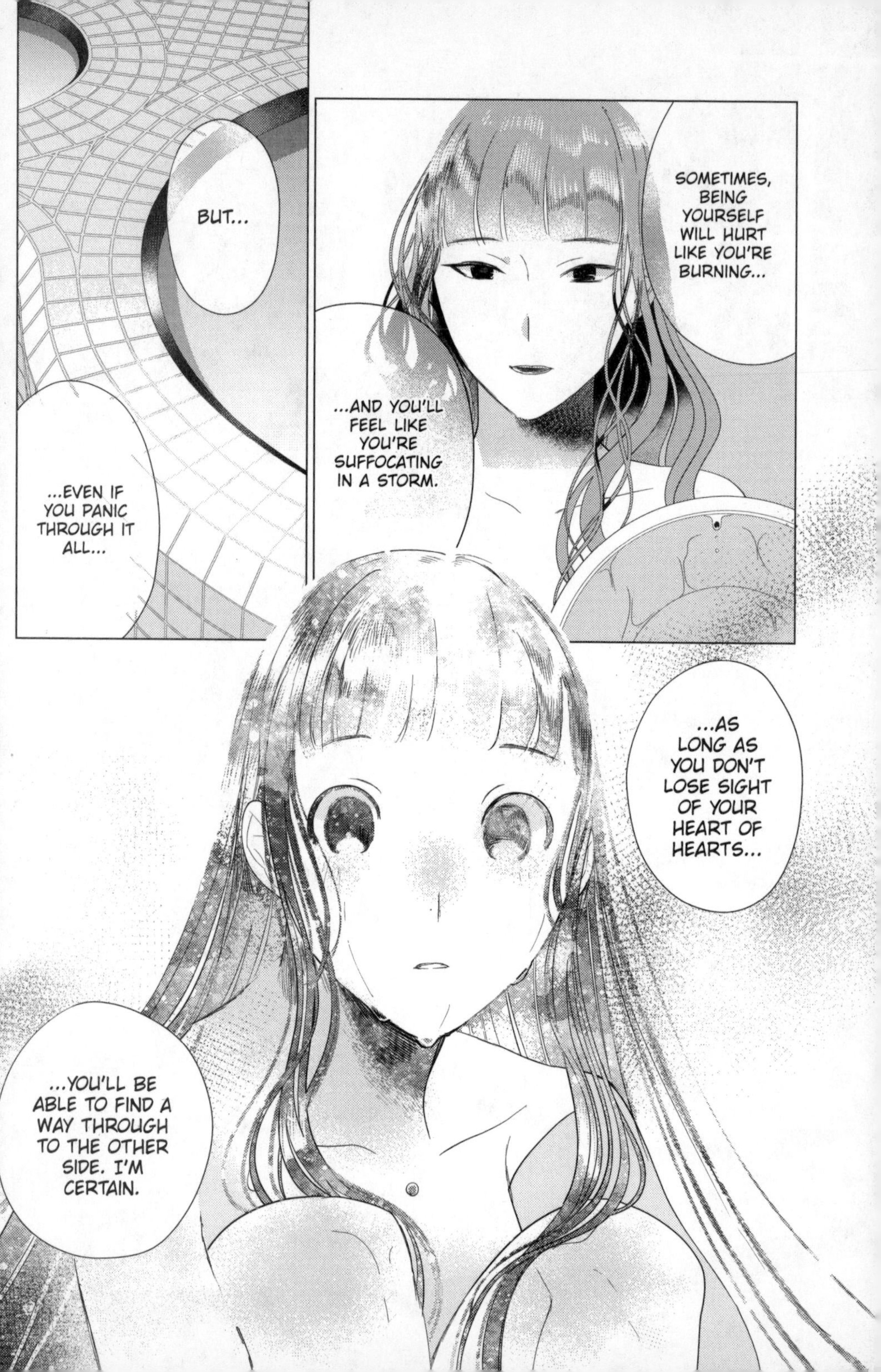
SOMETIMES, BEING YOURSELF WILL HURT LIKE YOU'RE BURNING...
...AND YOU'LL FEEL LIKE YOU'RE SUFFOCATING IN A STORM.
BUT...
...EVEN IF YOU PANIC THROUGH IT ALL...
...AS LONG AS YOU DON'T LOSE SIGHT OF YOUR HEART OF HEARTS...
...YOU'LL BE ABLE TO FIND A WAY THROUGH TO THE OTHER SIDE. I'M CERTAIN.

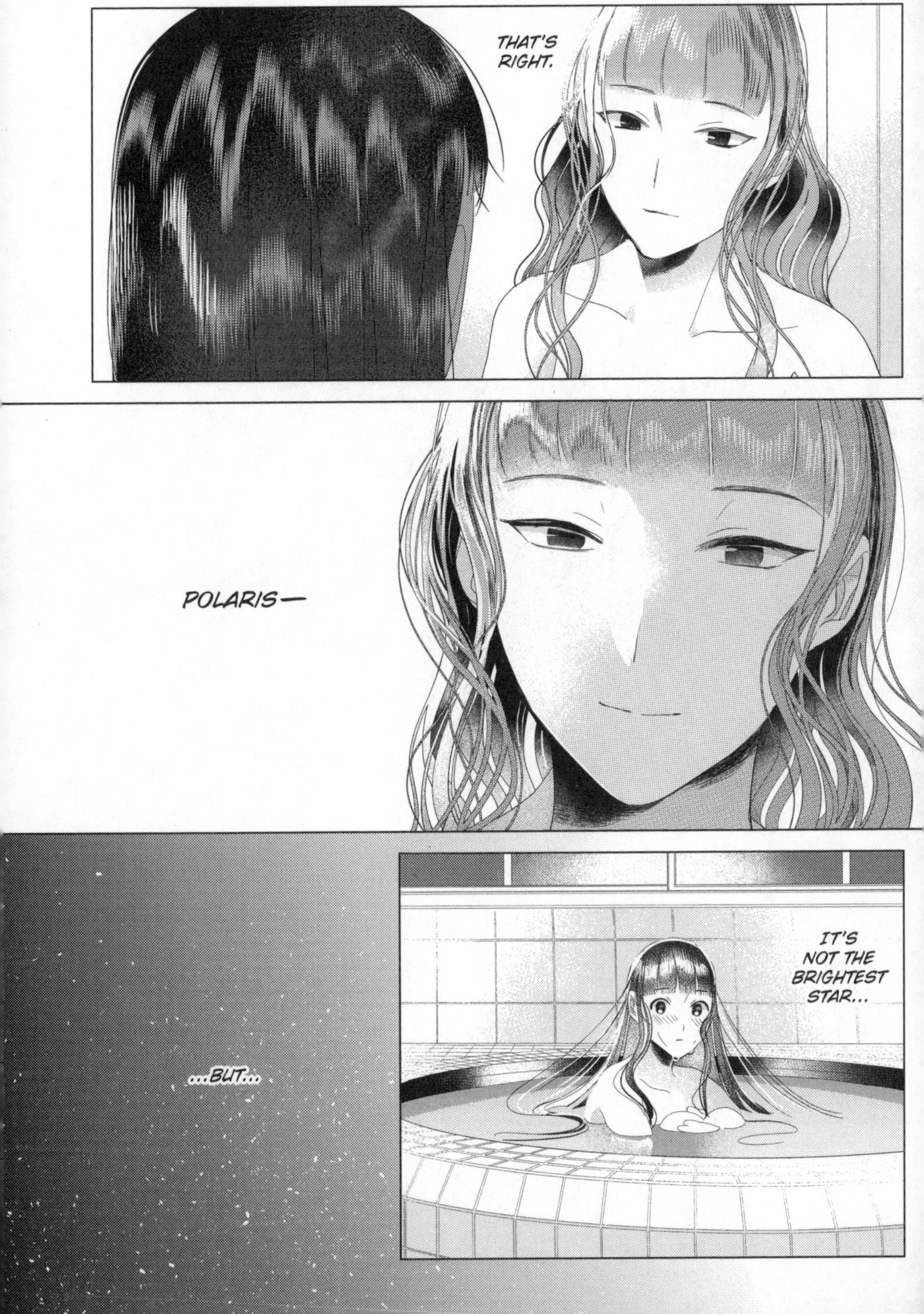
THAT'S RIGHT.
POLARIS—
IT'S NOT THE BRIGHTEST STAR...
...BUT...

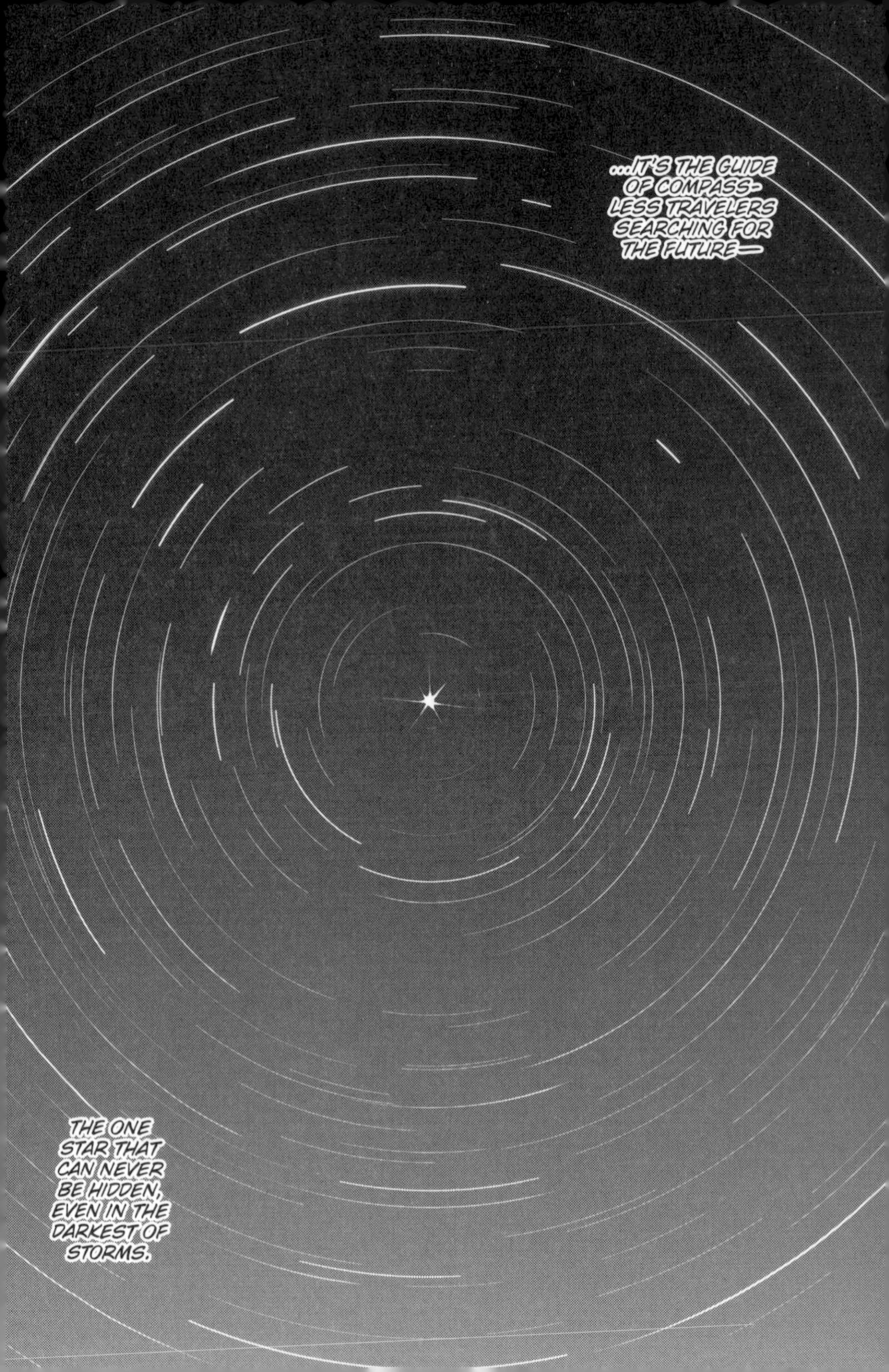
...IT'S THE GUIDE OF COMPASS-LESS TRAVELERS SEARCHING FOR THE FUTURE—
THE ONE STAR THAT CAN NEVER BE HIDDEN, EVEN IN THE DARKEST OF STORMS.

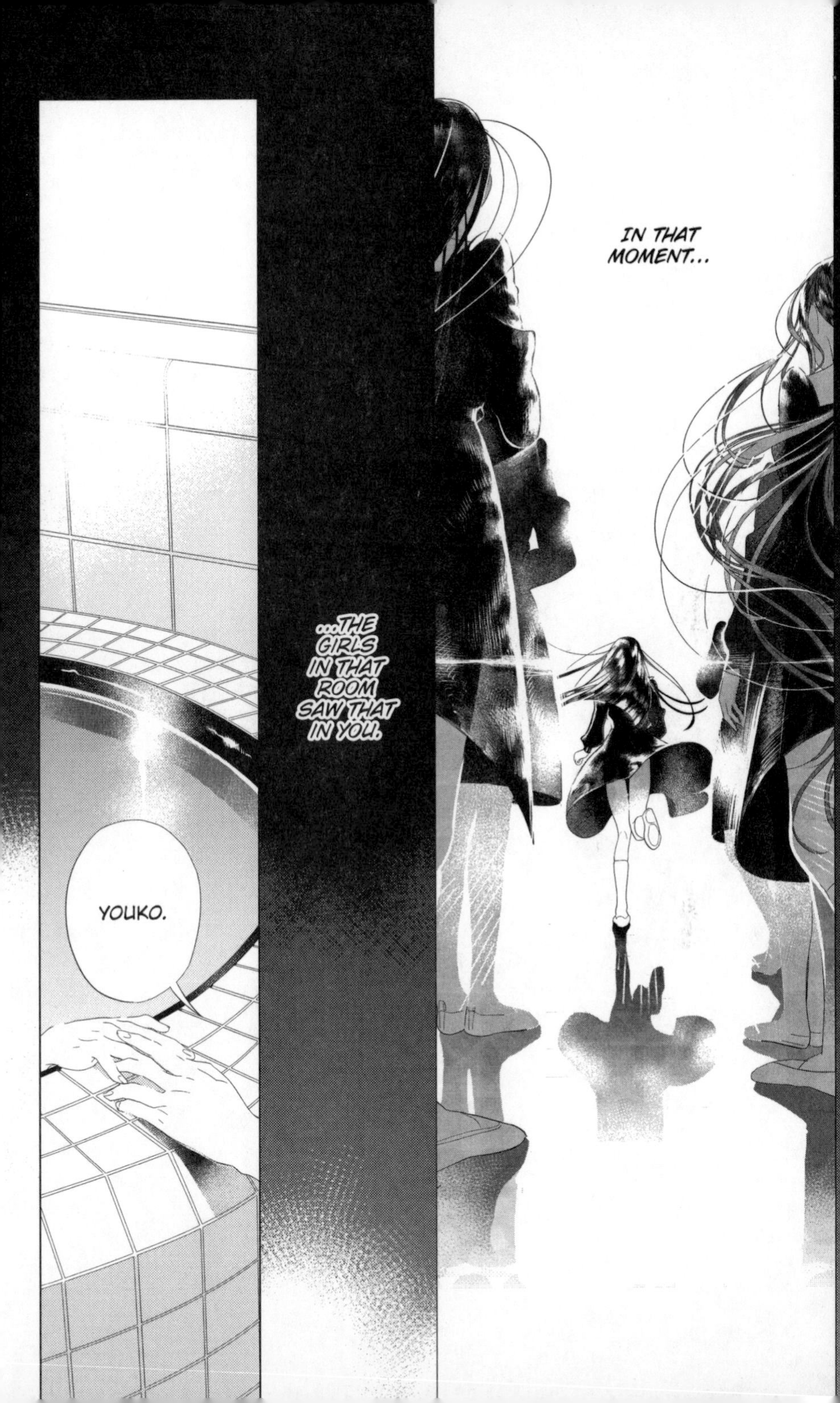
IN THAT MOMENT...
...THE GIRLS IN THAT ROOM SAW THAT IN YOU.
YOUKO.

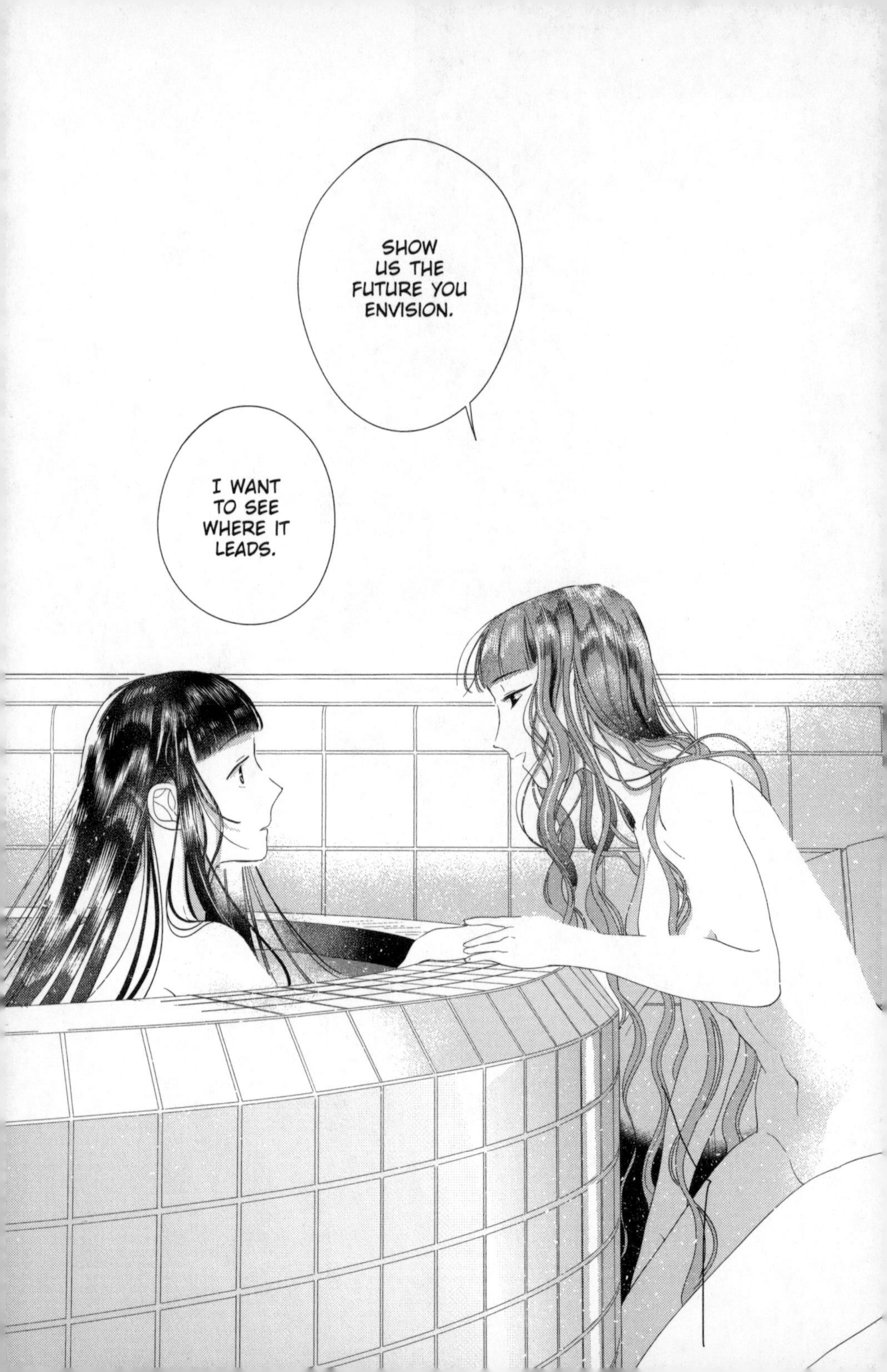
SHOW US THE FUTURE YOU ENVISION.
I WANT TO SEE WHERE IT LEADS.

Cocoon
Entwined

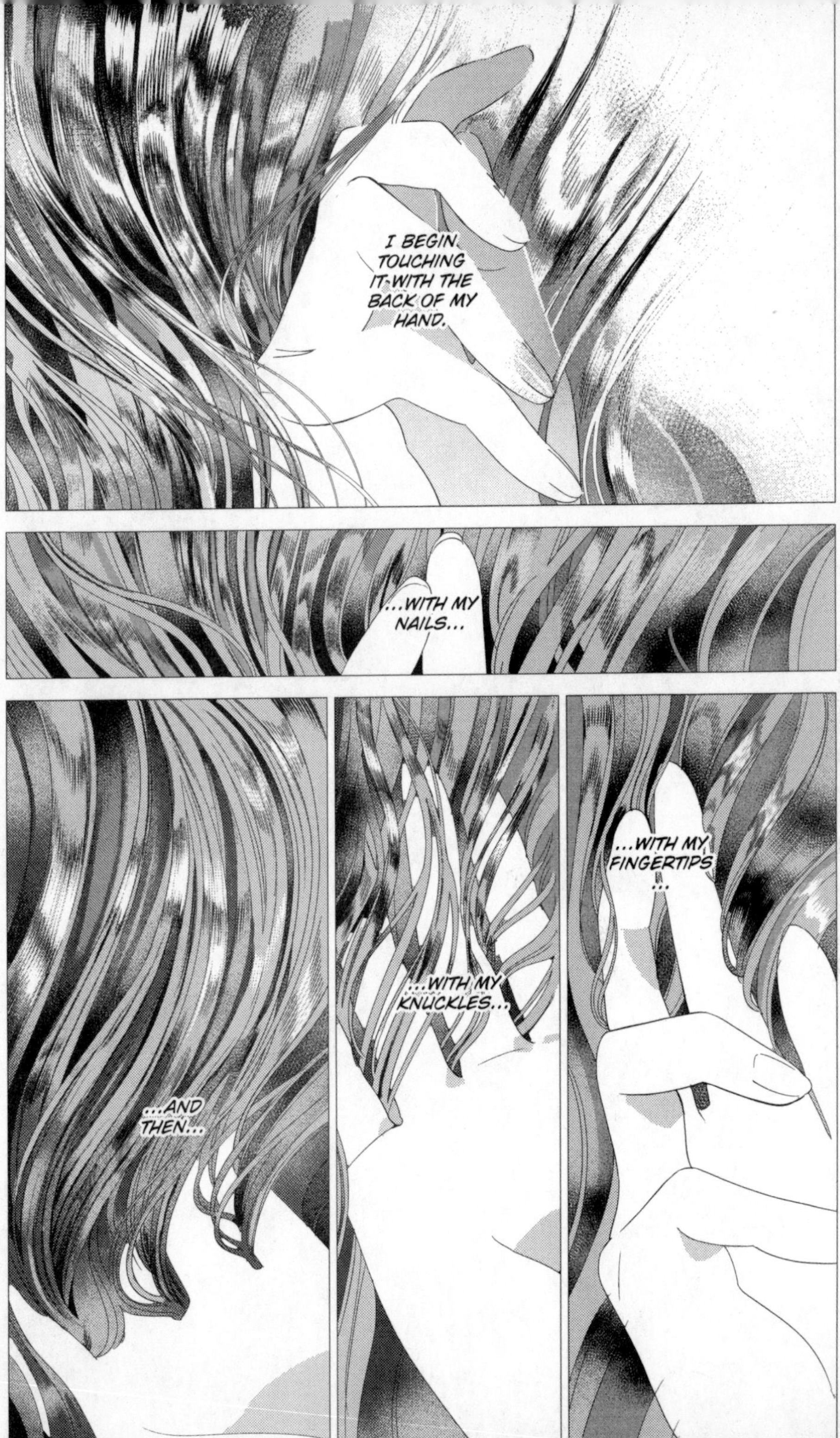
I BEGIN TOUCHING IT WITH THE BACK OF MY HAND.
...WITH MY NAILS...
...WITH MY FINGERTIPS...
...WITH MY KNUCKLES...
...AND THEN...

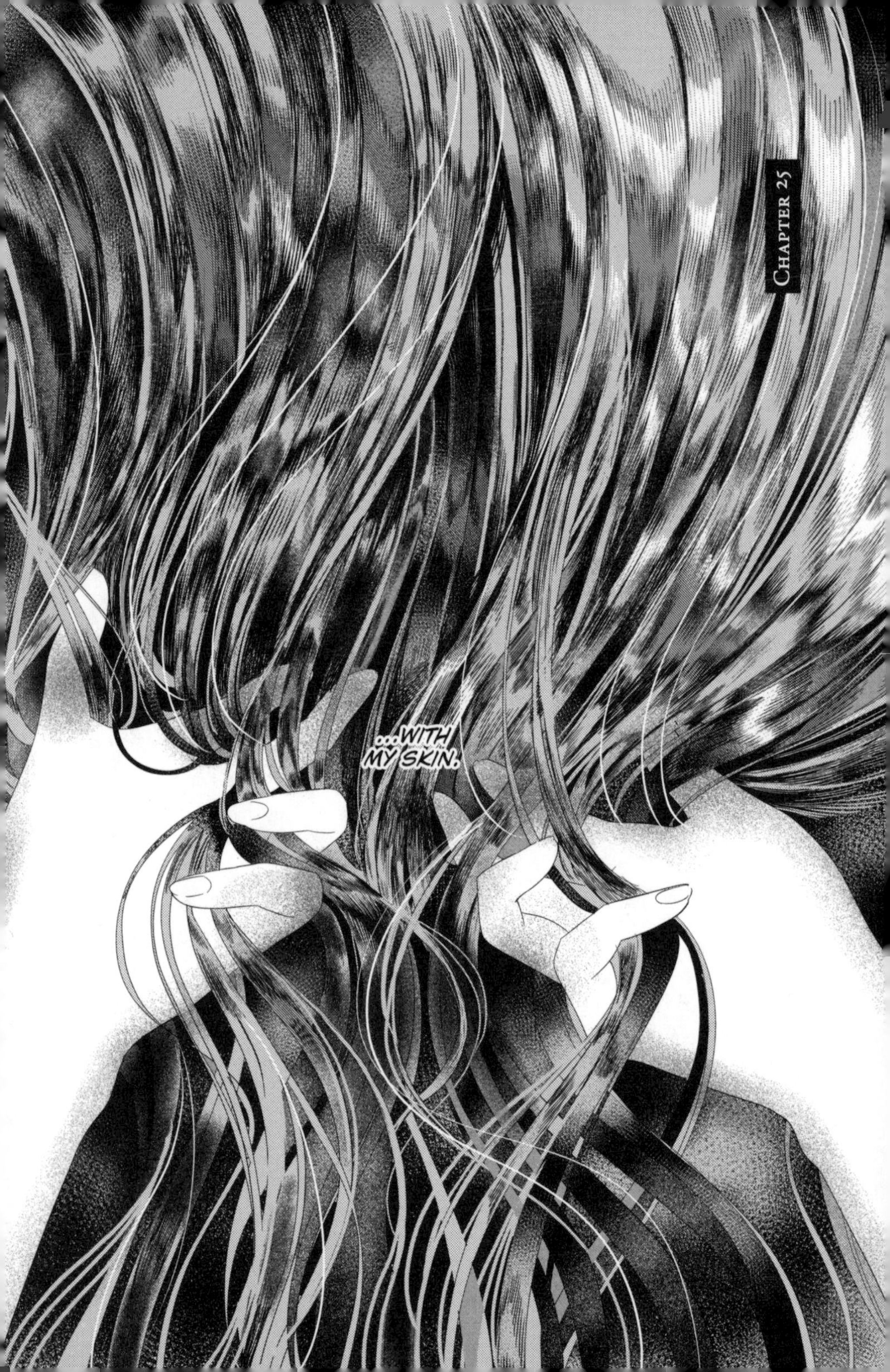
CHAPTER 25
...WITH MY SKIN.

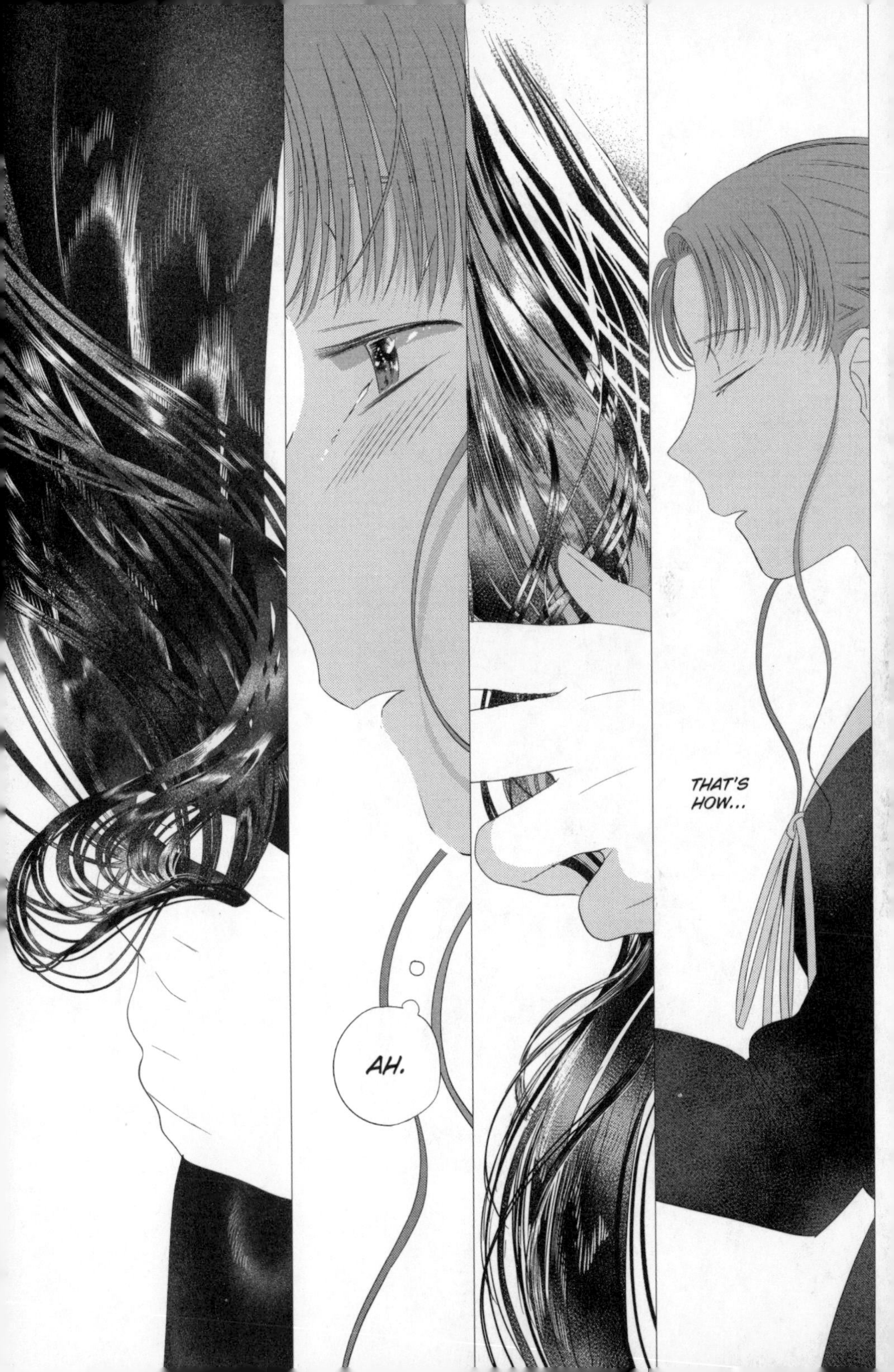
THAT'S HOW...
AH.

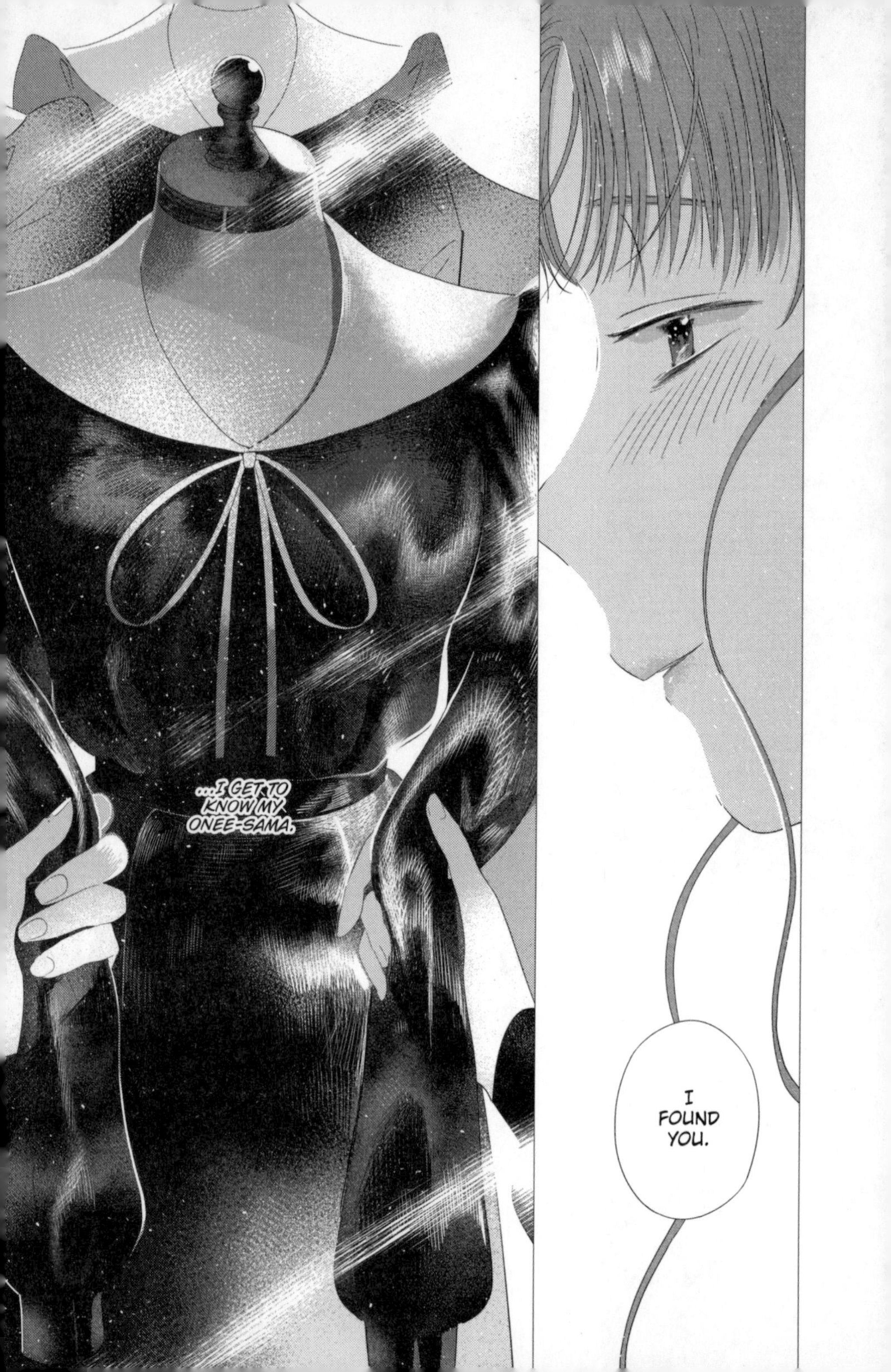
I FOUND YOU.
...I GET TO KNOW MY ONEE-SAMA.

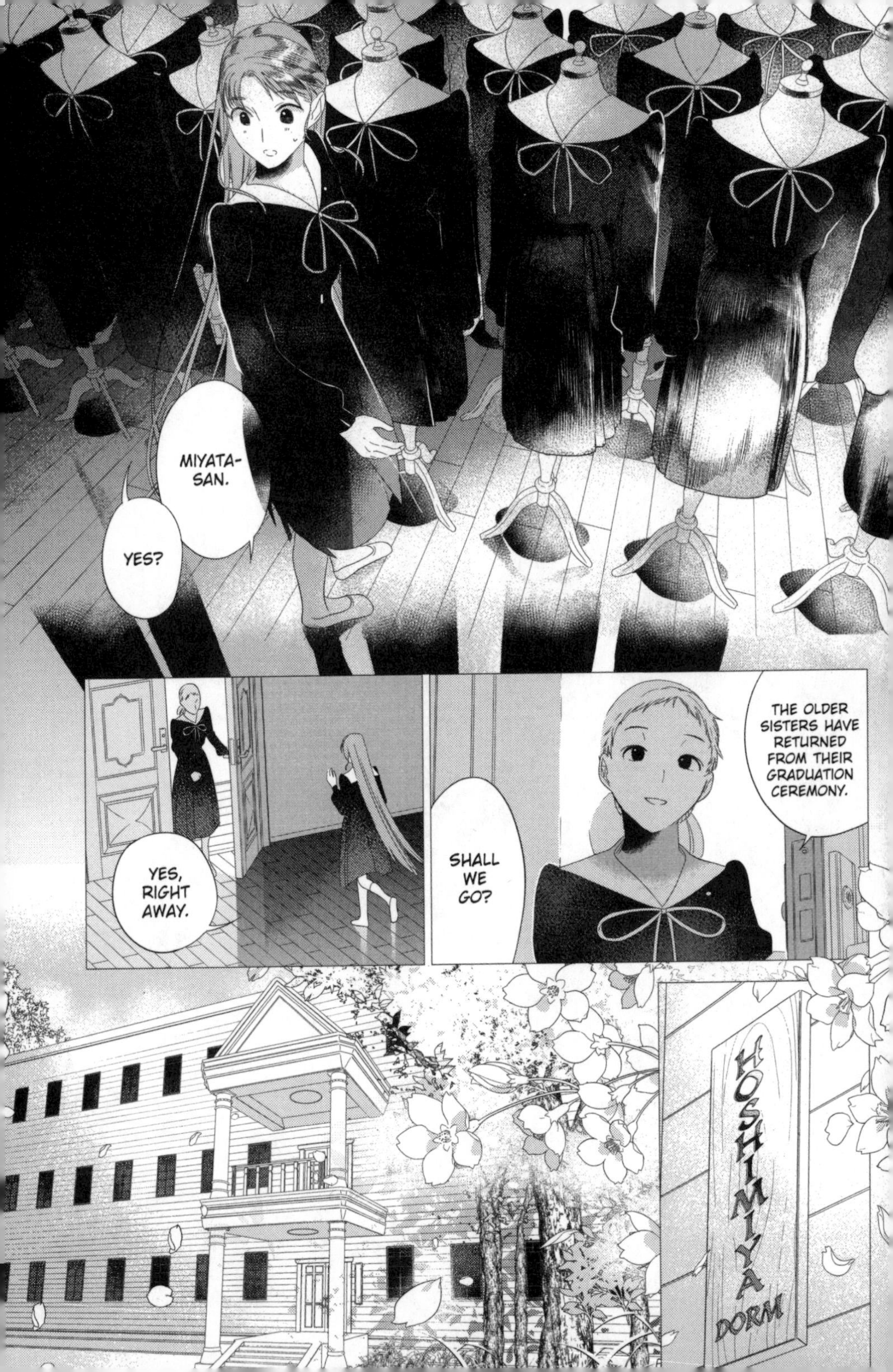
MIYATA-SAN.
YES?
THE OLDER SISTERS HAVE RETURNED FROM THEIR GRADUATION CEREMONY.
SHALL WE GO?
YES, RIGHT AWAY.
HOSHIMIYA DORM

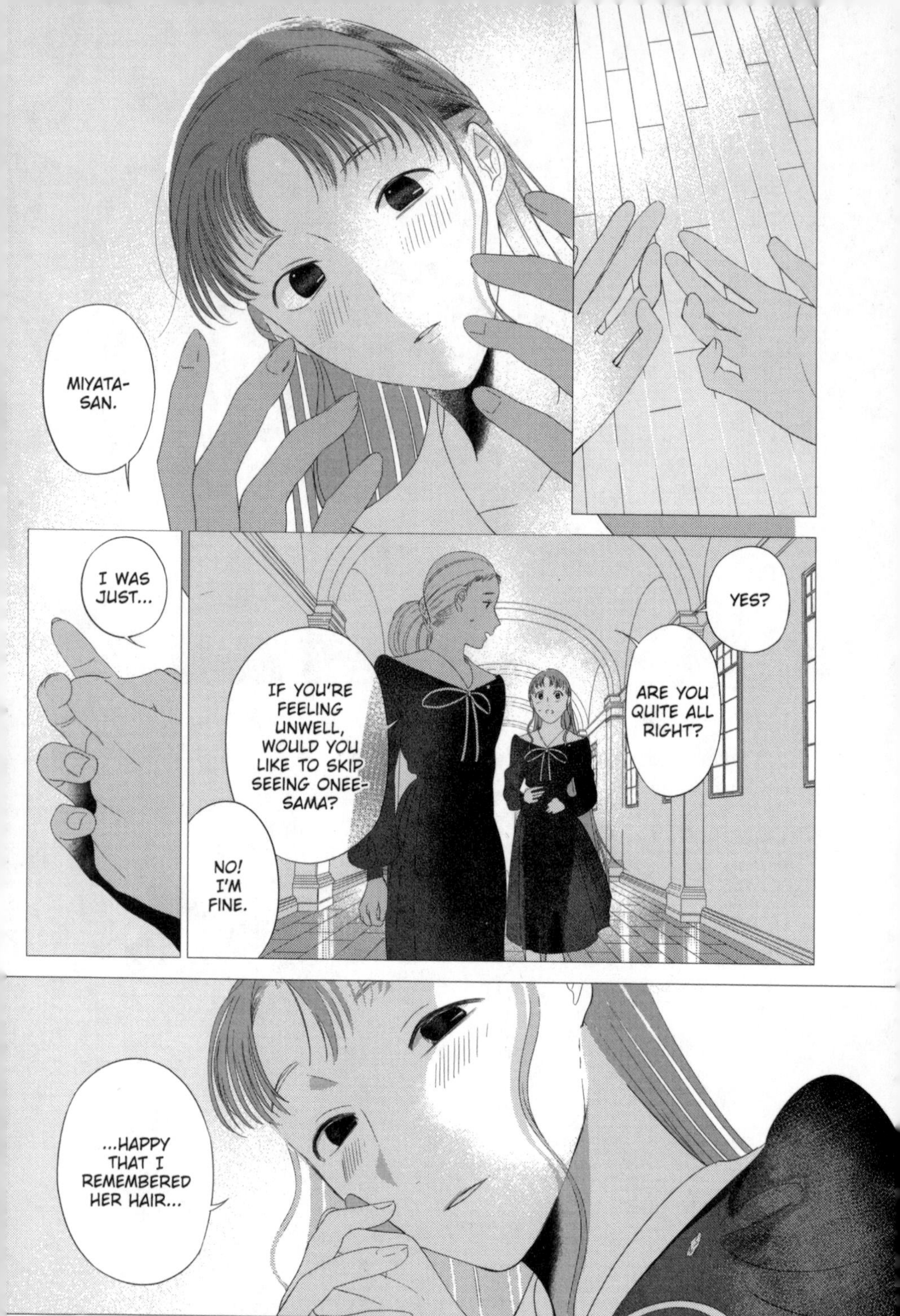
MIYATA-SAN.
YES?
ARE YOU QUITE ALL RIGHT?
IF YOU'RE FEELING UNWELL, WOULD YOU LIKE TO SKIP SEEING ONEE-SAMA?
NO! I'M FINE.
I WAS JUST...
...HAPPY THAT I REMEMBERED HER HAIR...

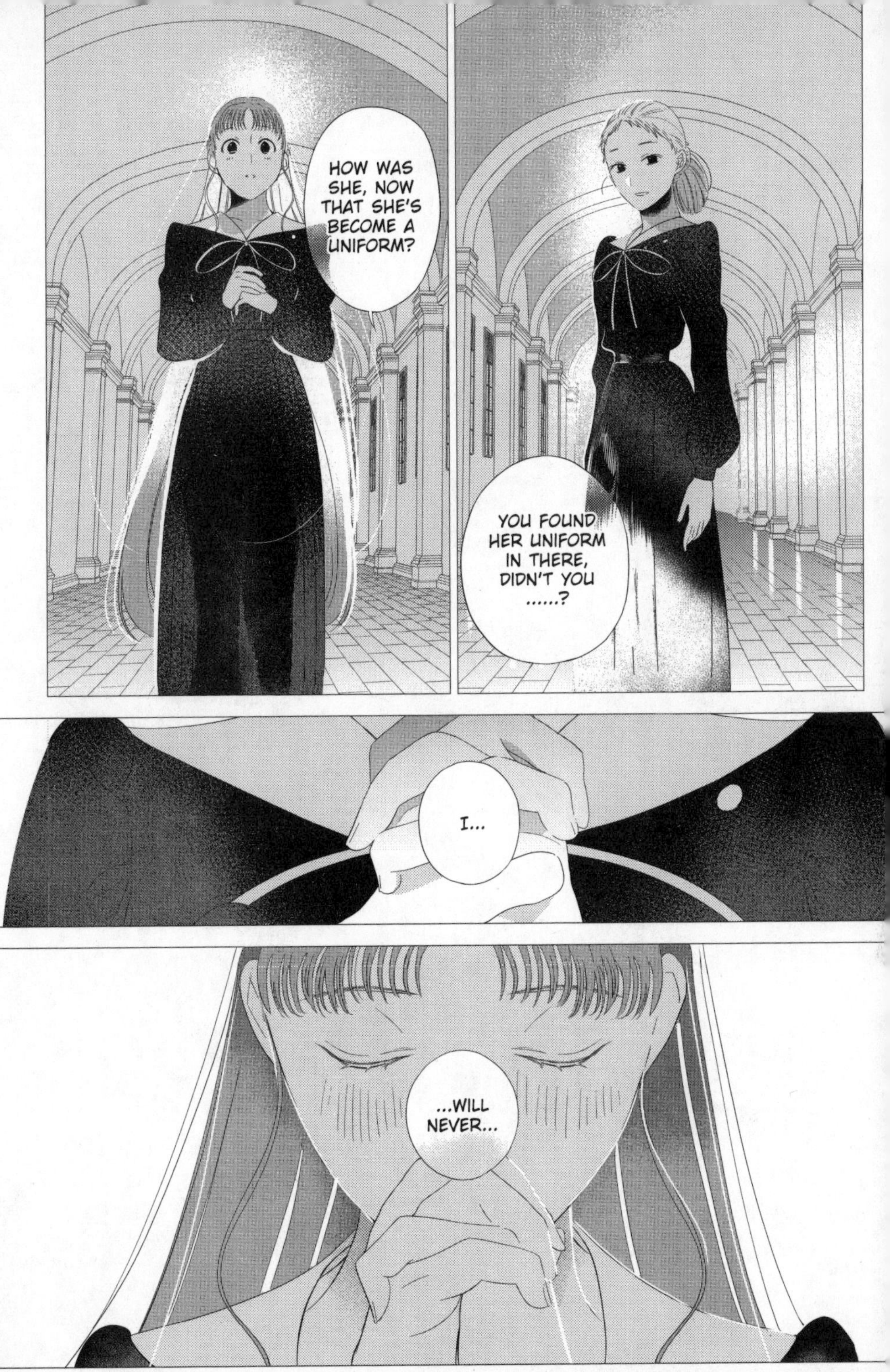
YOU FOUND HER UNIFORM IN THERE, DIDN'T YOU ......?
HOW WAS SHE, NOW THAT SHE'S BECOME A UNIFORM?
I...
...WILL NEVER...

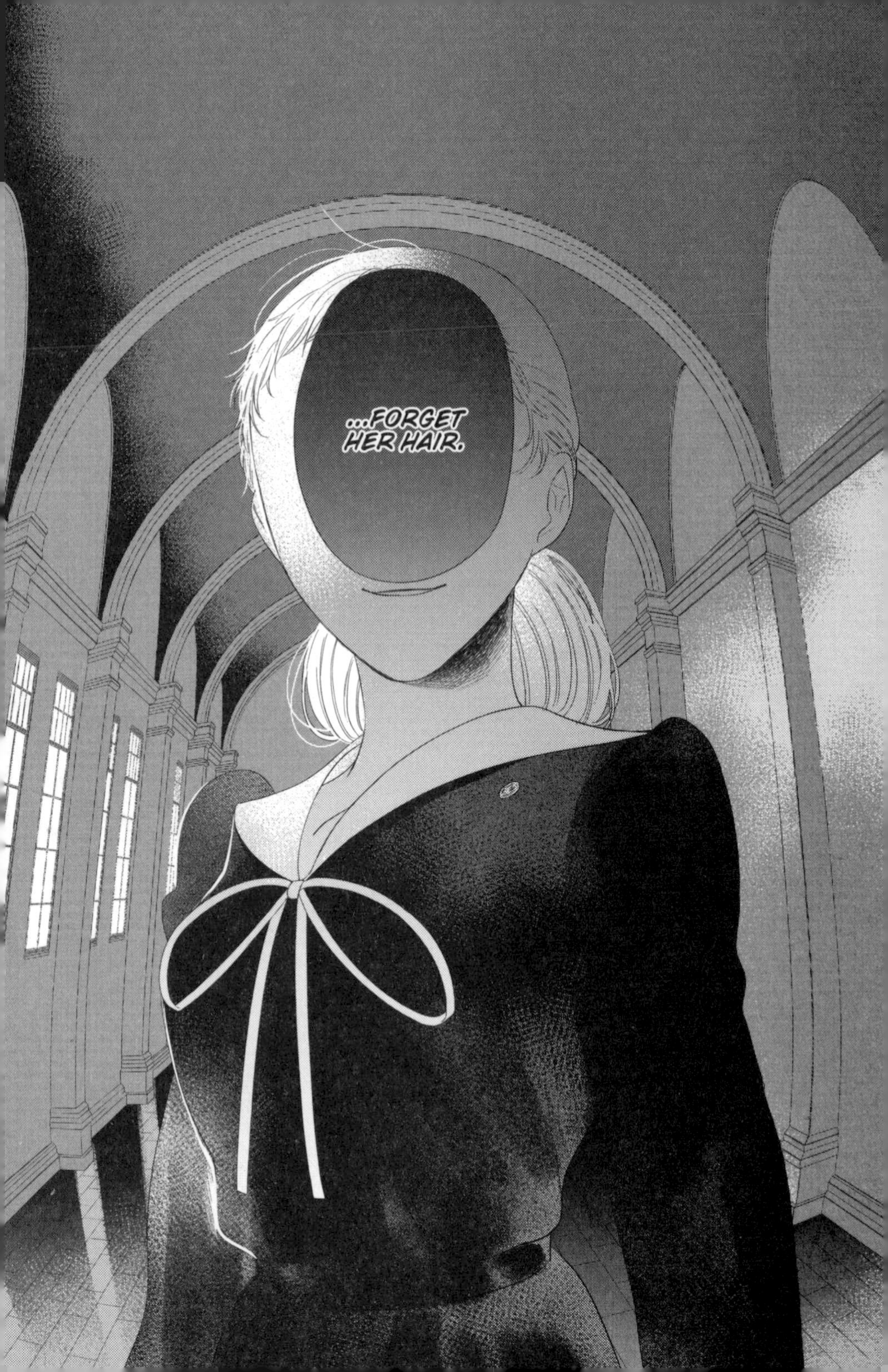
...FORGET
HER HAIR.

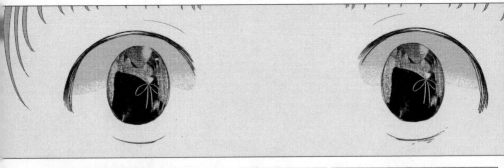

IS SOMETHING THE MATTER?

MIYATA-SAN?

LET'S GO TO HER, THEN.

NOT AT ALL.

WHAT DID I JUST—

ONE THING.

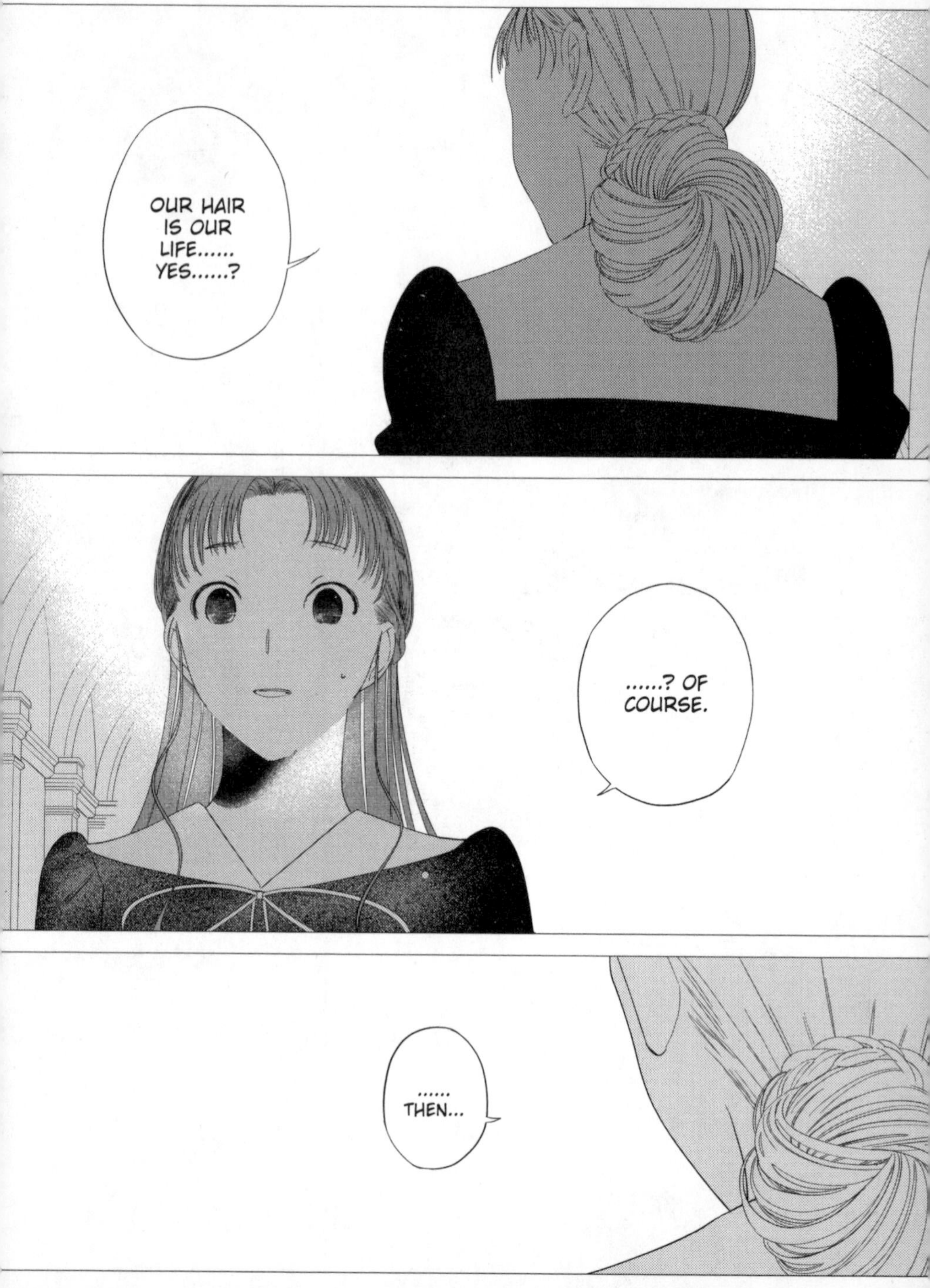
OUR HAIR IS OUR LIFE...... YES......?
......? OF COURSE.
...... THEN...

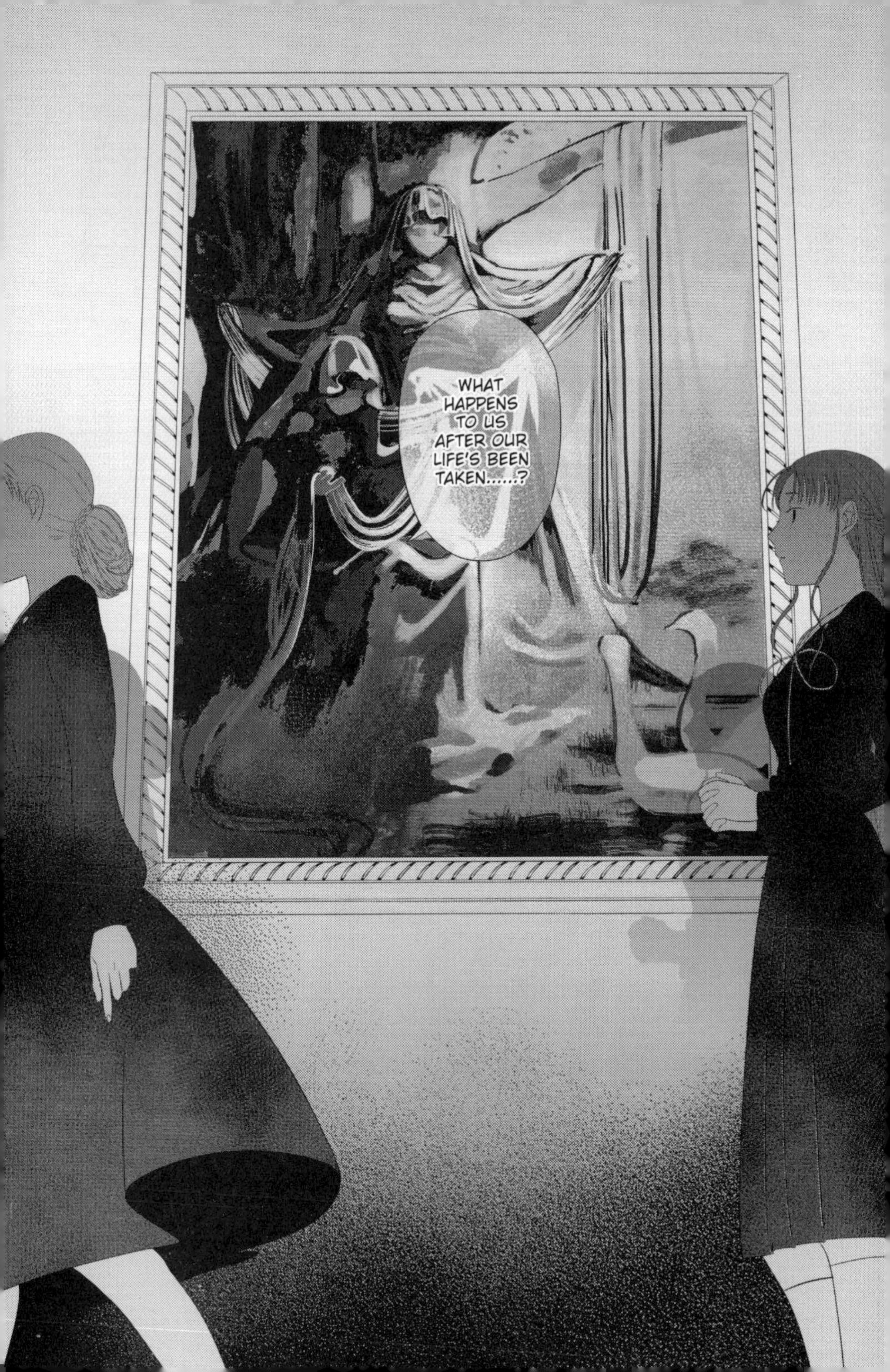
WHAT HAPPENS TO US AFTER OUR LIFE'S BEEN TAKEN......?

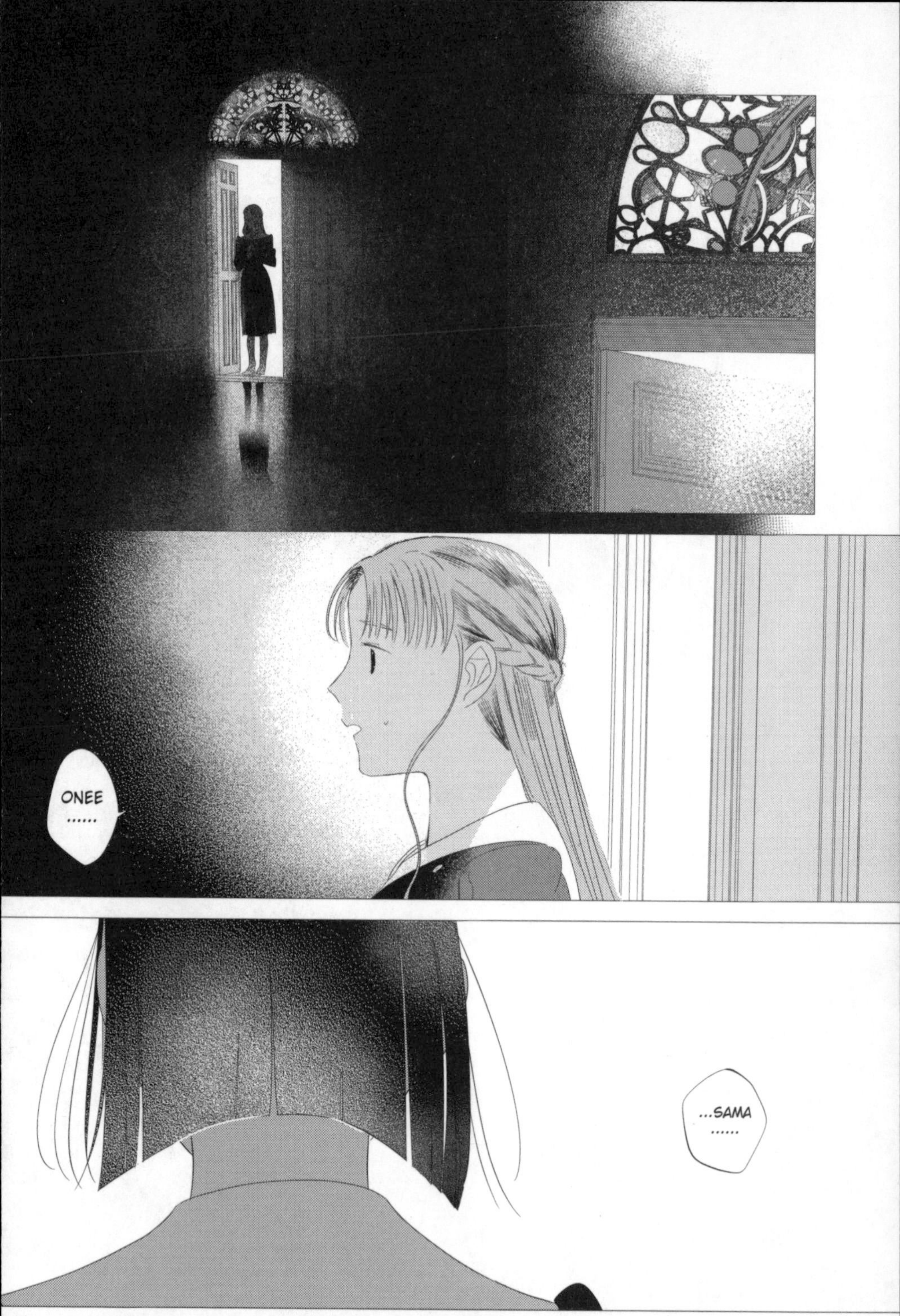
ONEE ......
...SAMA ......

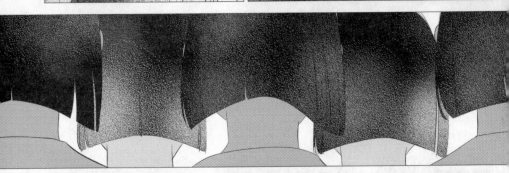

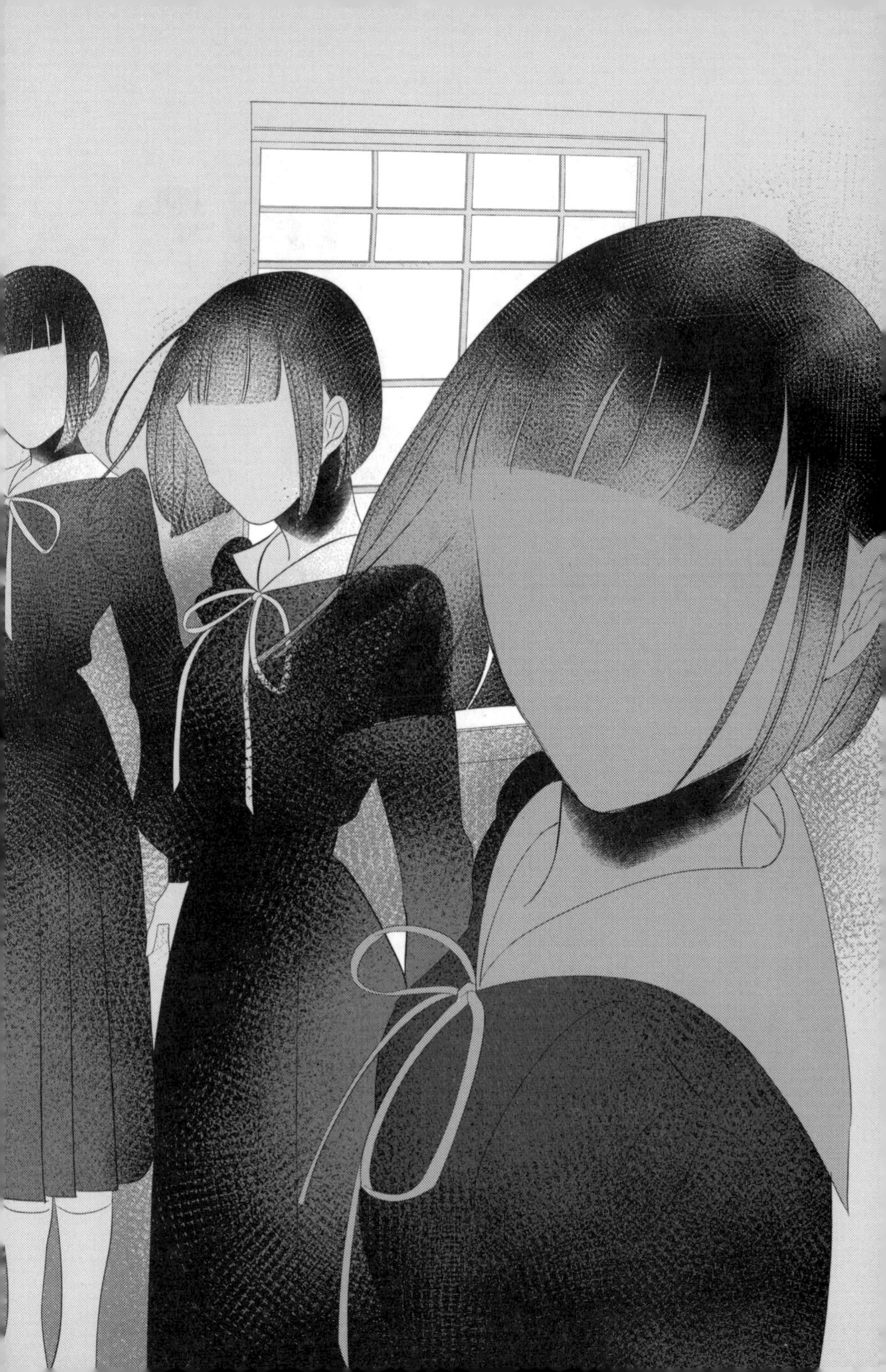

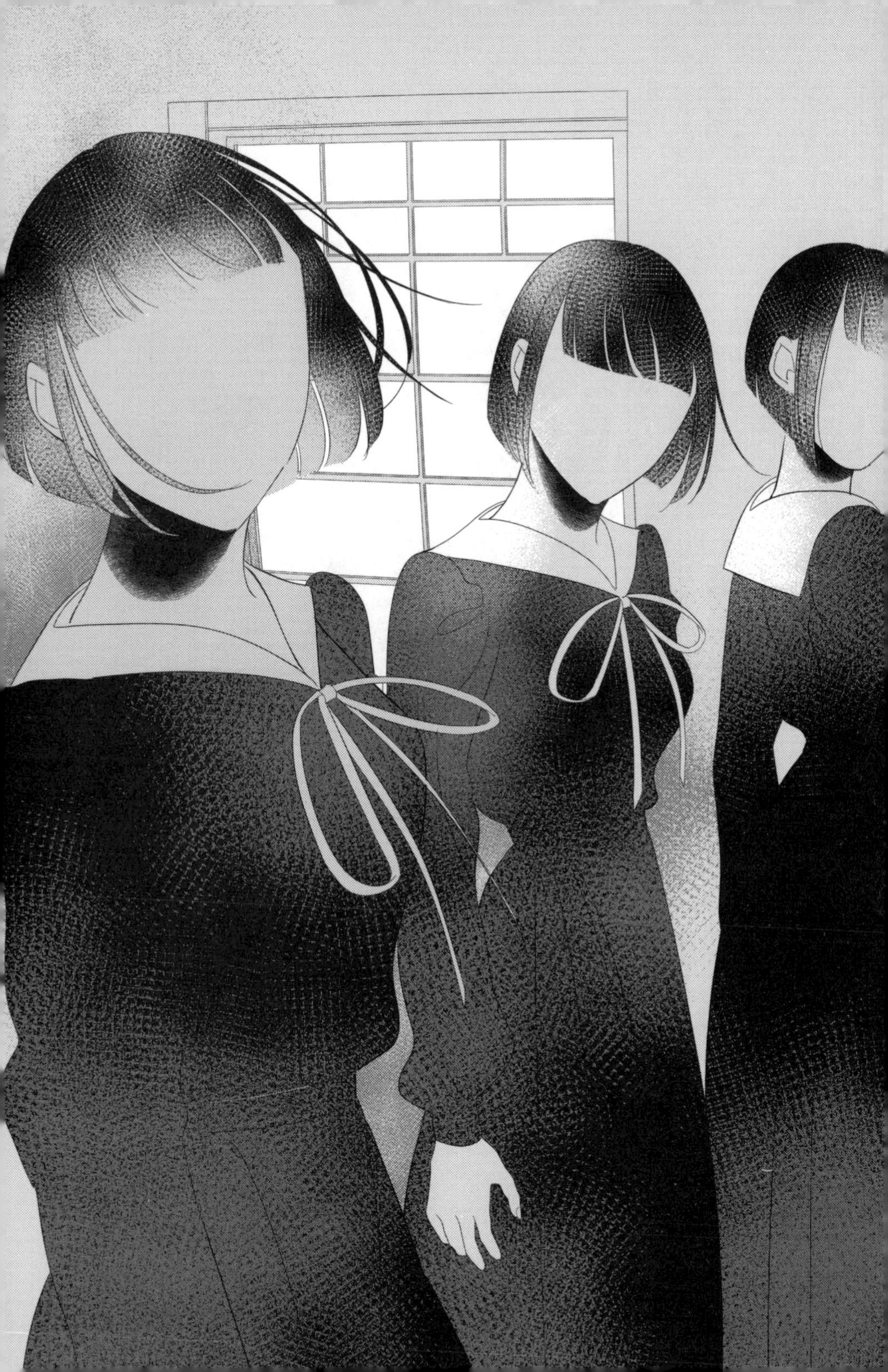

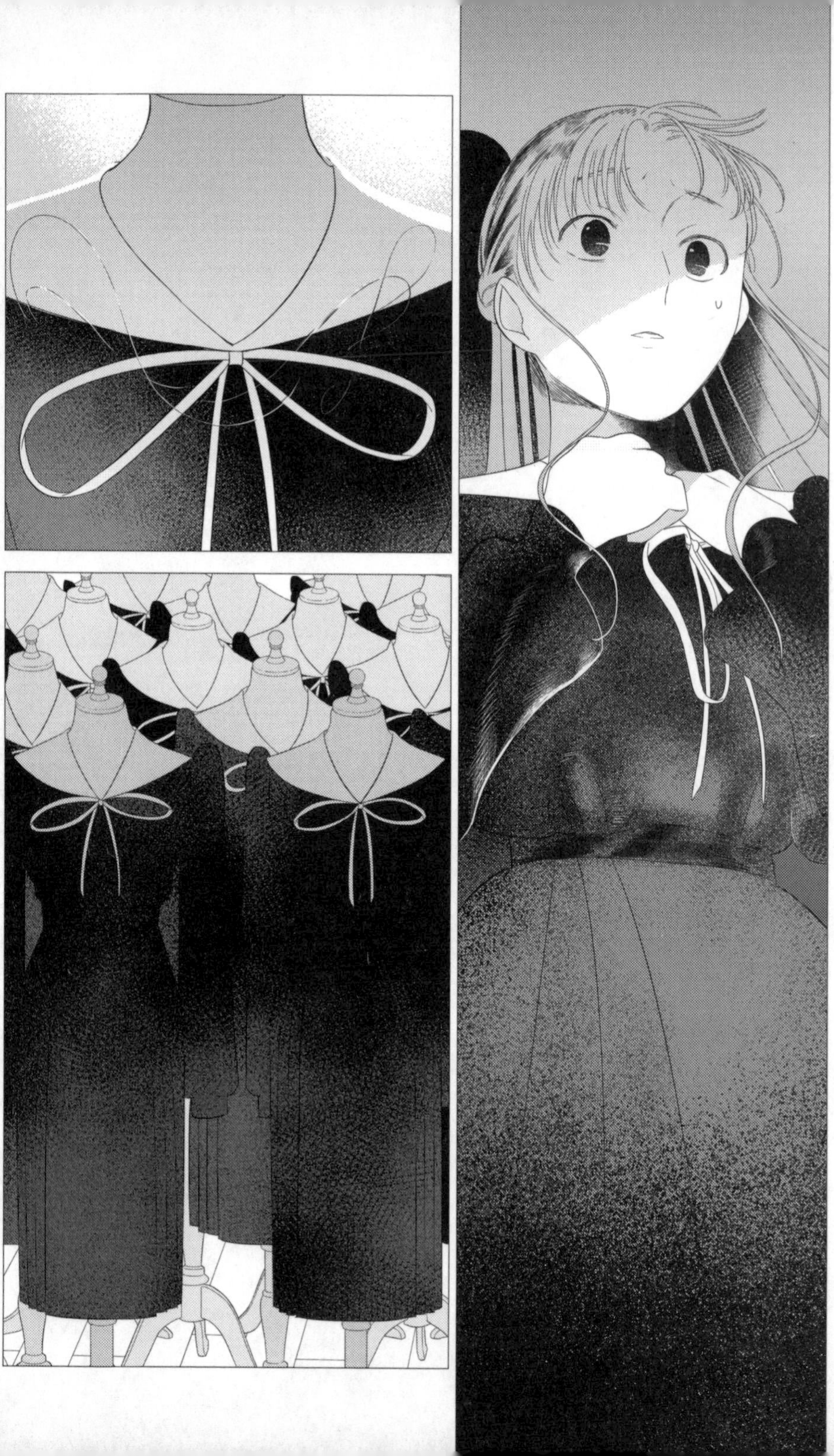

Cocoon
Entwined

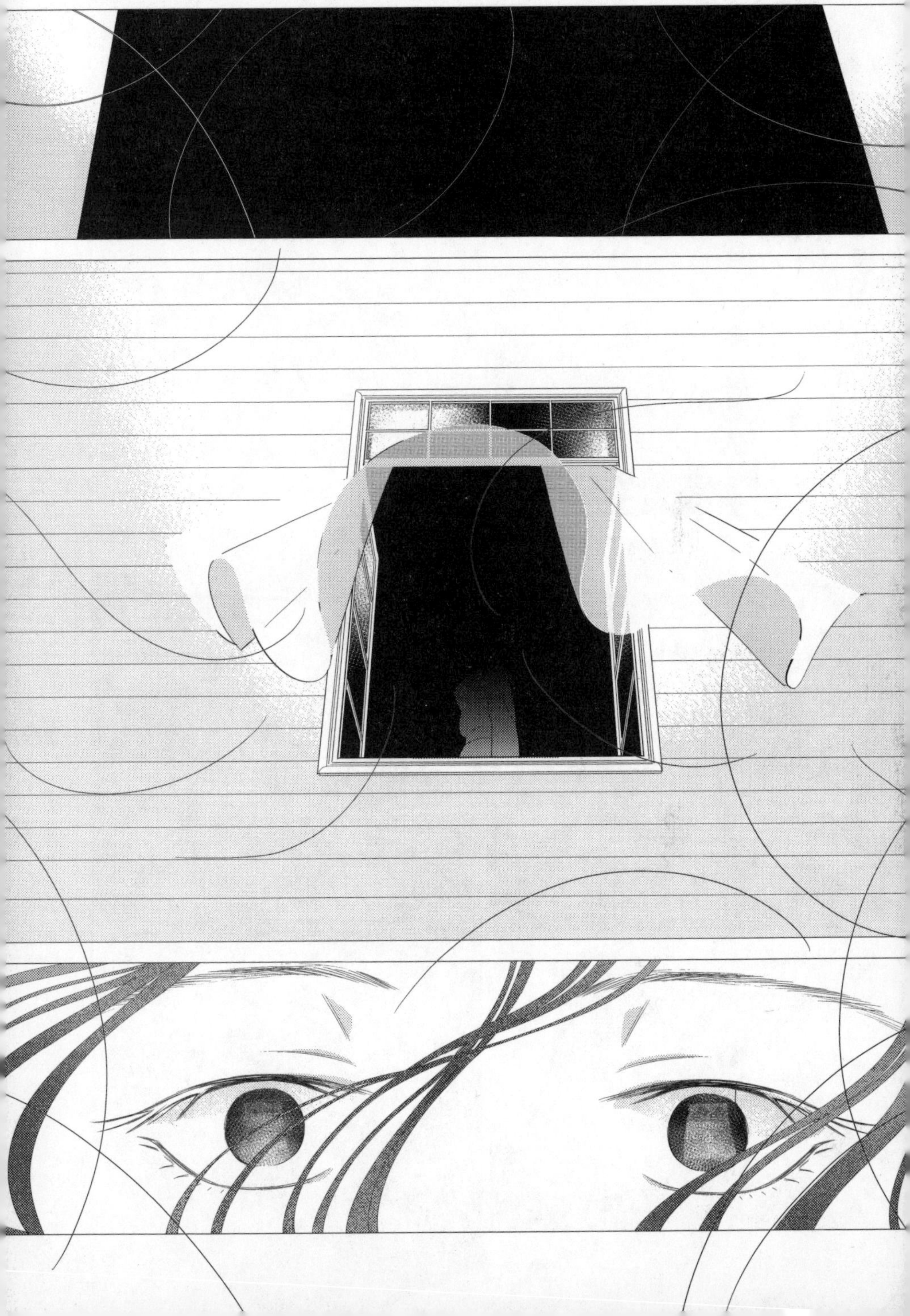

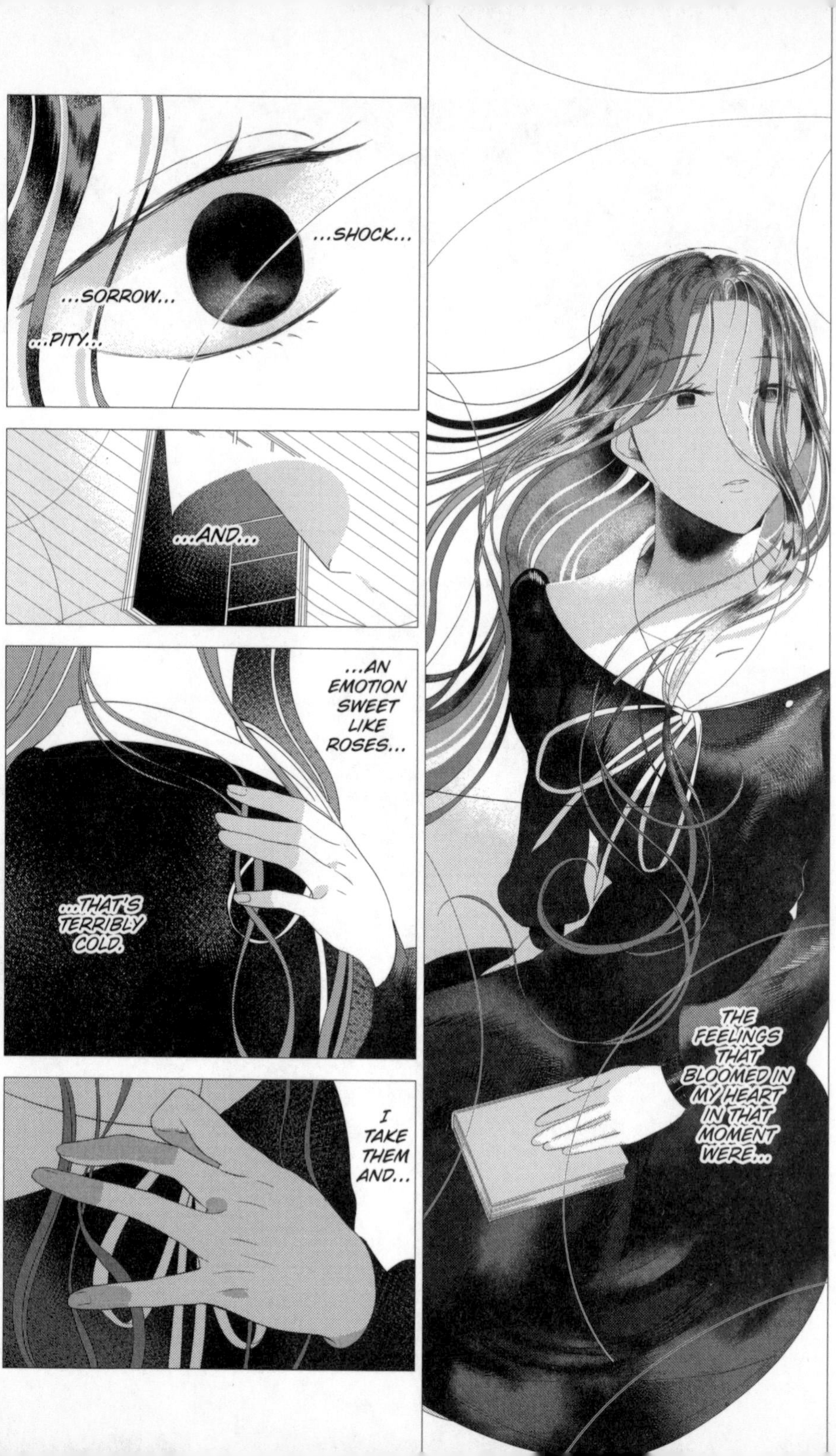
THE FEELINGS THAT BLOOMED IN MY HEART IN THAT MOMENT WERE...
...SHOCK...
...SORROW...
...PITY...
...AND...
...AN EMOTION SWEET LIKE ROSES...
...THAT'S TERRIBLY COLD.
I TAKE THEM AND...

Chapter 26

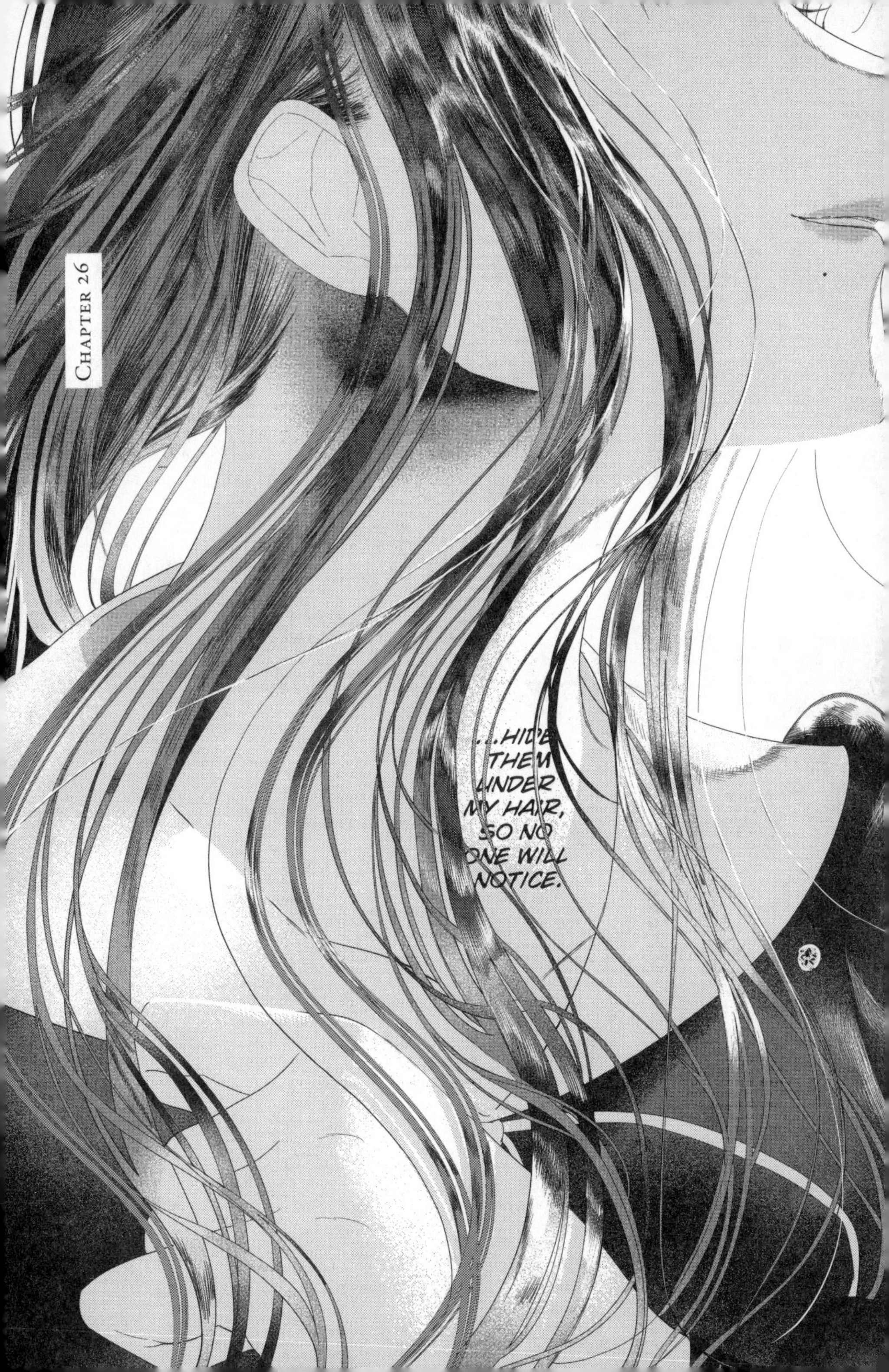
...HIDE THEM UNDER MY HAIR, SO NO ONE WILL NOTICE.

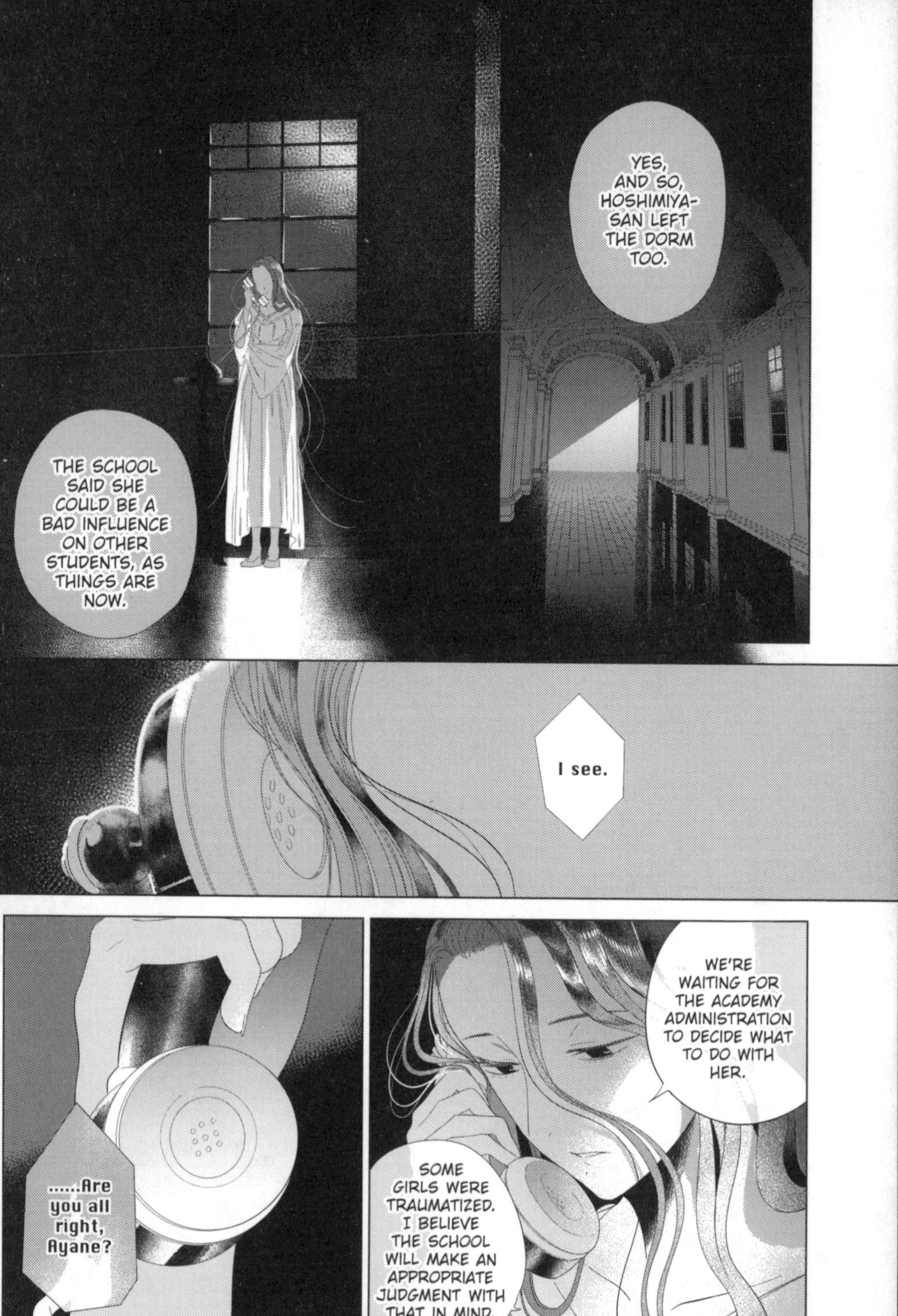
YES, AND SO, HOSHIMIYA-SAN LEFT THE DORM TOO.
THE SCHOOL SAID SHE COULD BE A BAD INFLUENCE ON OTHER STUDENTS, AS THINGS ARE NOW.
I see.
WE'RE WAITING FOR THE ACADEMY ADMINISTRATION TO DECIDE WHAT TO DO WITH HER.
SOME GIRLS WERE TRAUMATIZED. I BELIEVE THE SCHOOL WILL MAKE AN APPROPRIATE JUDGMENT WITH THAT IN MIND.
......Are you all right, Ayane?

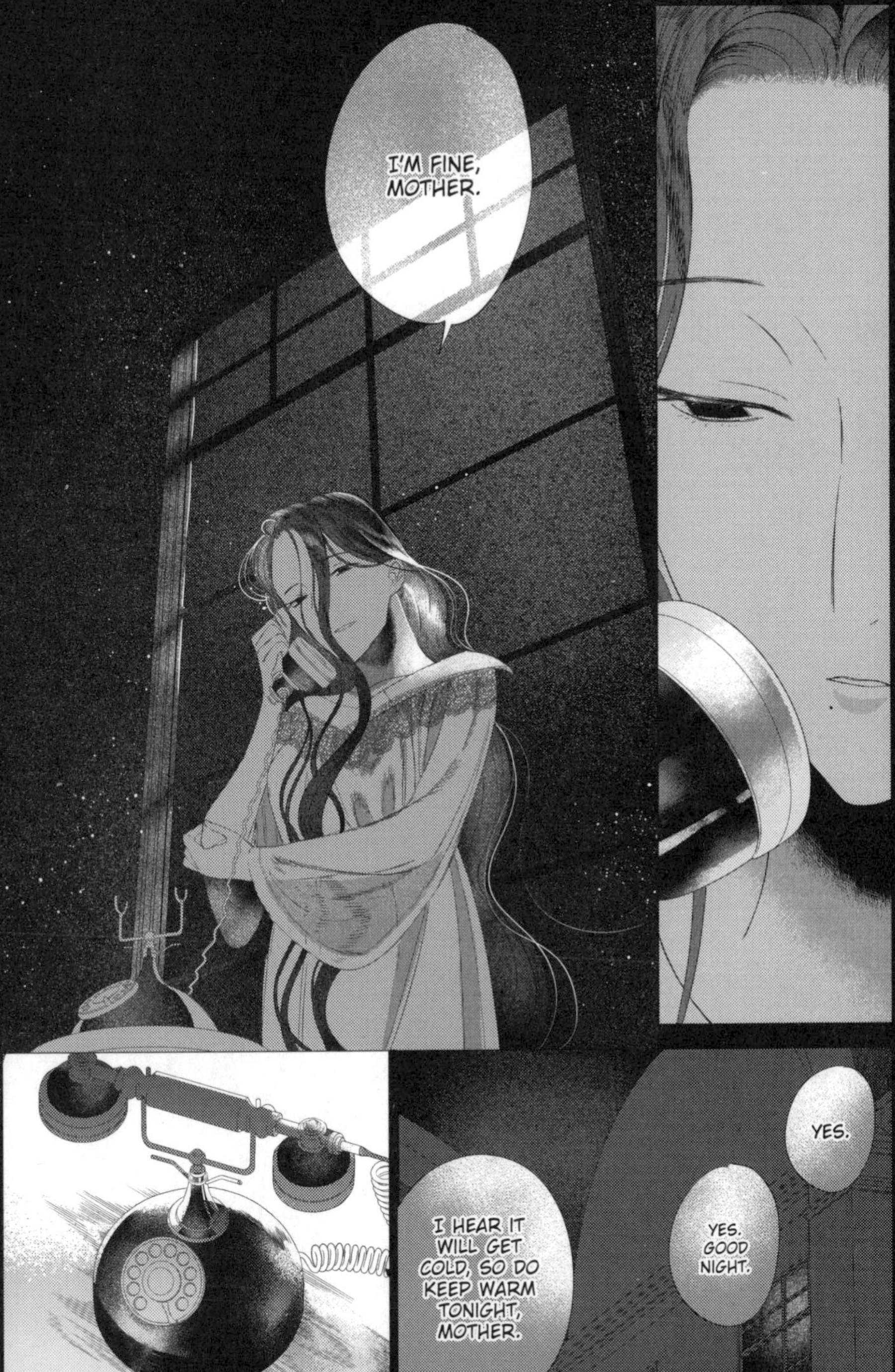
I'M FINE, MOTHER.
YES.
YES. GOOD NIGHT.
I HEAR IT WILL GET COLD, SO DO KEEP WARM TONIGHT, MOTHER.

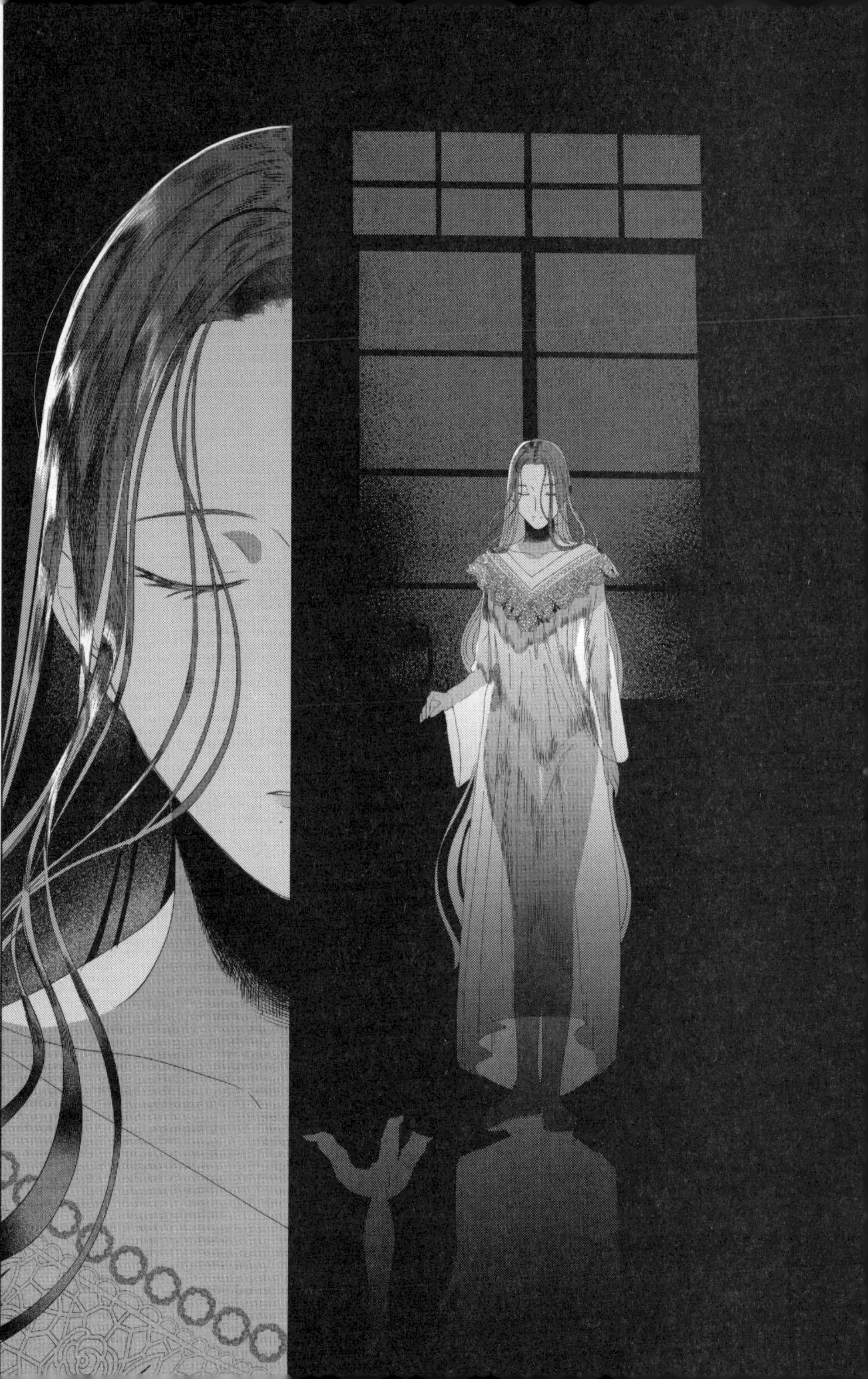

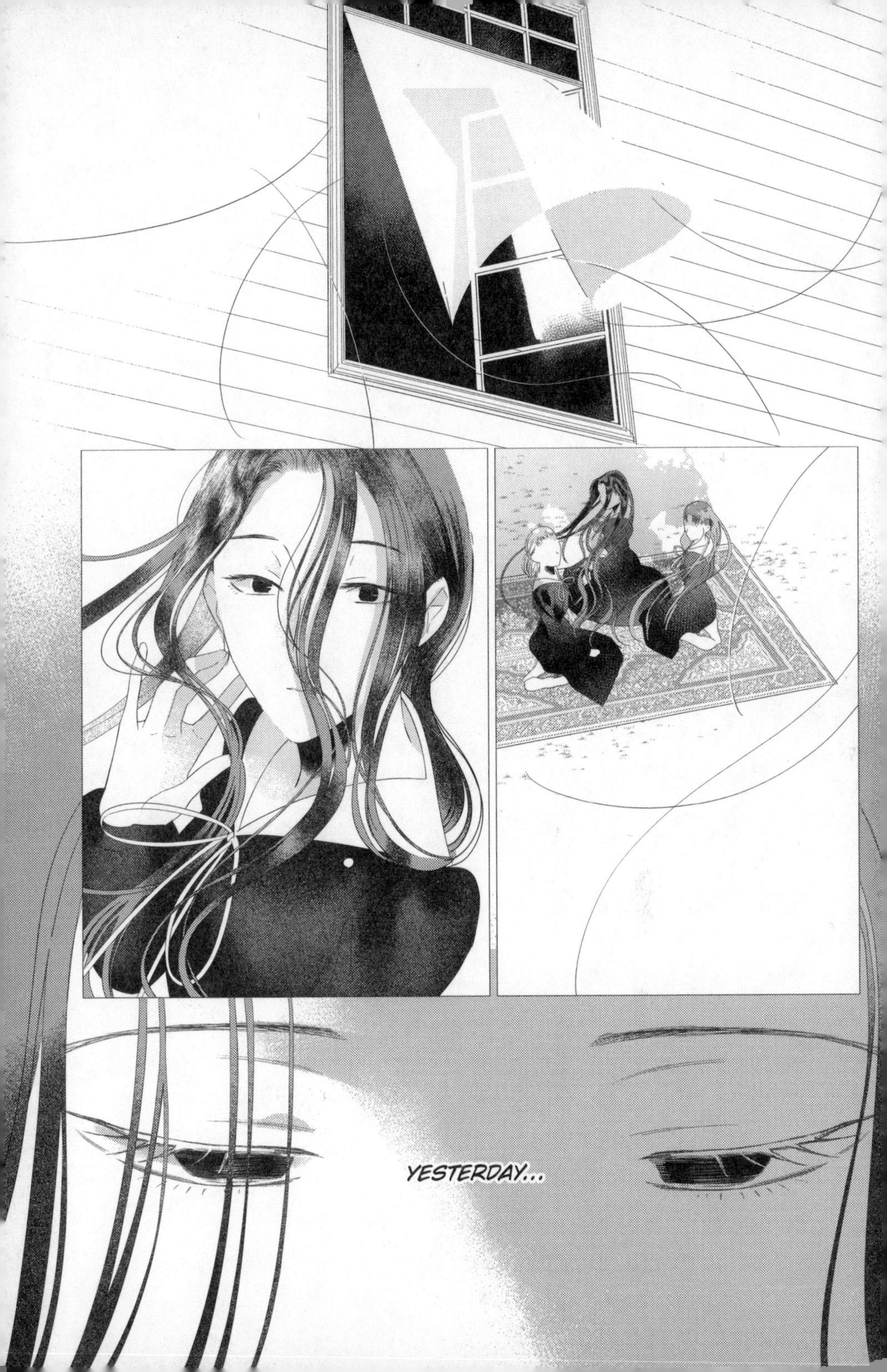
YESTERDAY...

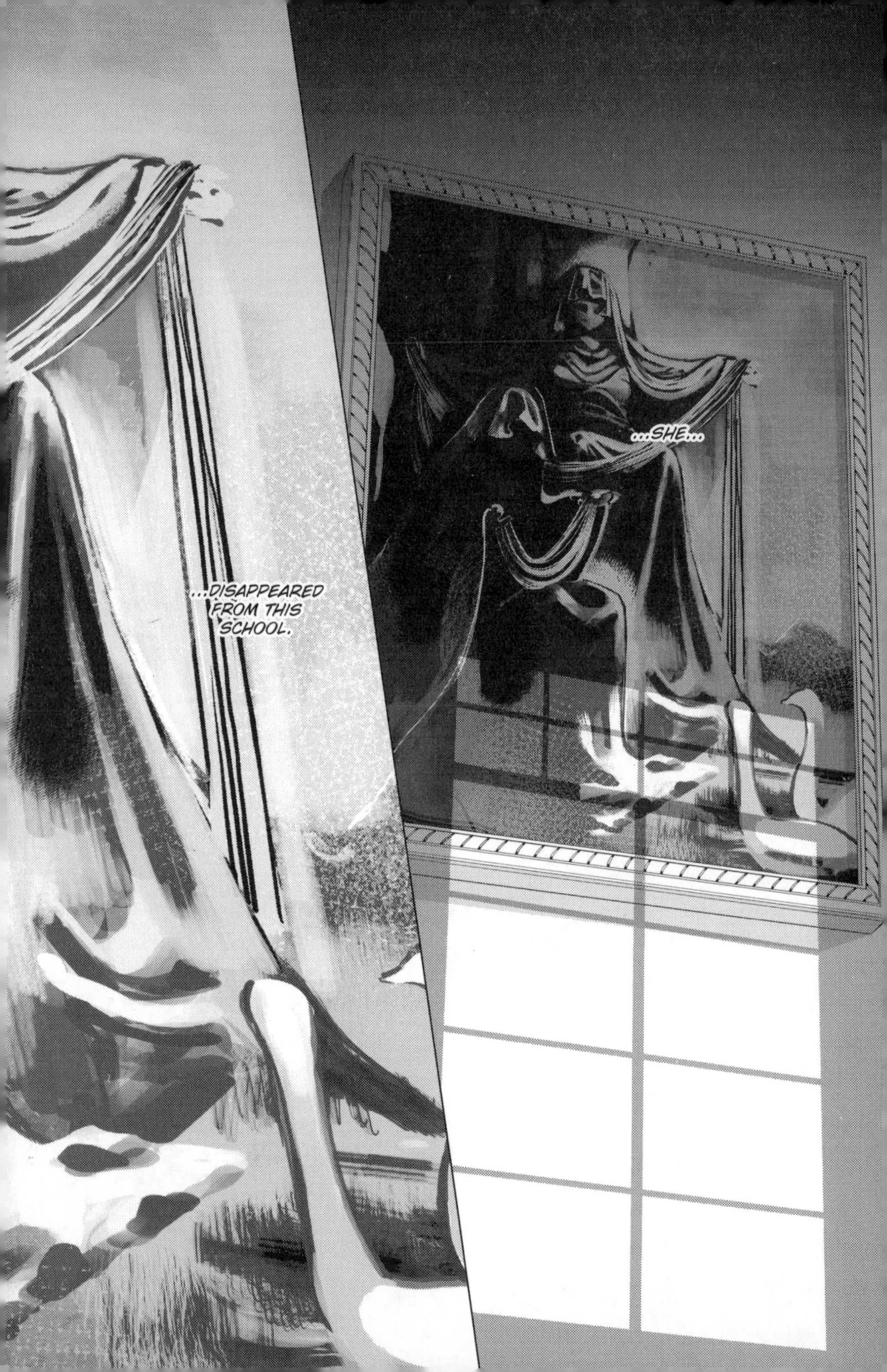
...SHE...
...DISAPPEARED FROM THIS SCHOOL.

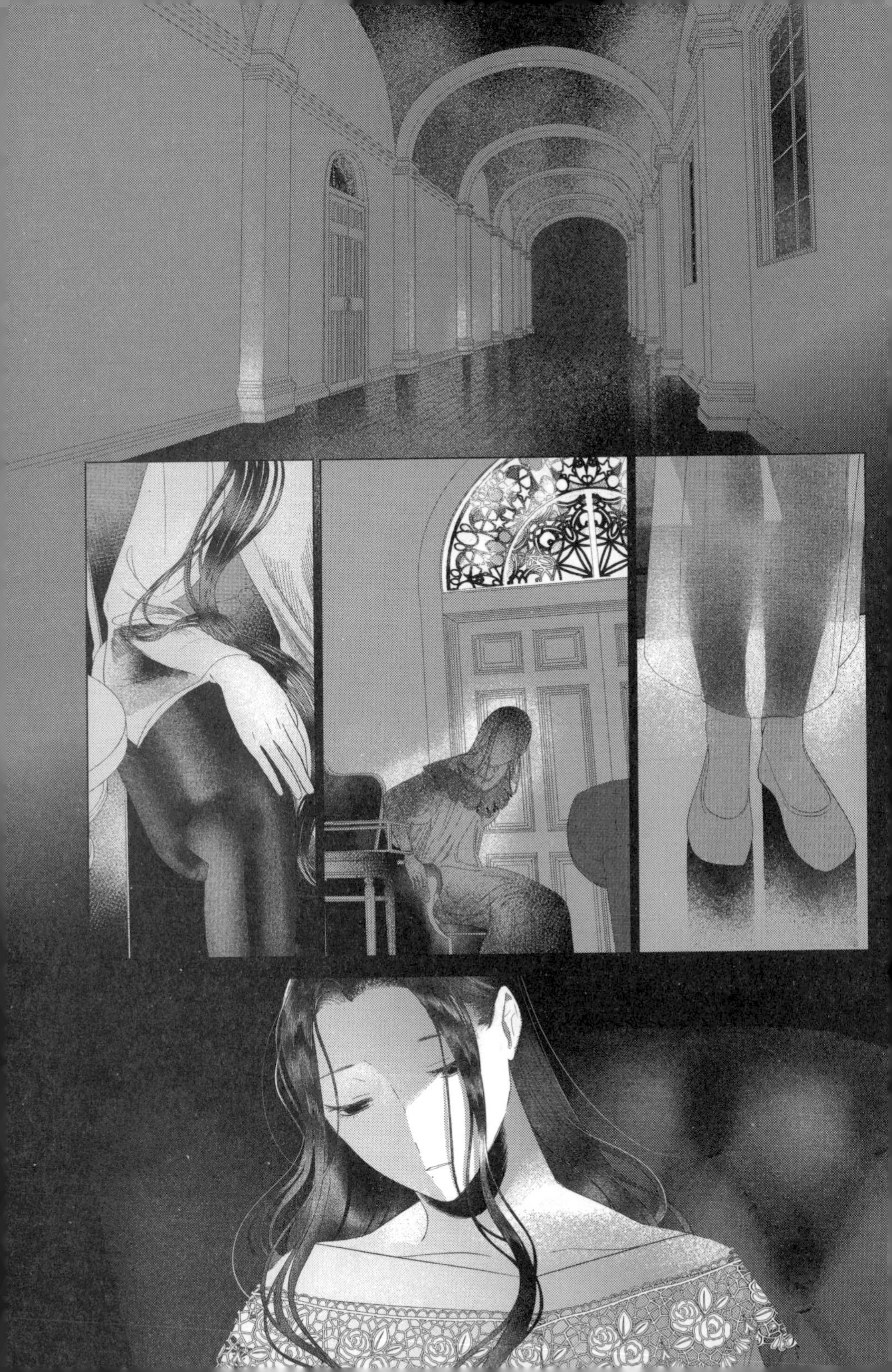

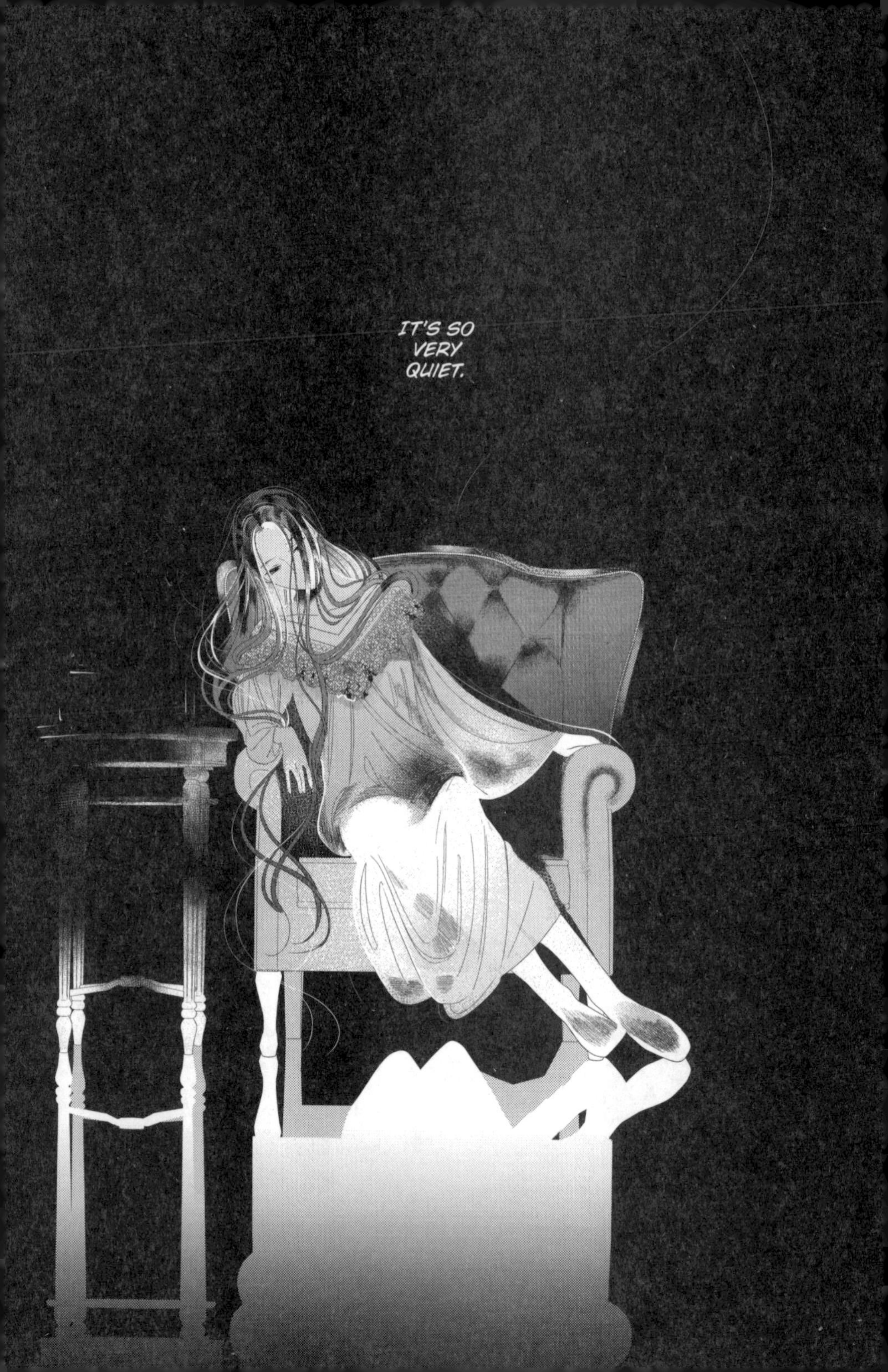
IT'S SO VERY QUIET.

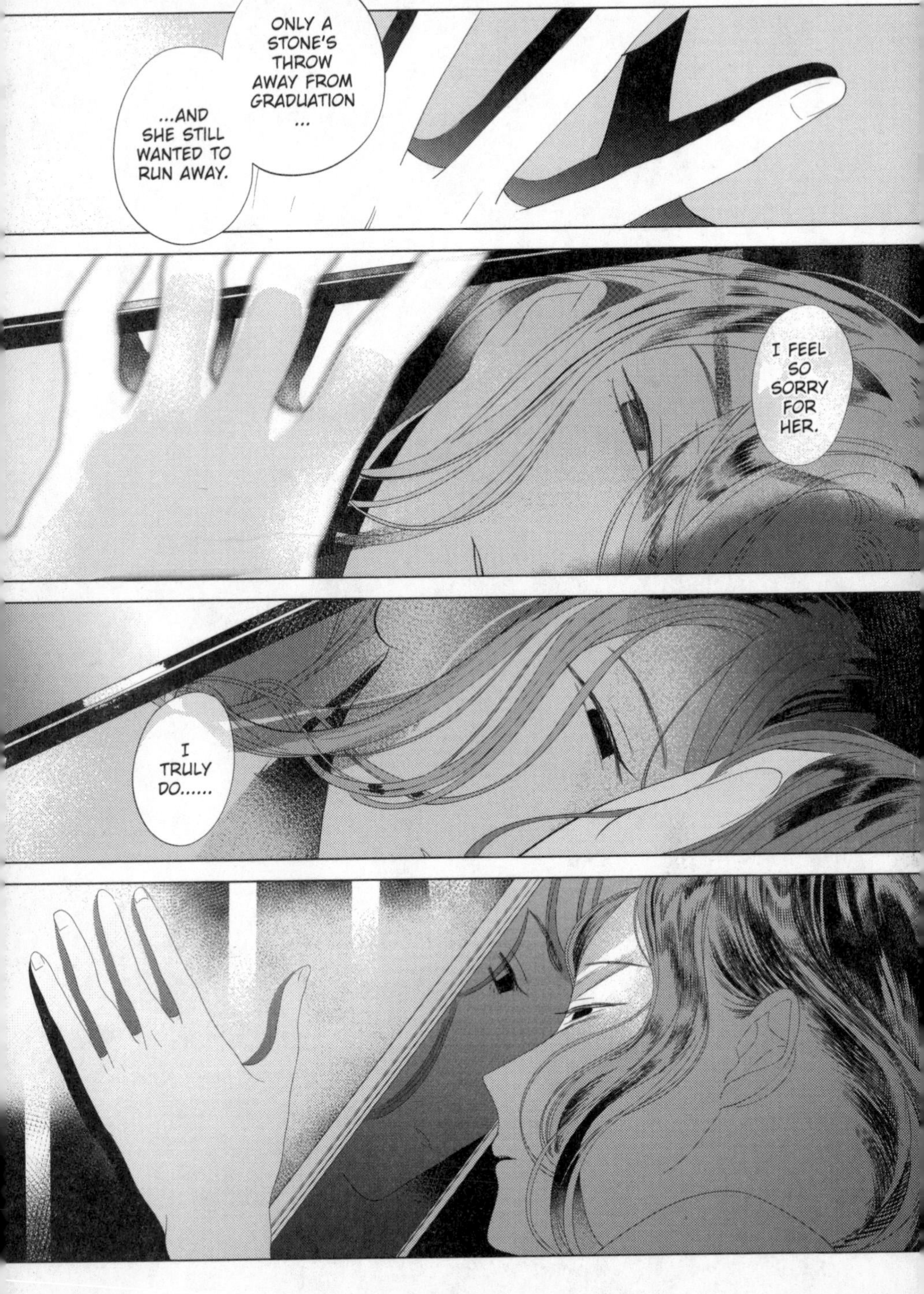
ONLY A STONE'S THROW AWAY FROM GRADUATION ...
...AND SHE STILL WANTED TO RUN AWAY.
I FEEL SO SORRY FOR HER.
I TRULY DO......

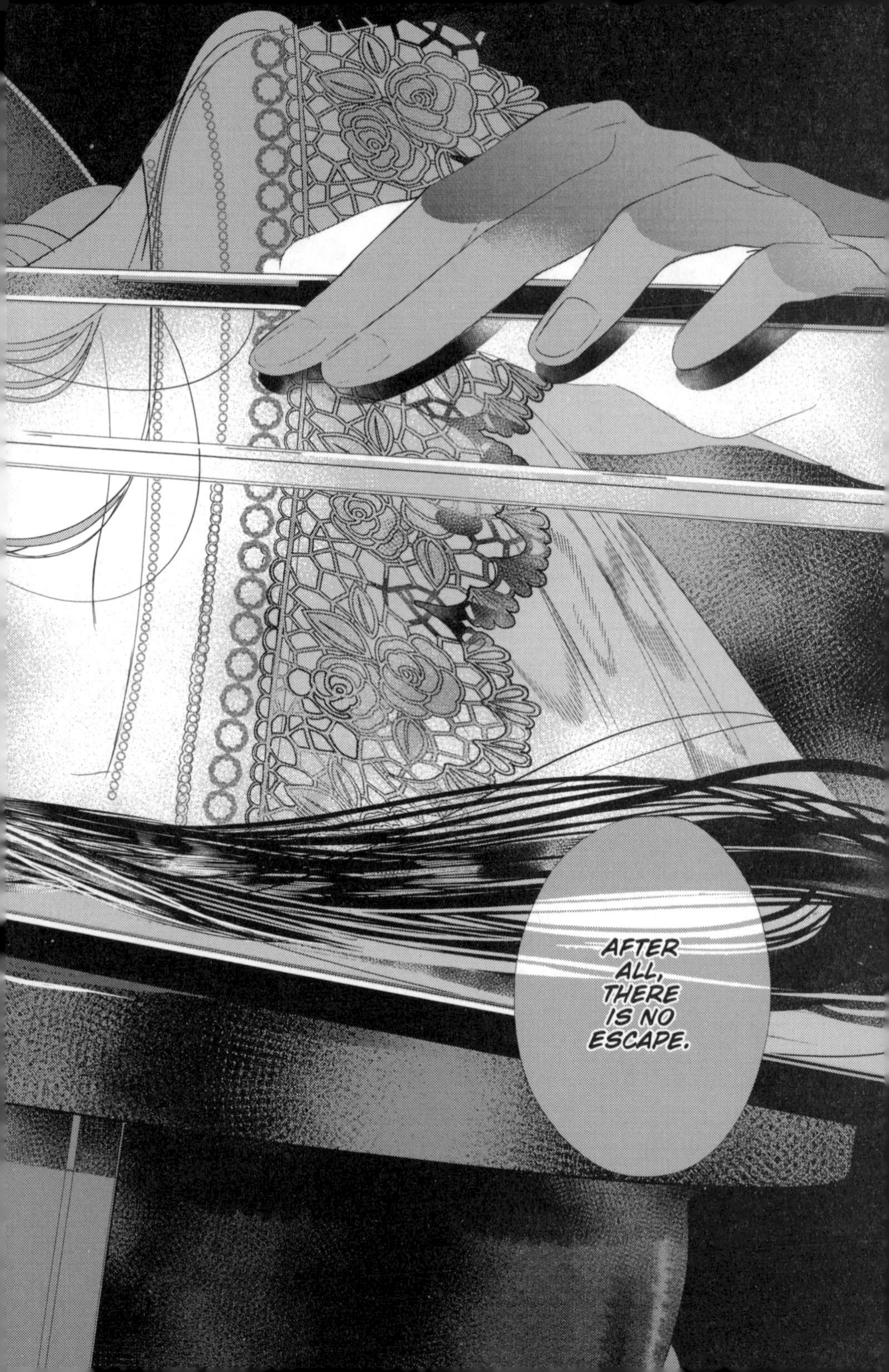
AFTER ALL, THERE IS NO ESCAPE.

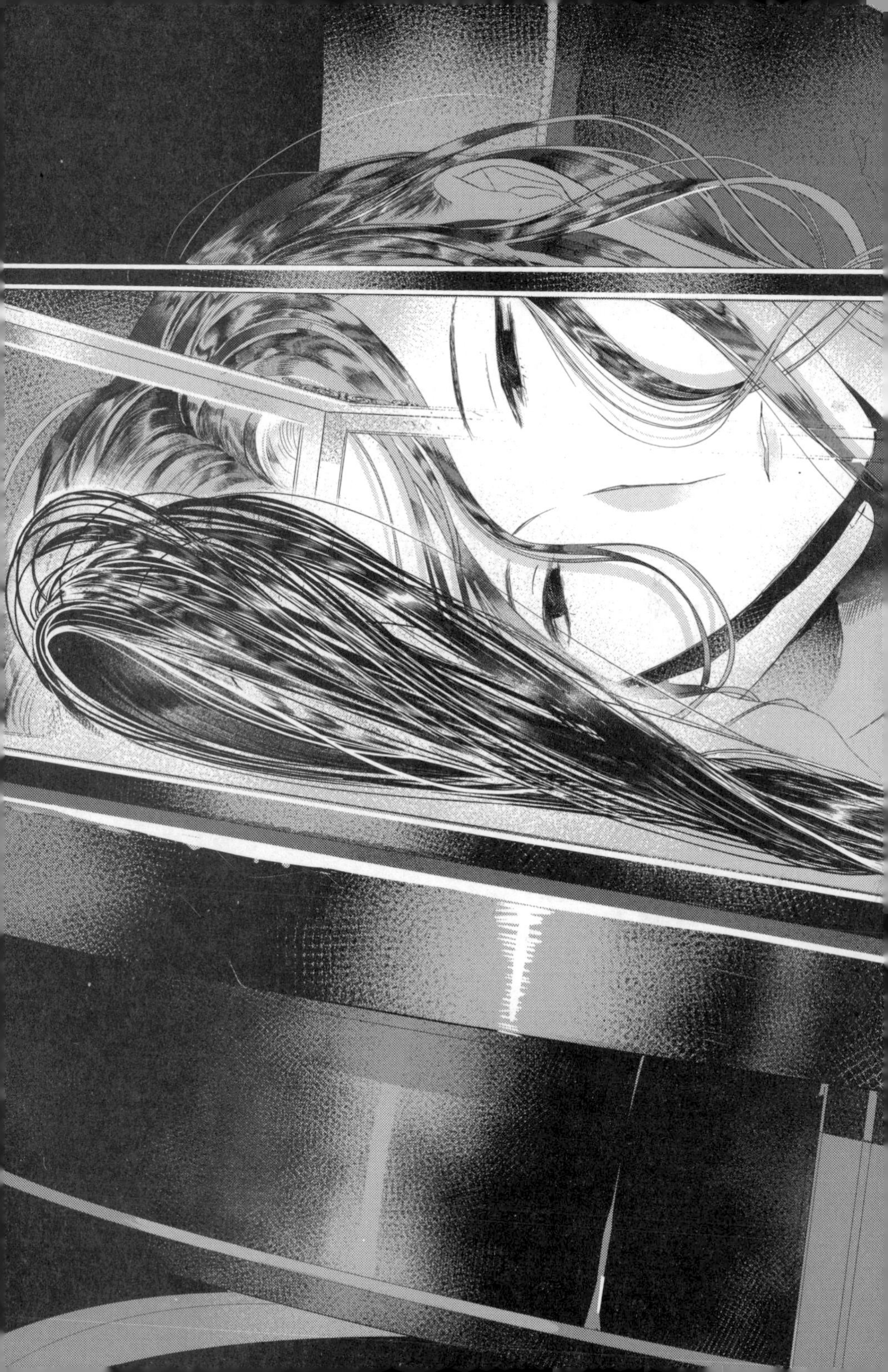

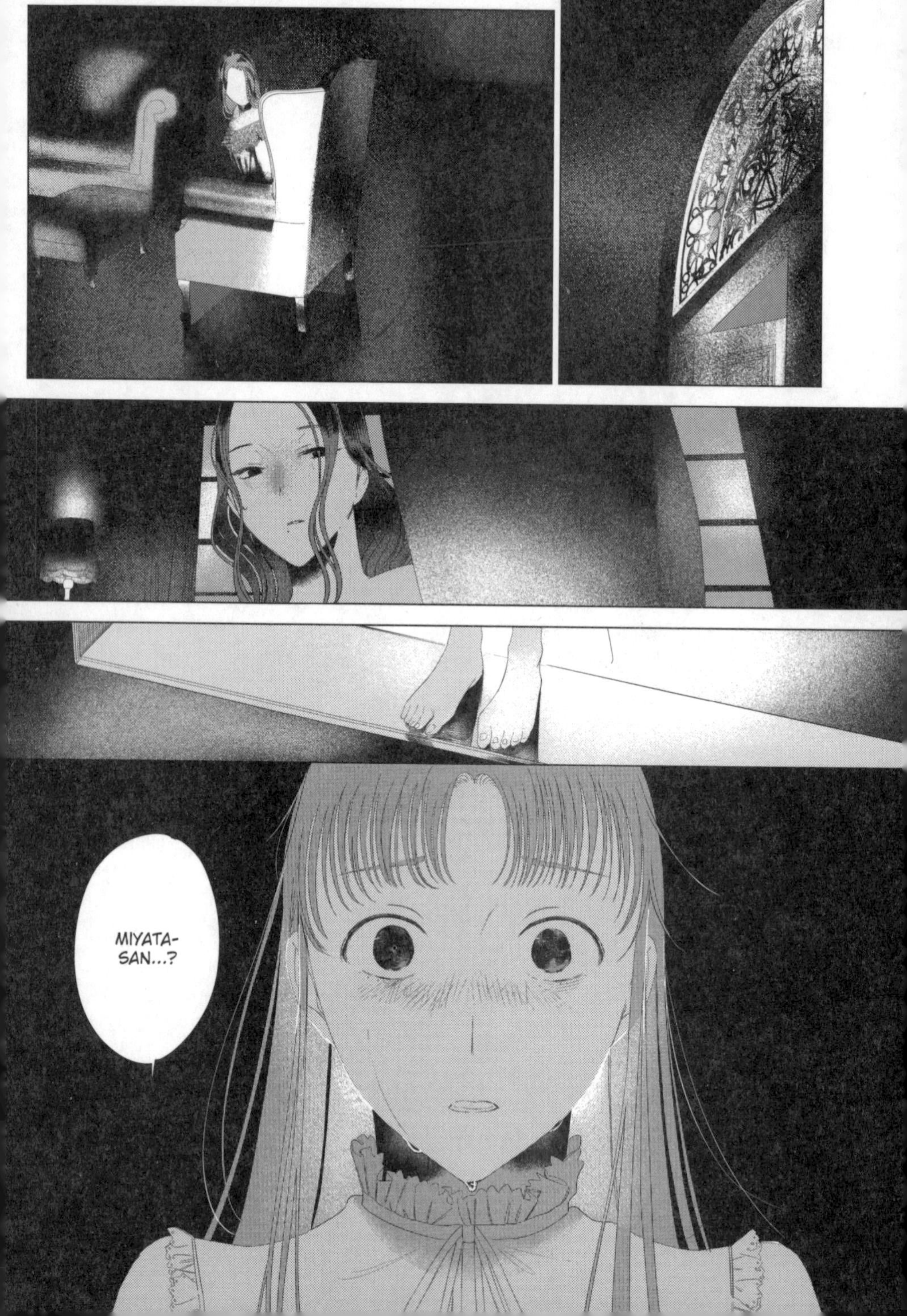
MIYATA-SAN...?

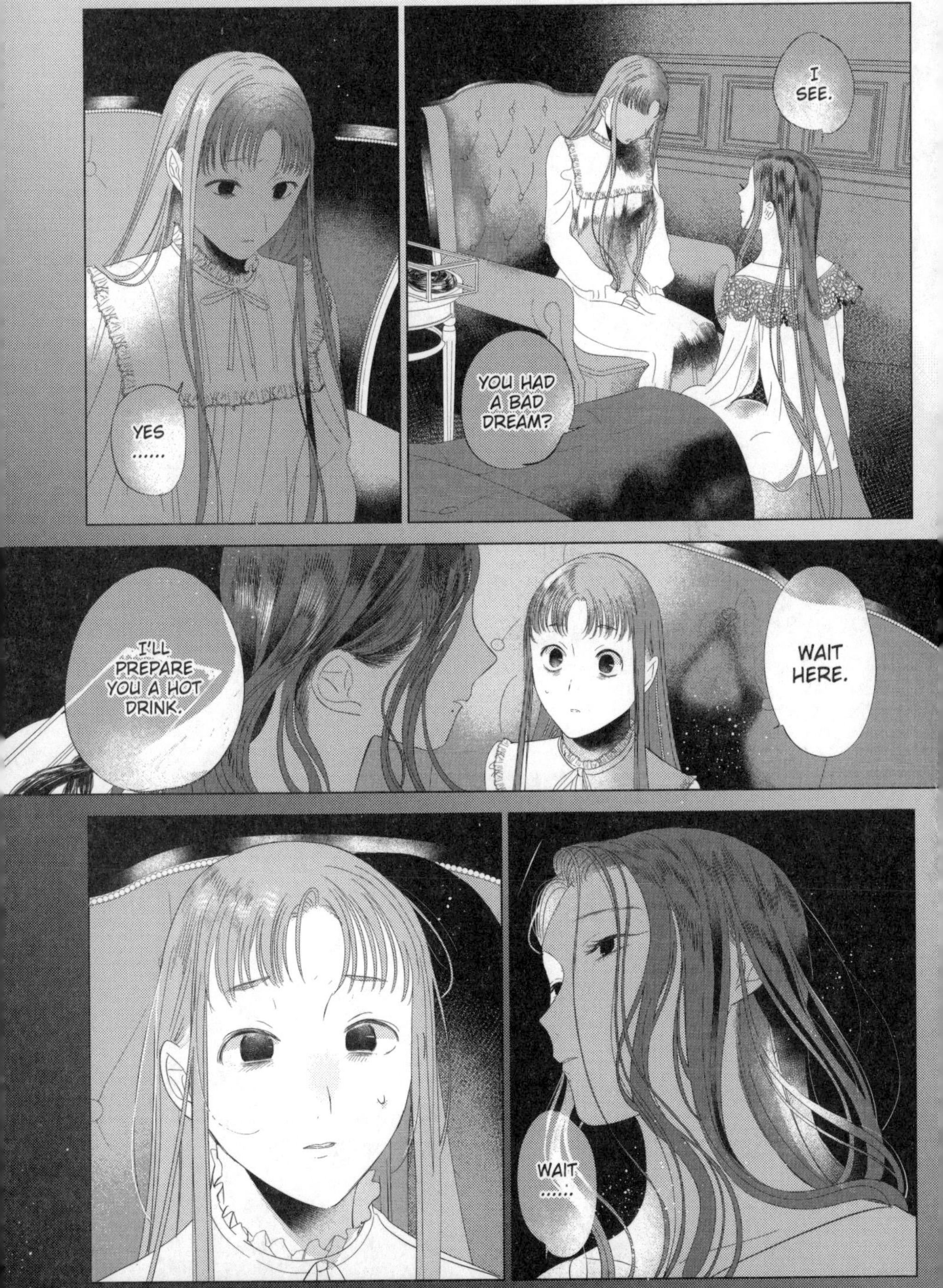
I SEE.
YOU HAD A BAD DREAM?
YES ......
I'LL PREPARE YOU A HOT DRINK.
WAIT HERE.
WAIT ......

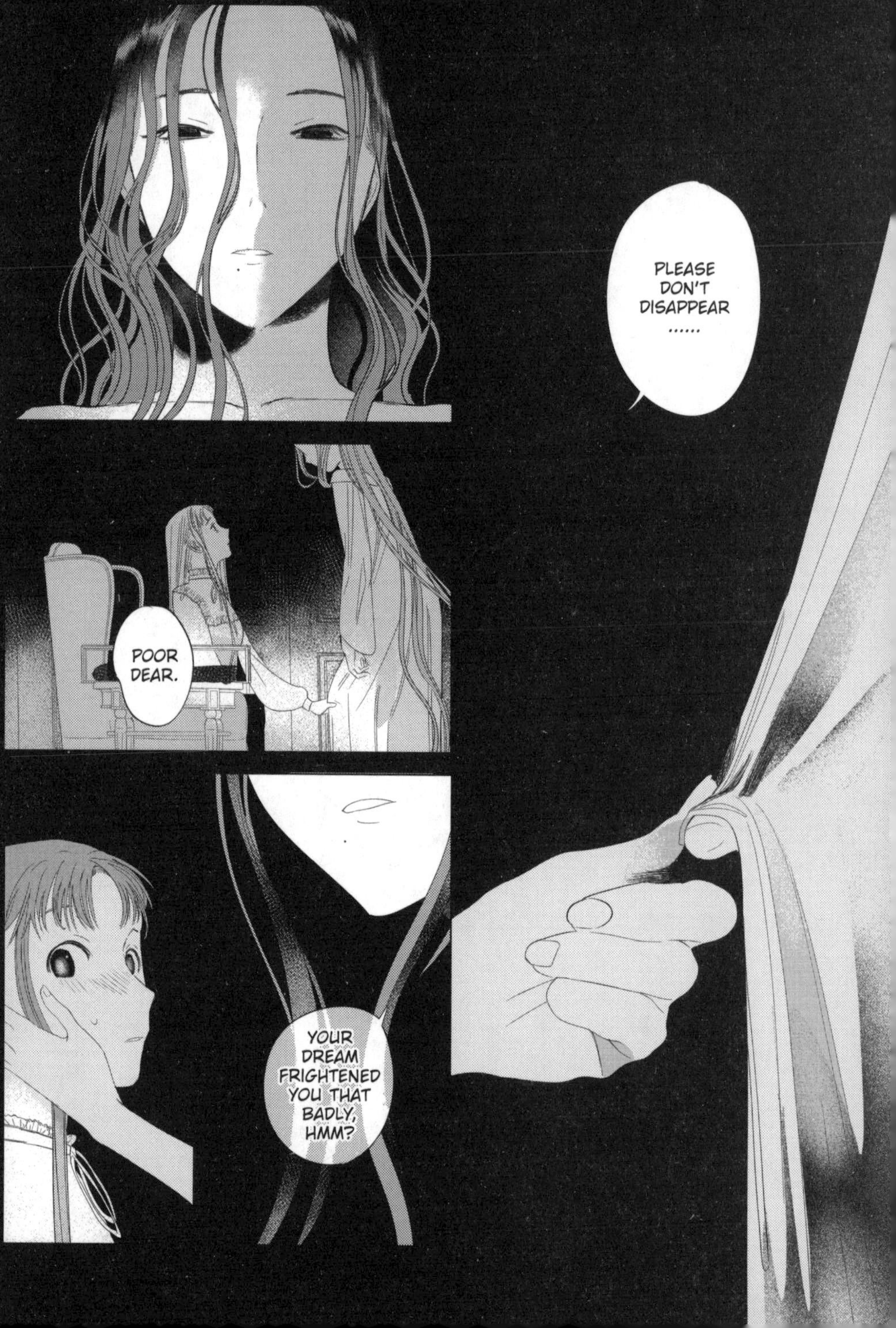
PLEASE DON'T DISAPPEAR ......
POOR DEAR.
YOUR DREAM FRIGHTENED YOU THAT BADLY, HMM?

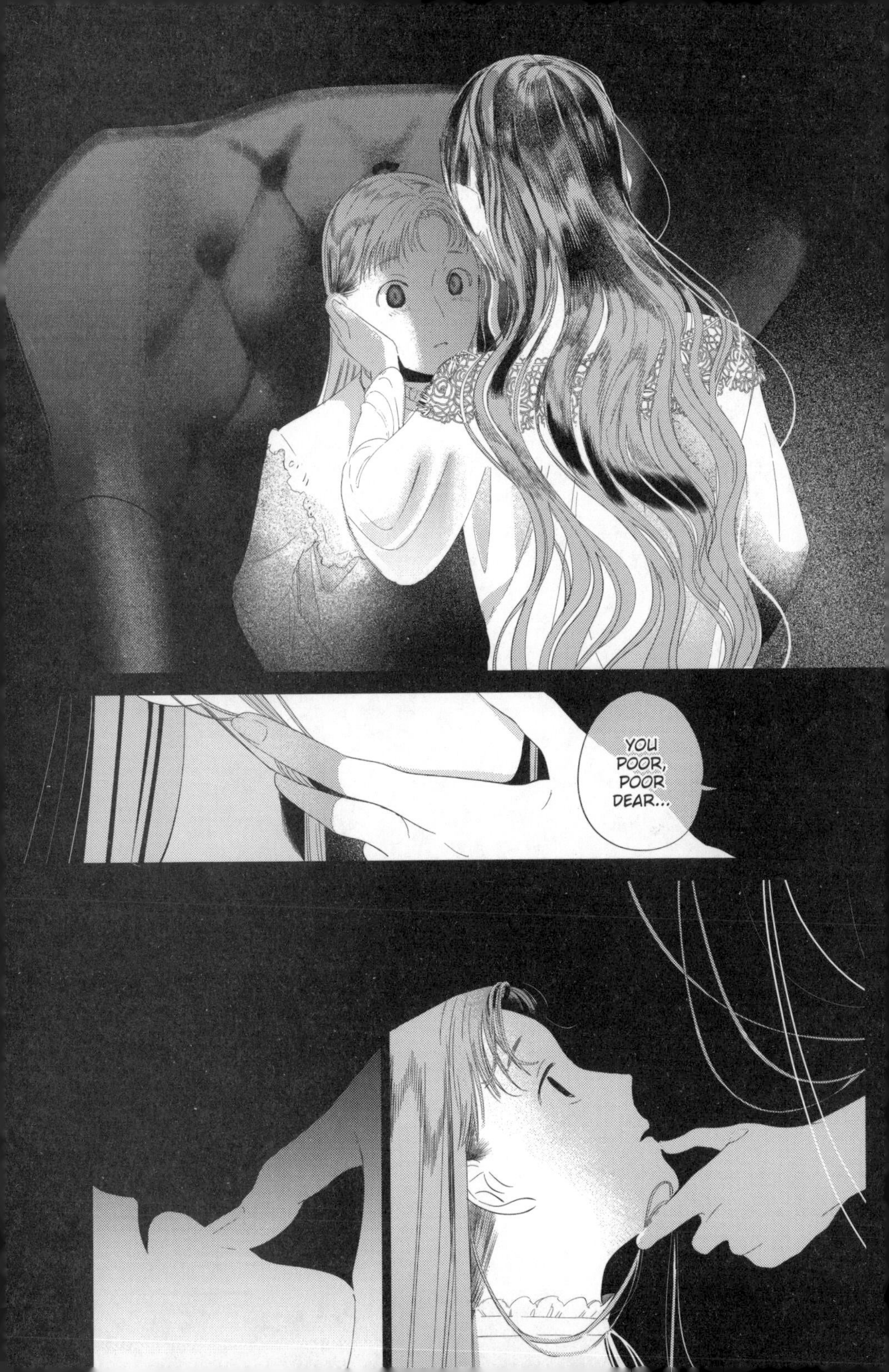
YOU POOR, POOR DEAR...

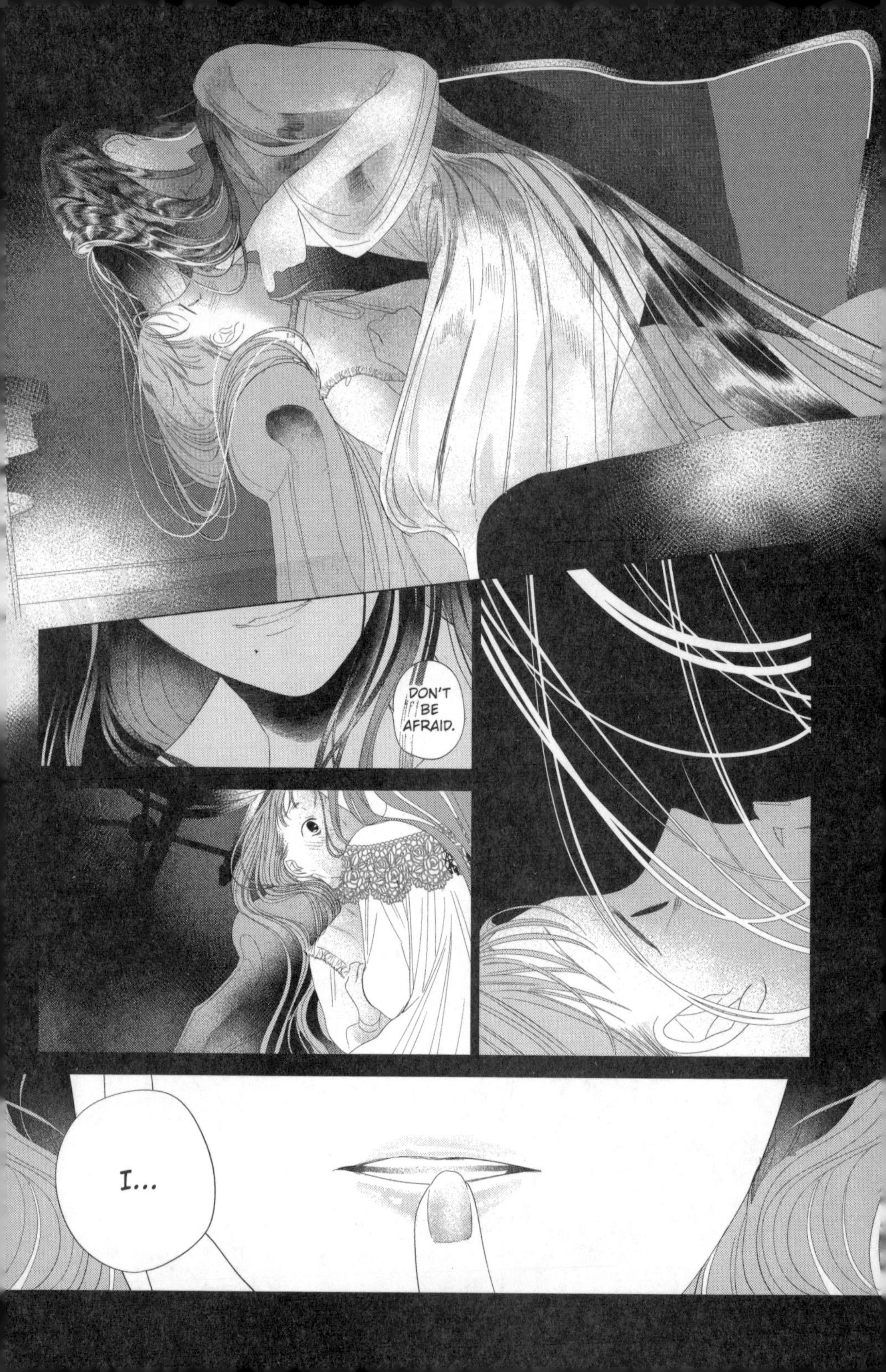
DON'T BE AFRAID.
I...

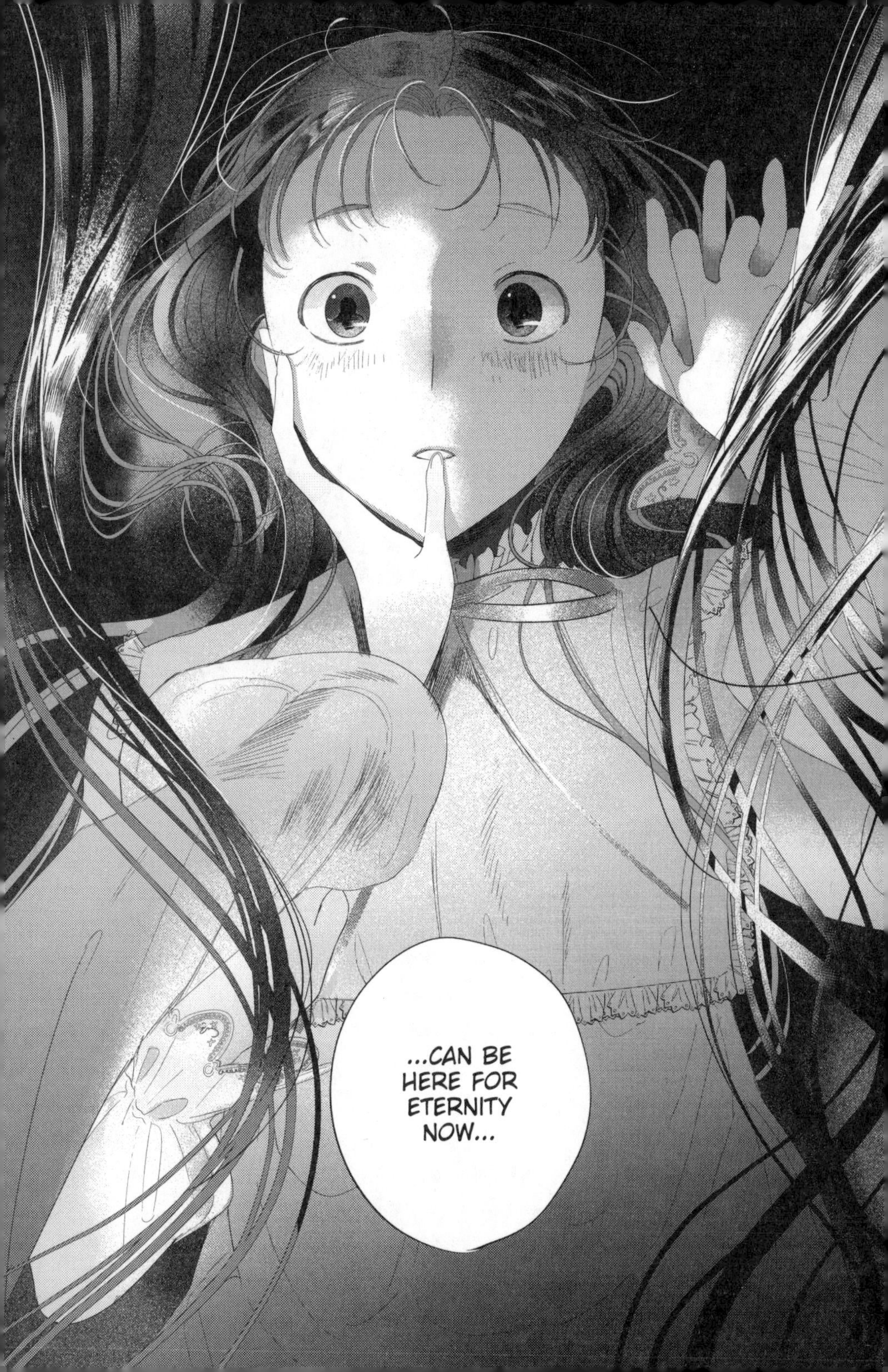
...CAN BE HERE FOR ETERNITY NOW...

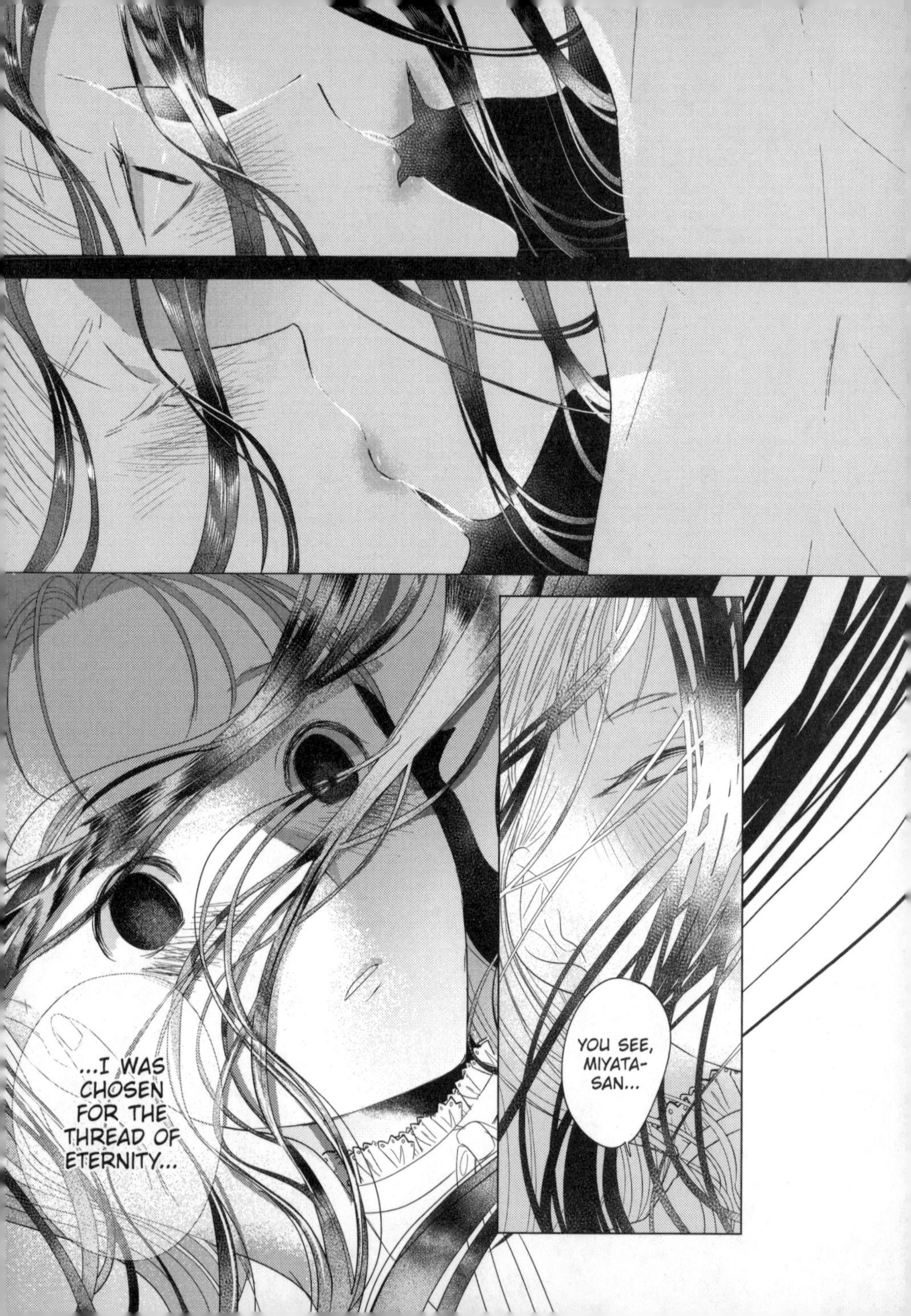
YOU SEE, MIYATA-SAN...
...I WAS CHOSEN FOR THE THREAD OF ETERNITY...

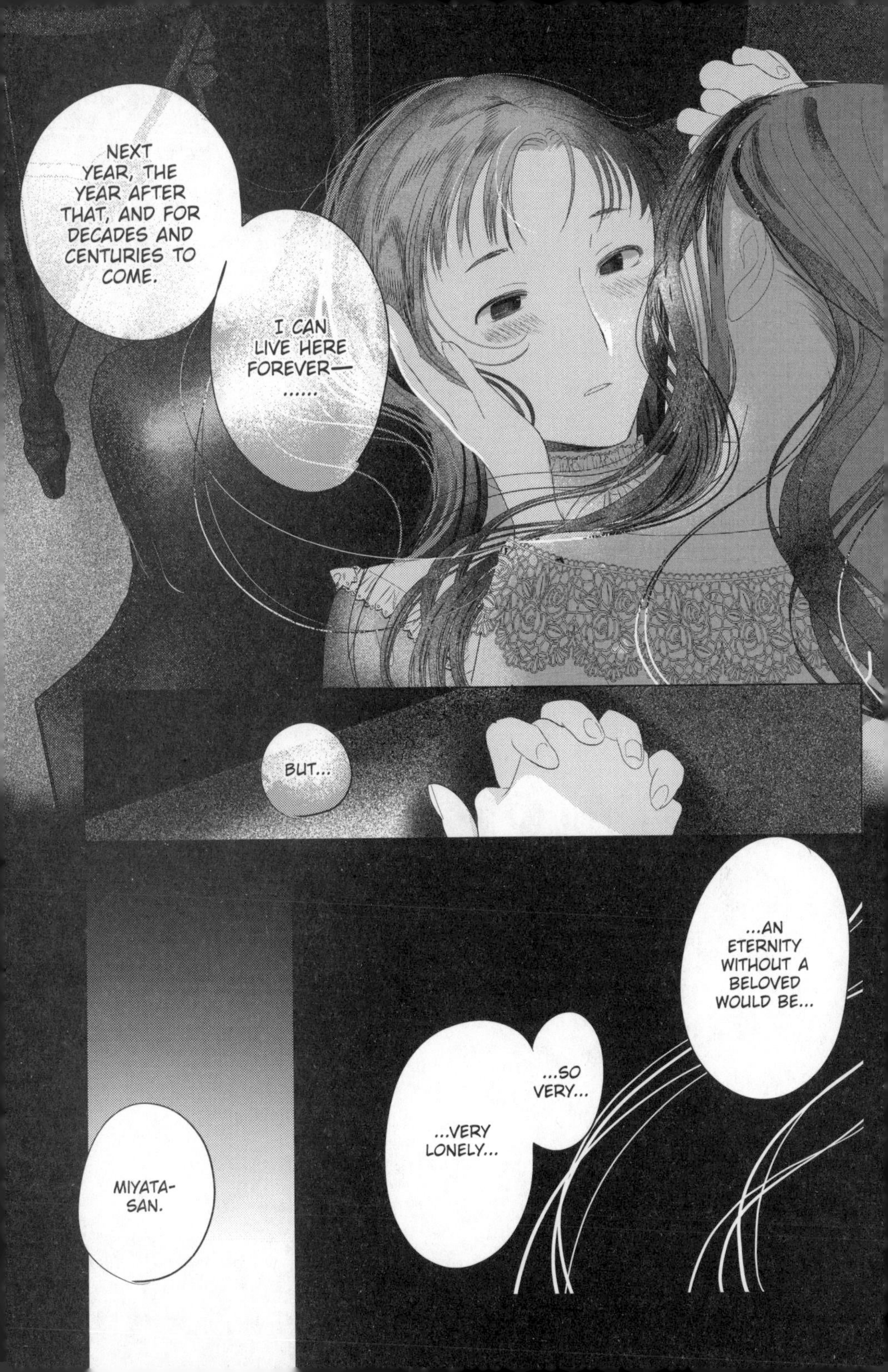
NEXT YEAR, THE YEAR AFTER THAT, AND FOR DECADES AND CENTURIES TO COME.
I CAN LIVE HERE FOREVER— ......
BUT...
...AN ETERNITY WITHOUT A BELOVED WOULD BE...
...SO VERY...
...VERY LONELY...
MIYATA-SAN.

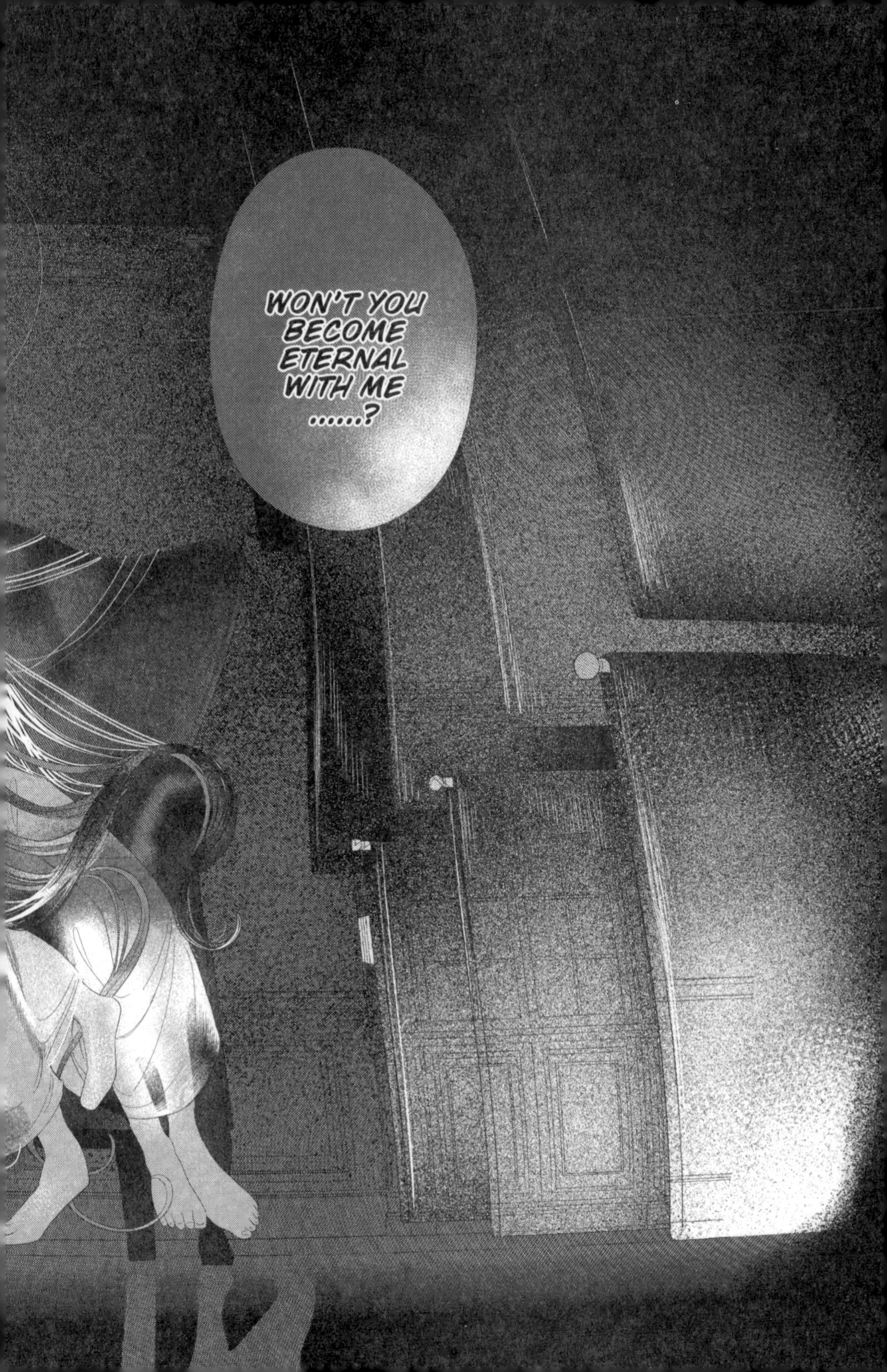
WON'T YOU BECOME ETERNAL WITH ME ......?

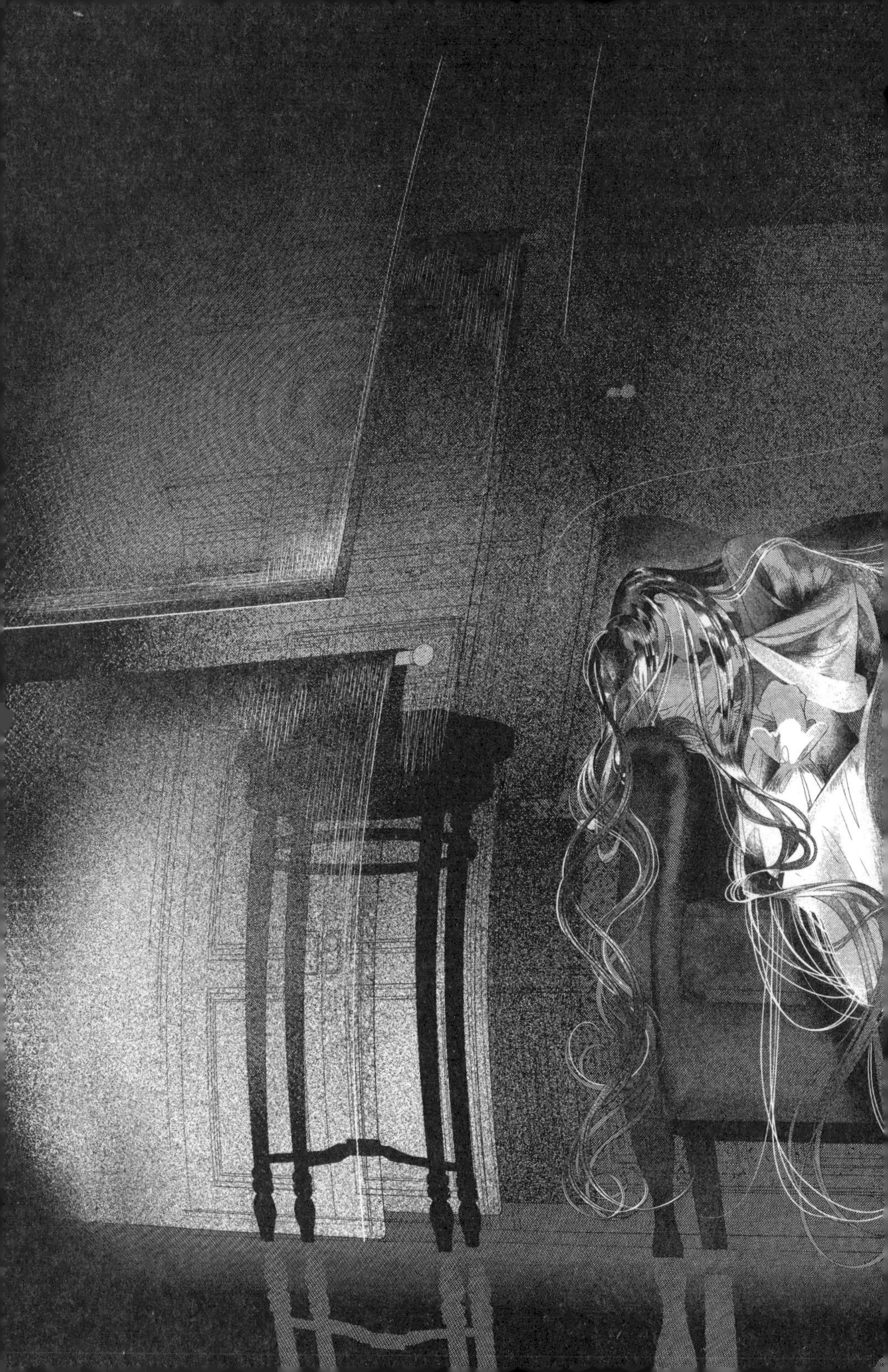

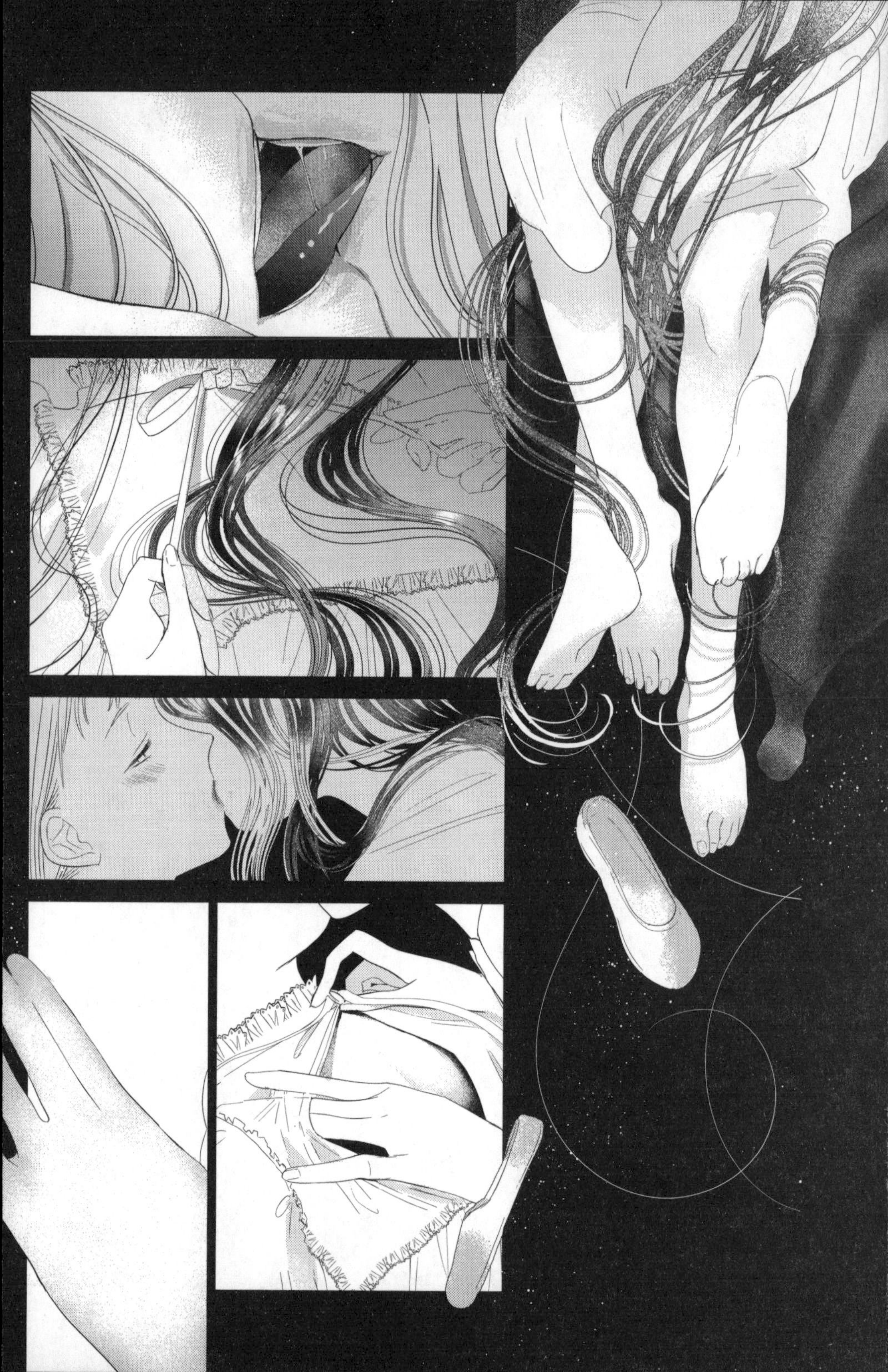

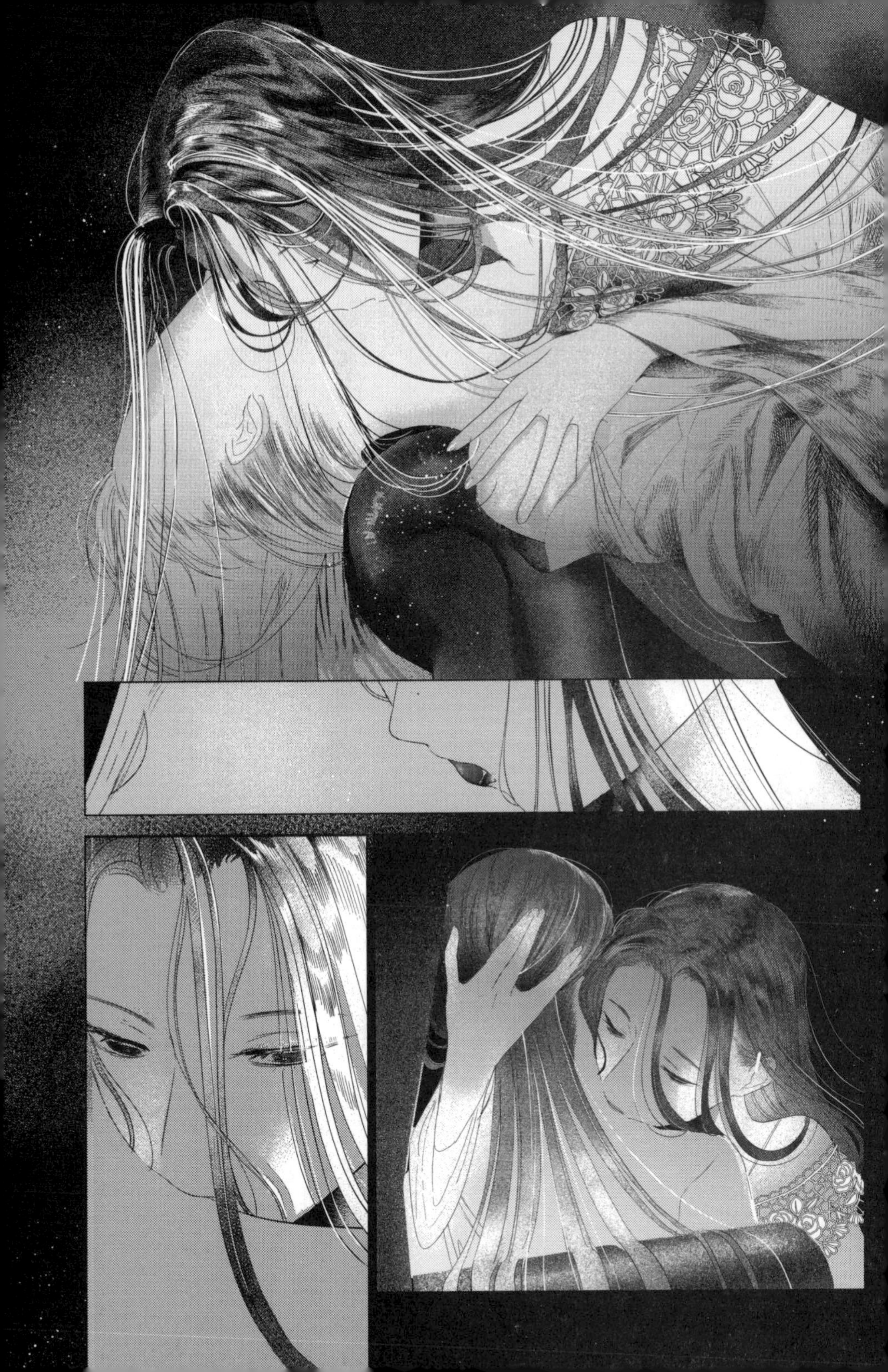

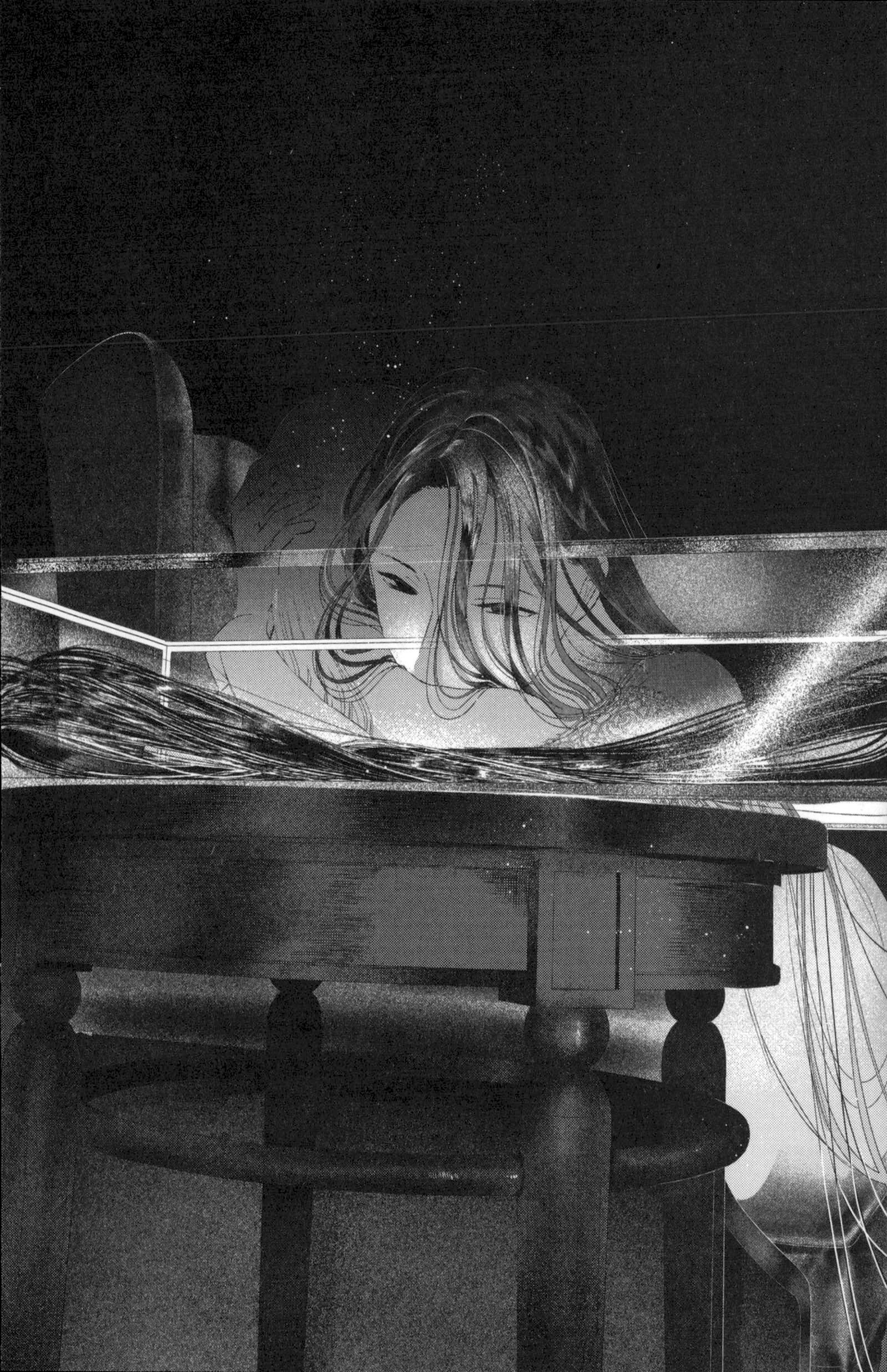

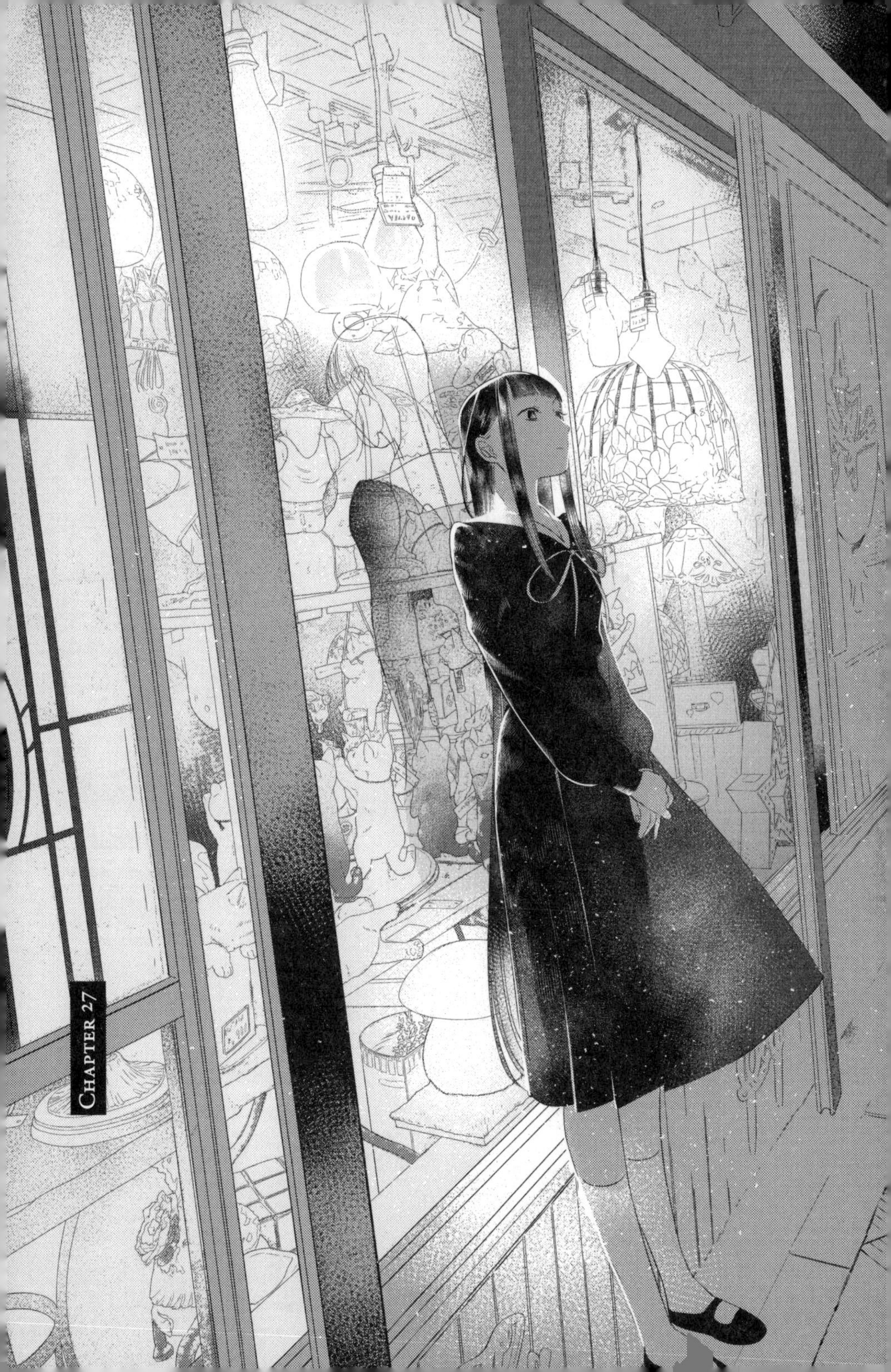
CHAPTER 27

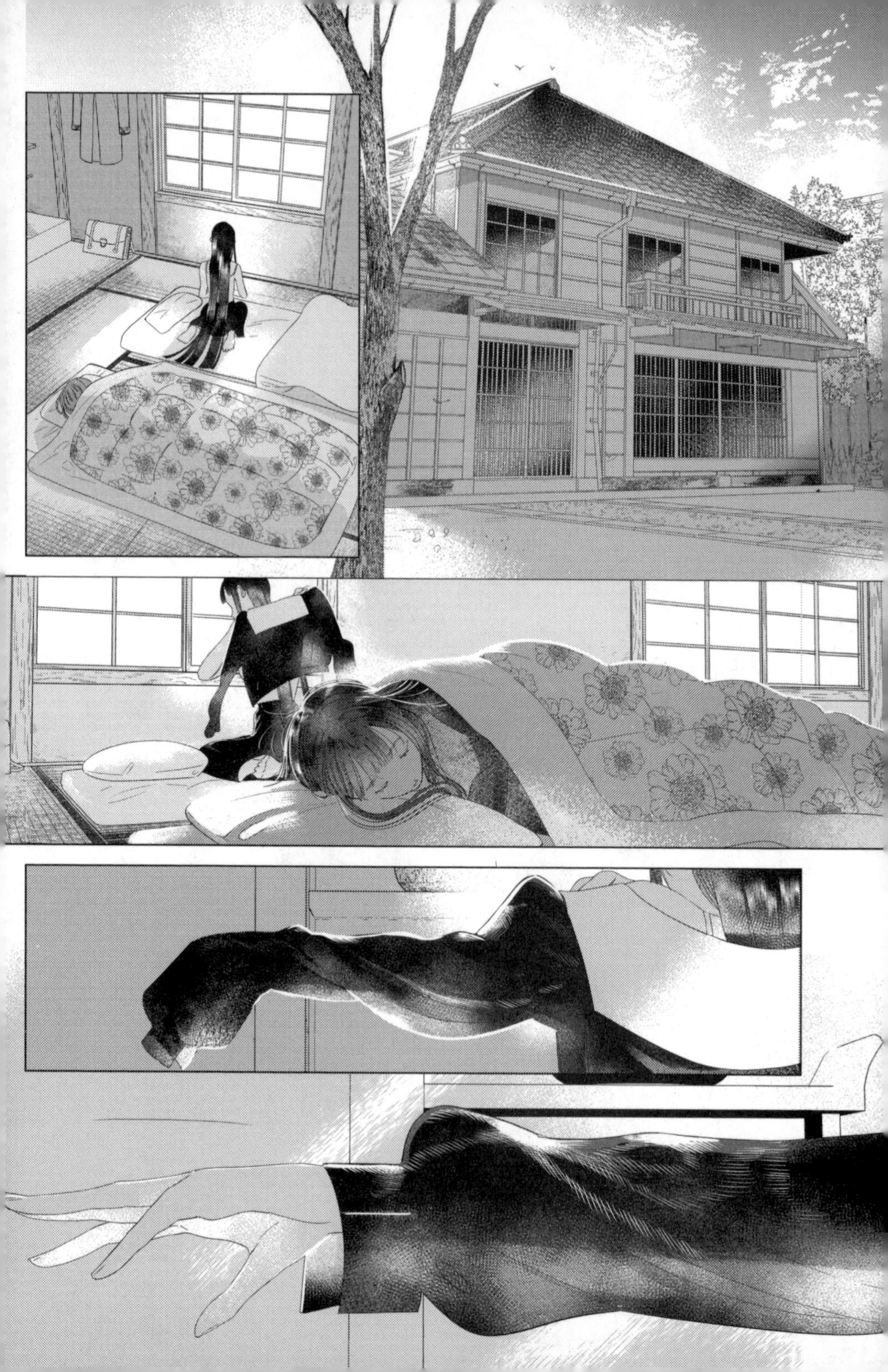

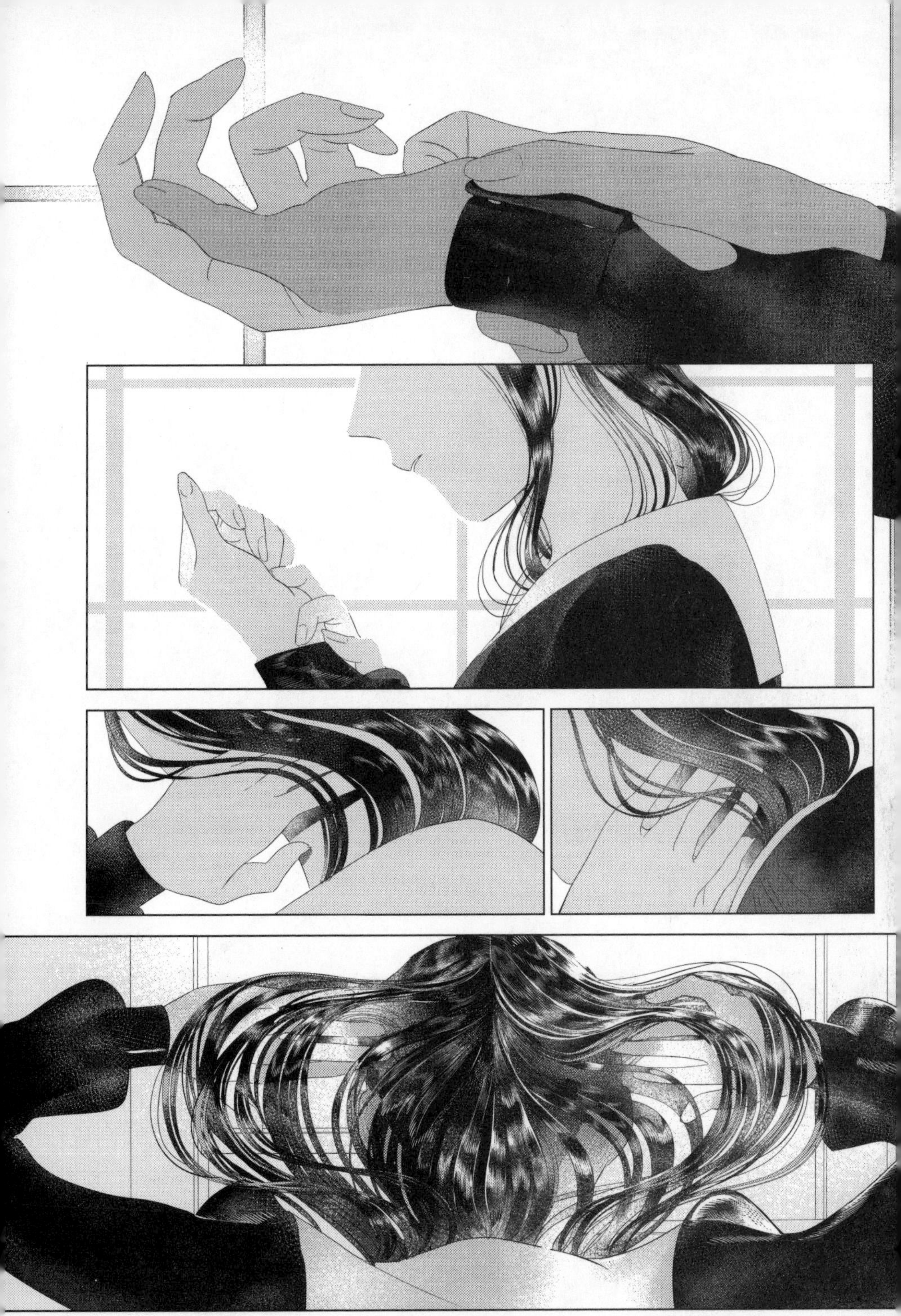

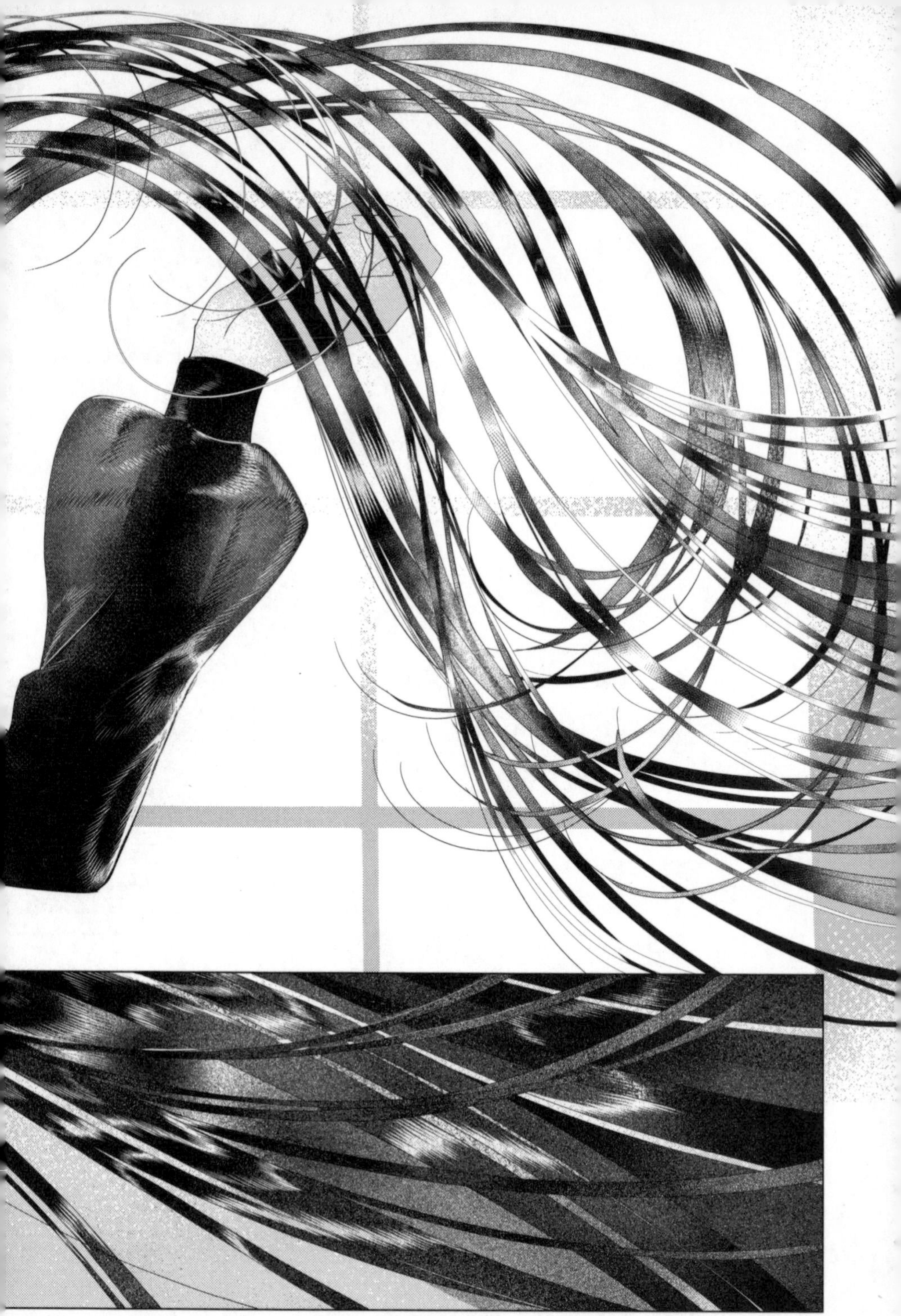

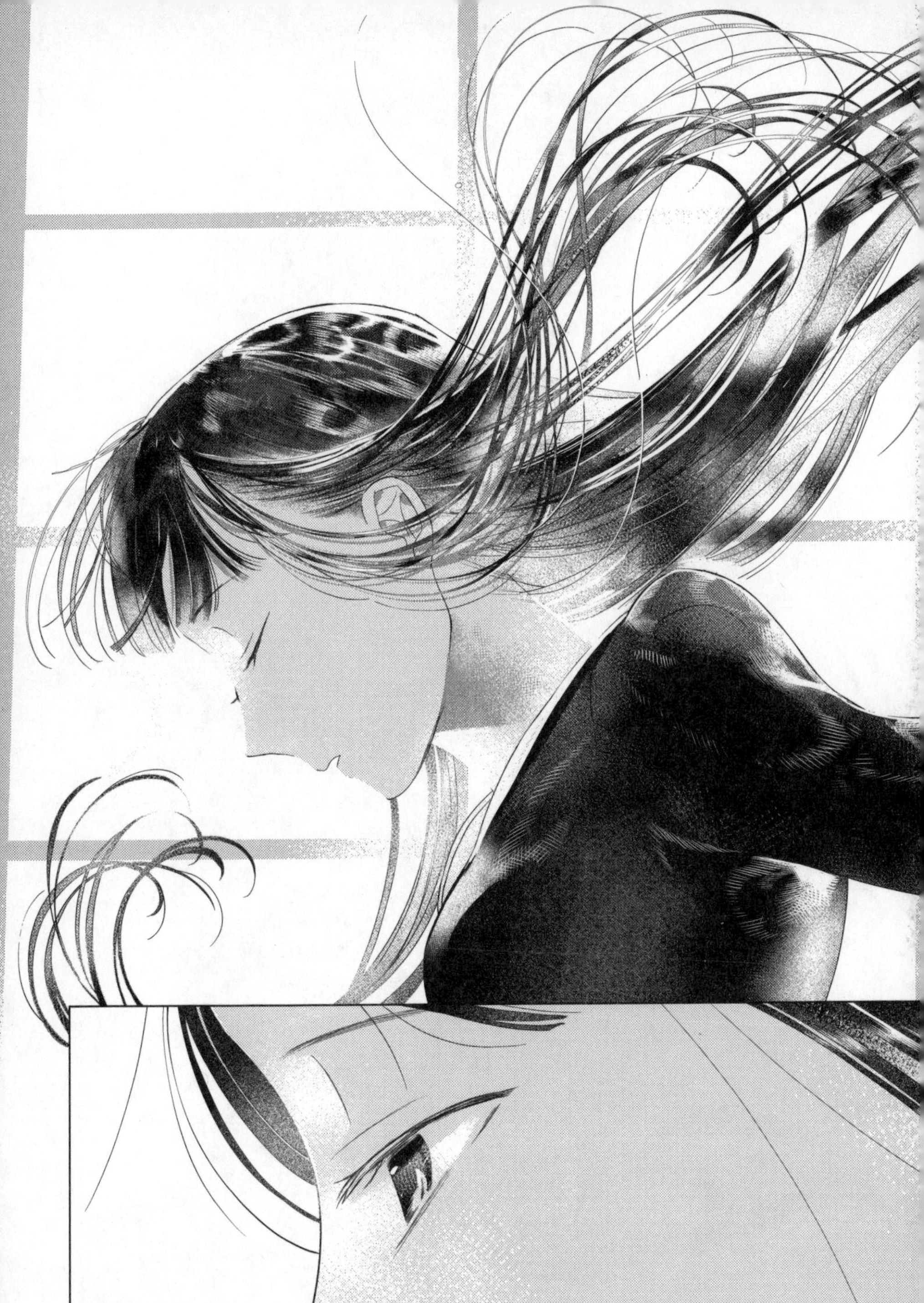

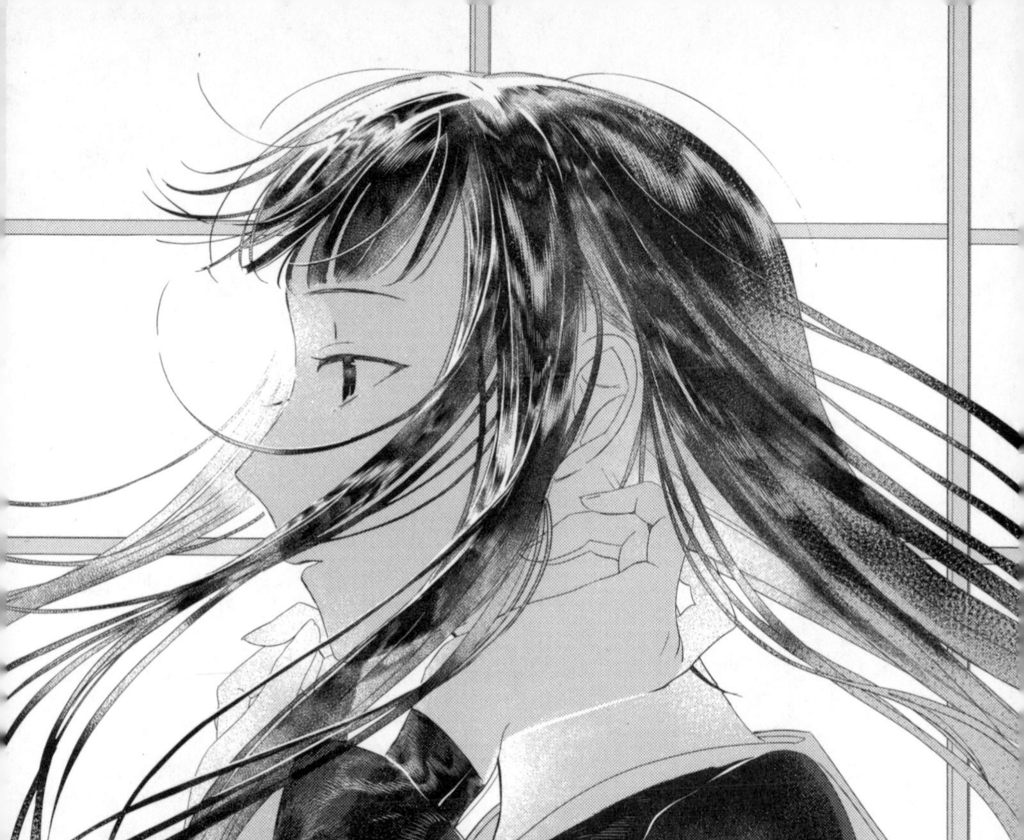

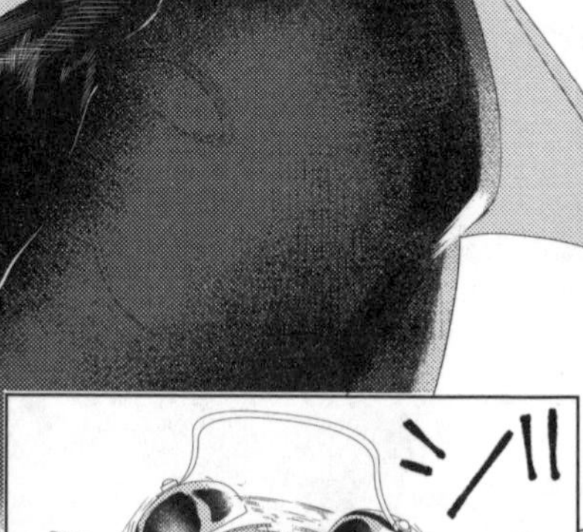
RIRIRI
JIRIRIRIRI
(RIIING)

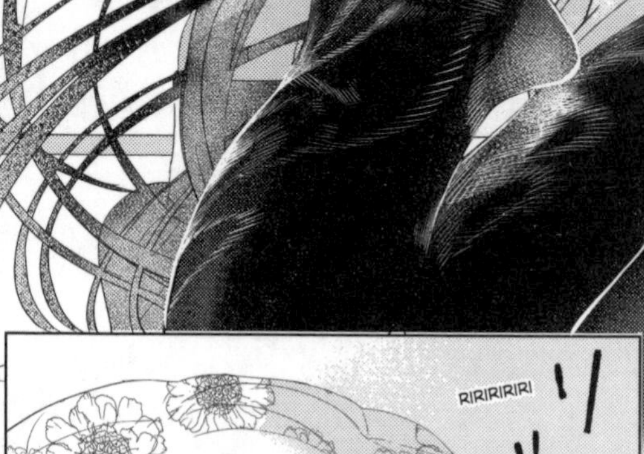
RIRIRIRIRI

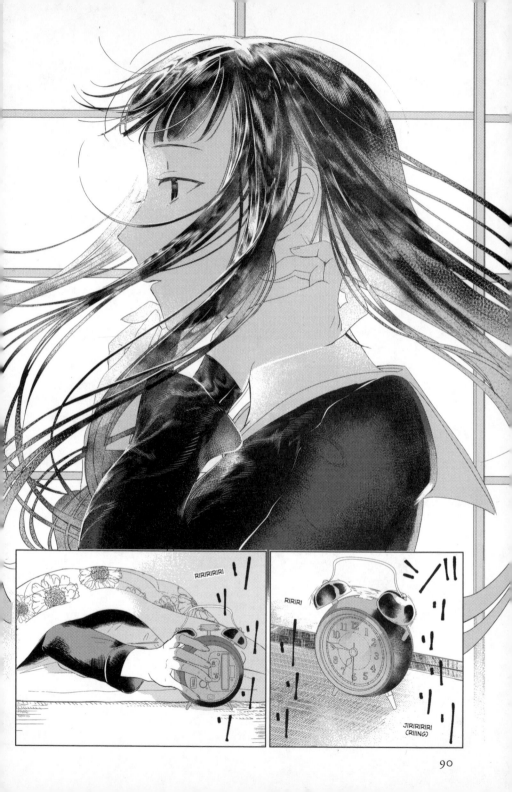

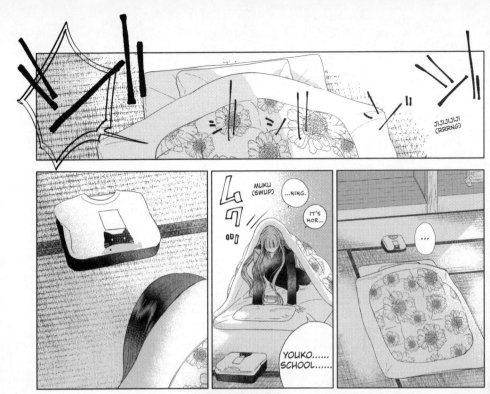

JIJIJIJIJI
(RRRNG)

MUKU
(SWUP)

...NING.

IT'S MOR...

...

YOUKO......
SCHOOL......

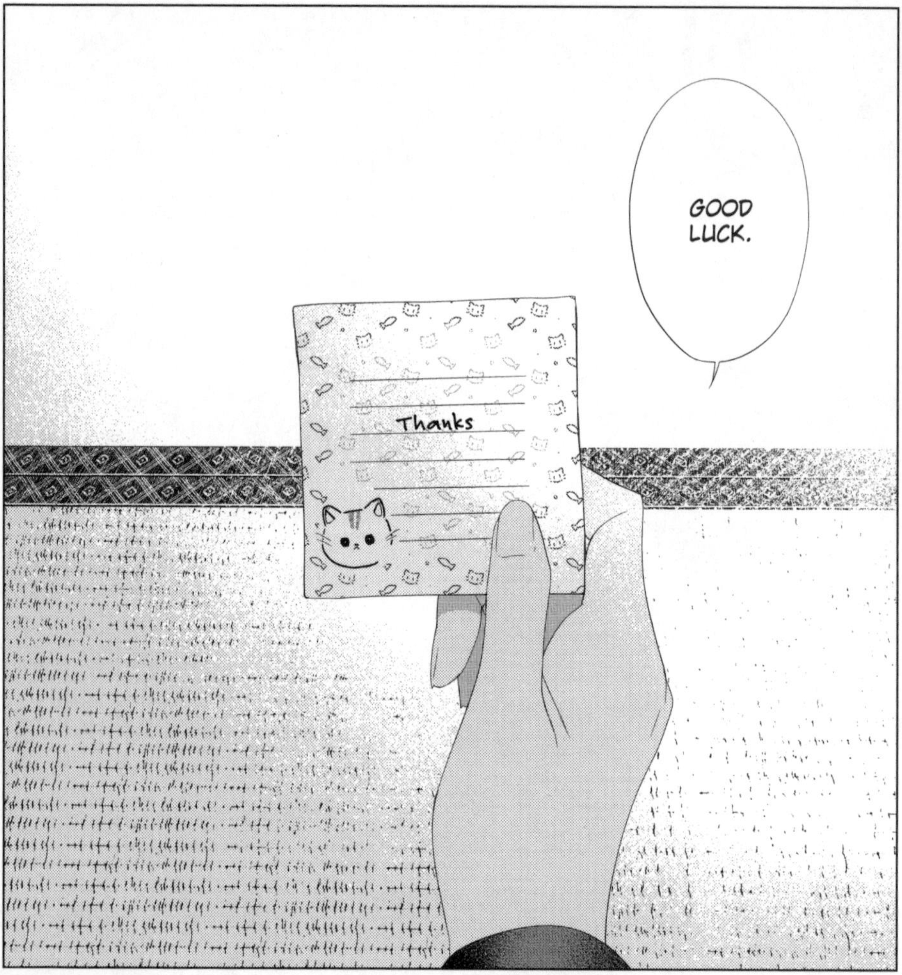
GOOD LUCK.
Thanks
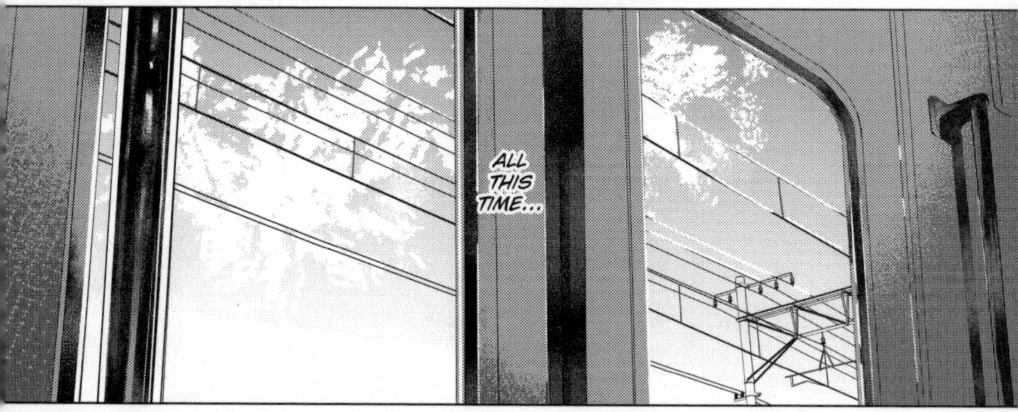
ALL THIS TIME...

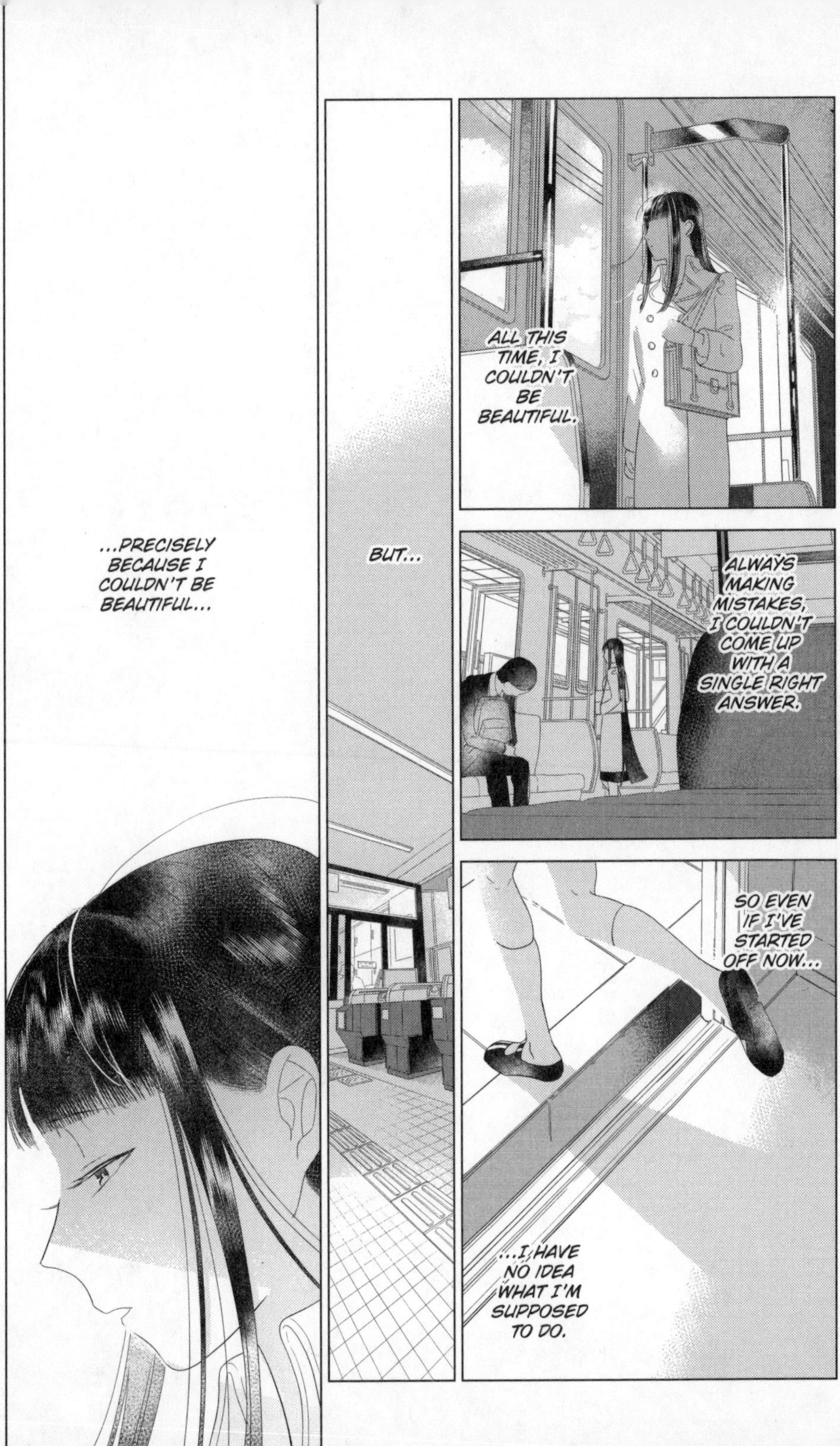
ALL THIS TIME, I COULDN'T BE BEAUTIFUL.
ALWAYS MAKING MISTAKES, I COULDN'T COME UP WITH A SINGLE RIGHT ANSWER.
SO EVEN IF I'VE STARTED OFF NOW...
...I HAVE NO IDEA WHAT I'M SUPPOSED TO DO.
BUT...
...PRECISELY BECAUSE I COULDN'T BE BEAUTIFUL...

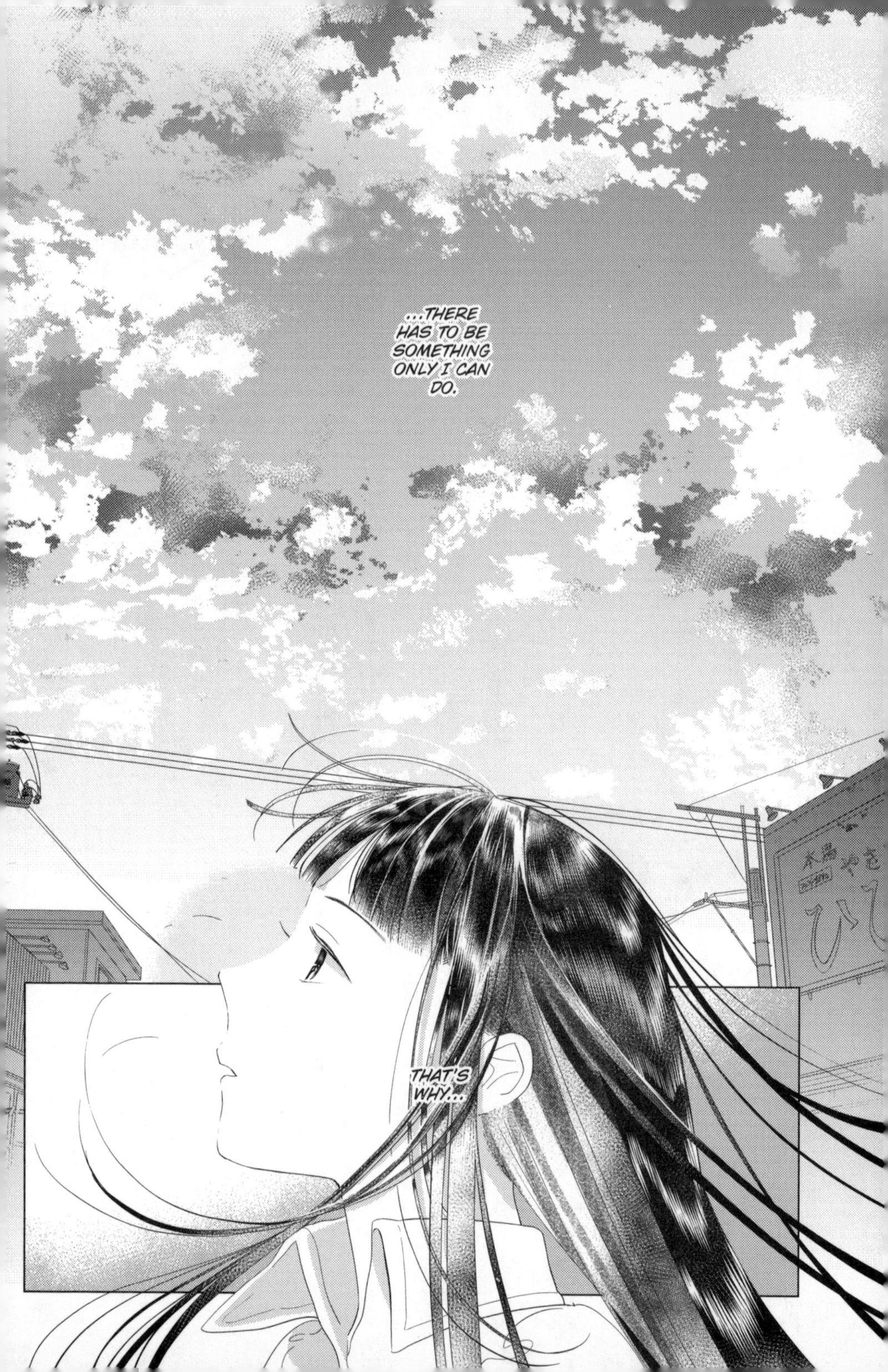
...THERE HAS TO BE SOMETHING ONLY I CAN DO.
THAT'S WHY...

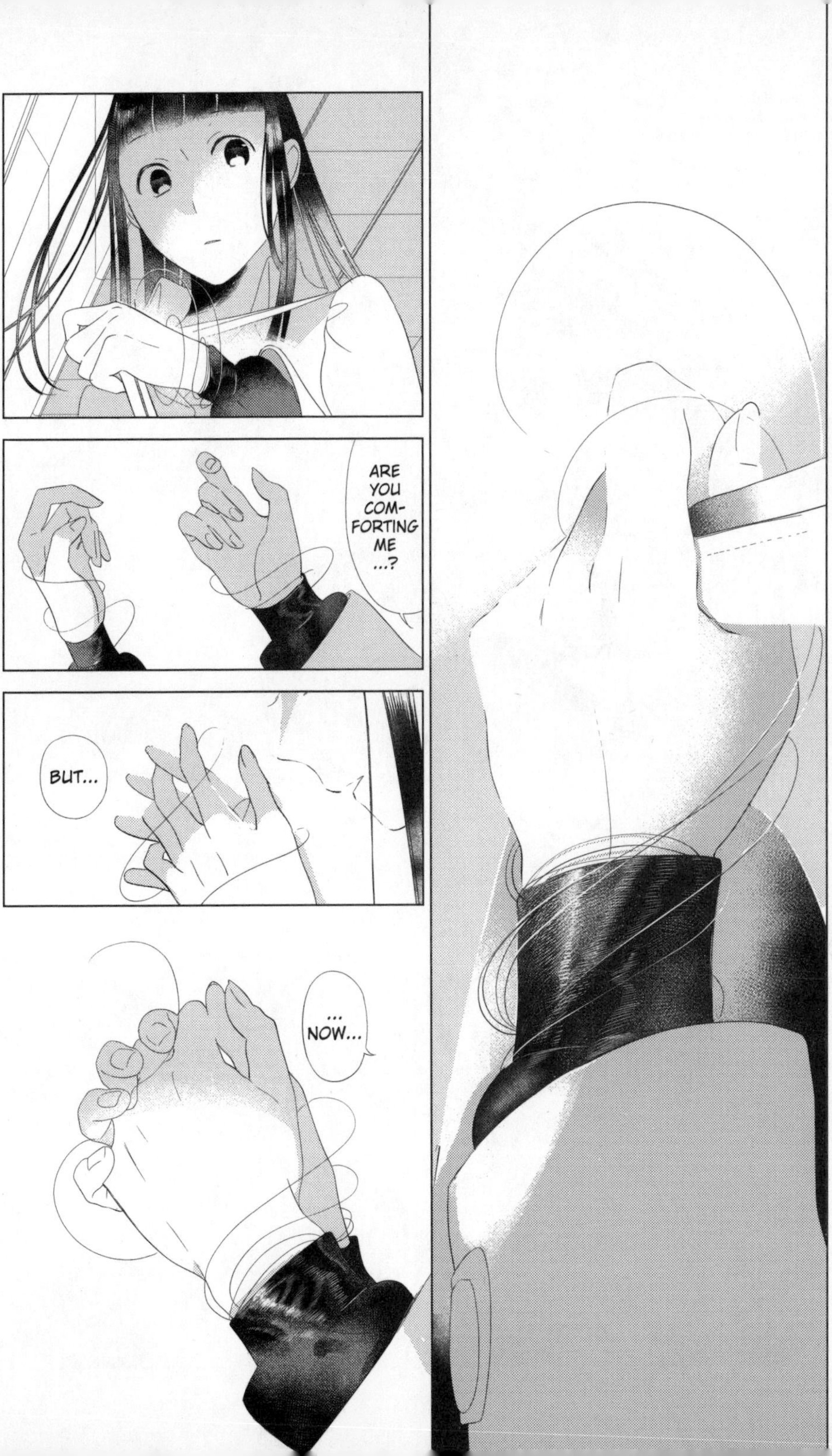
ARE YOU COM-FORTING ME ...?
BUT...
... NOW...

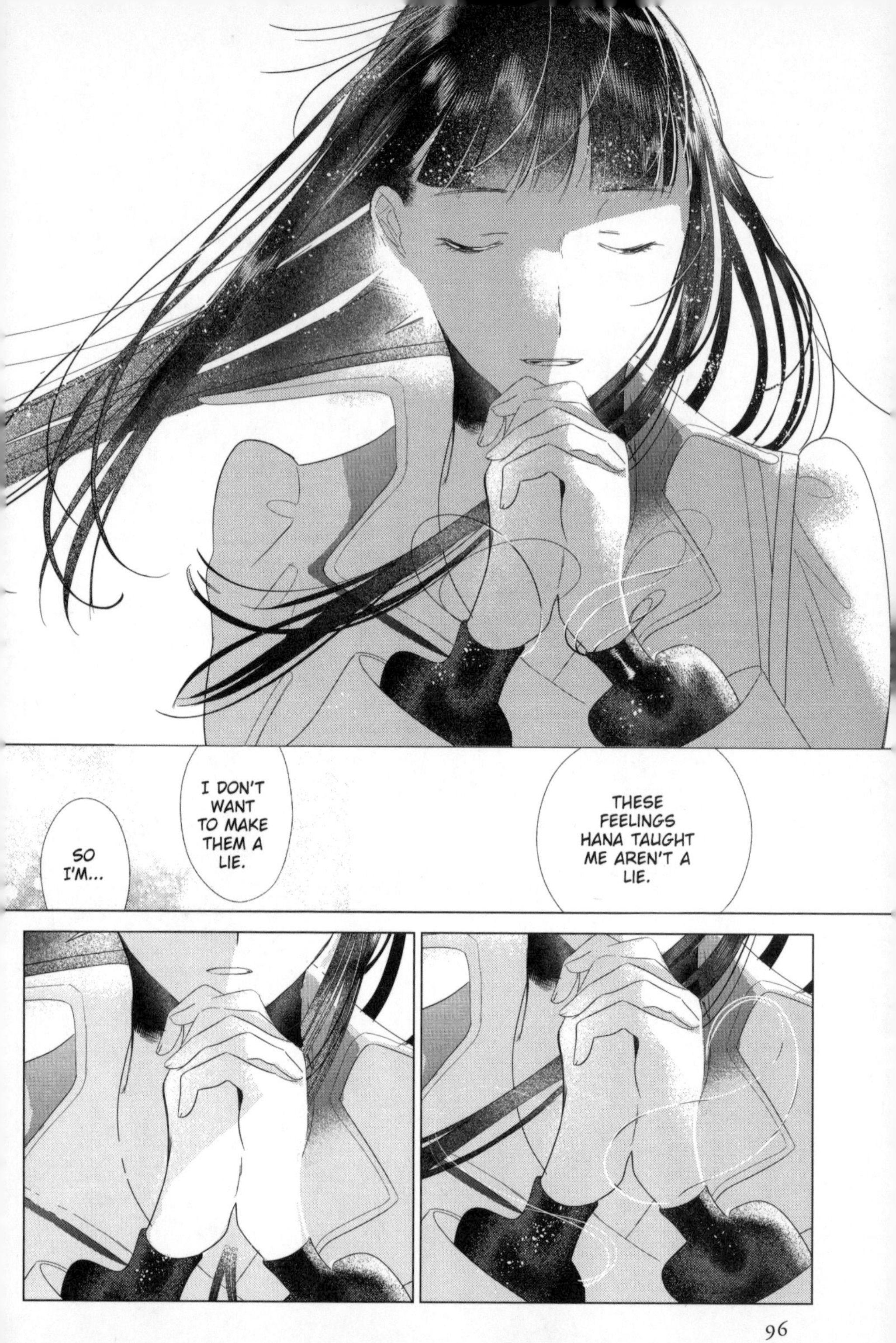
THESE FEELINGS HANA TAUGHT ME AREN'T A LIE.
I DON'T WANT TO MAKE THEM A LIE.
SO I'M...

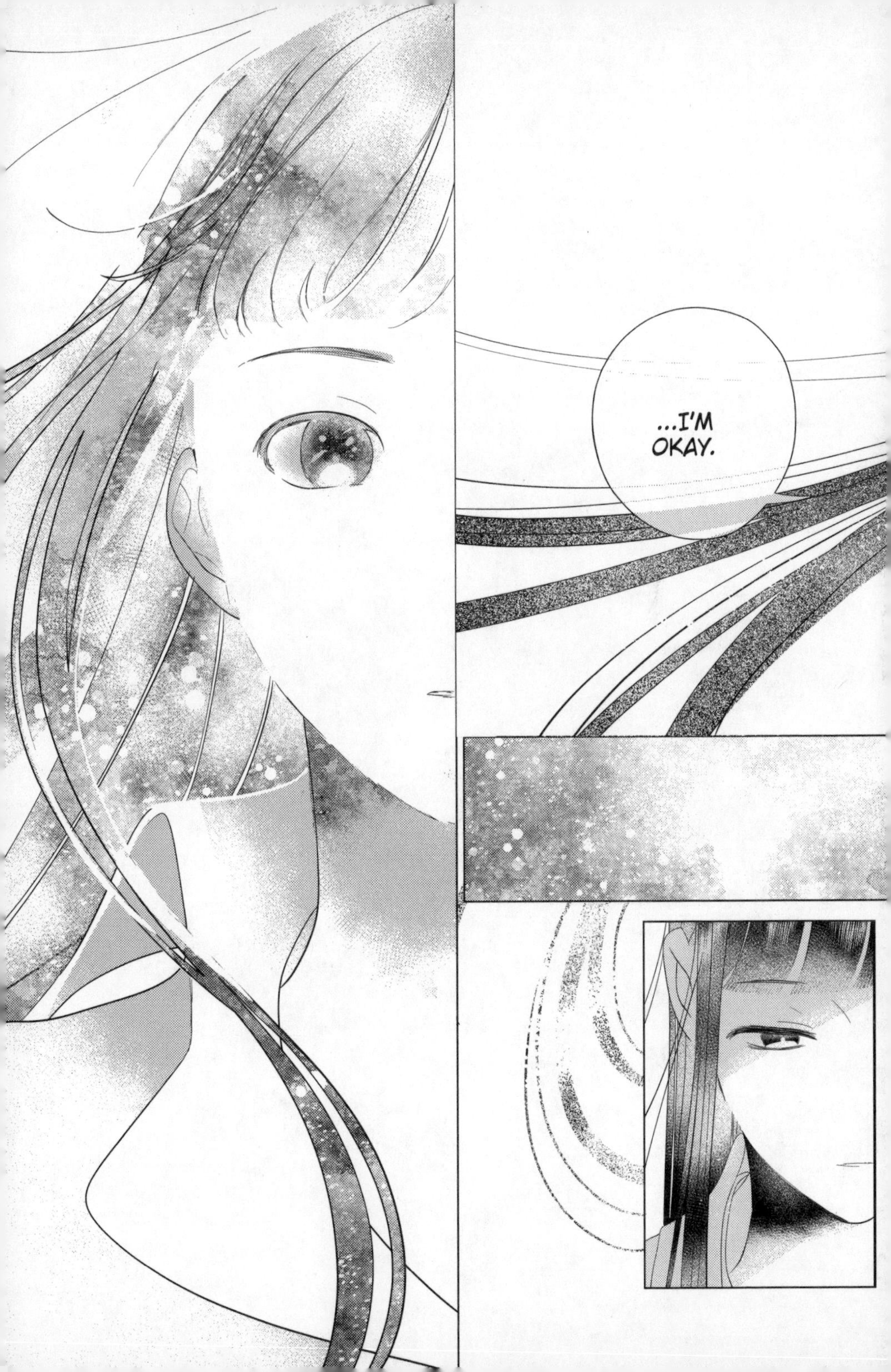
...I'M OKAY.

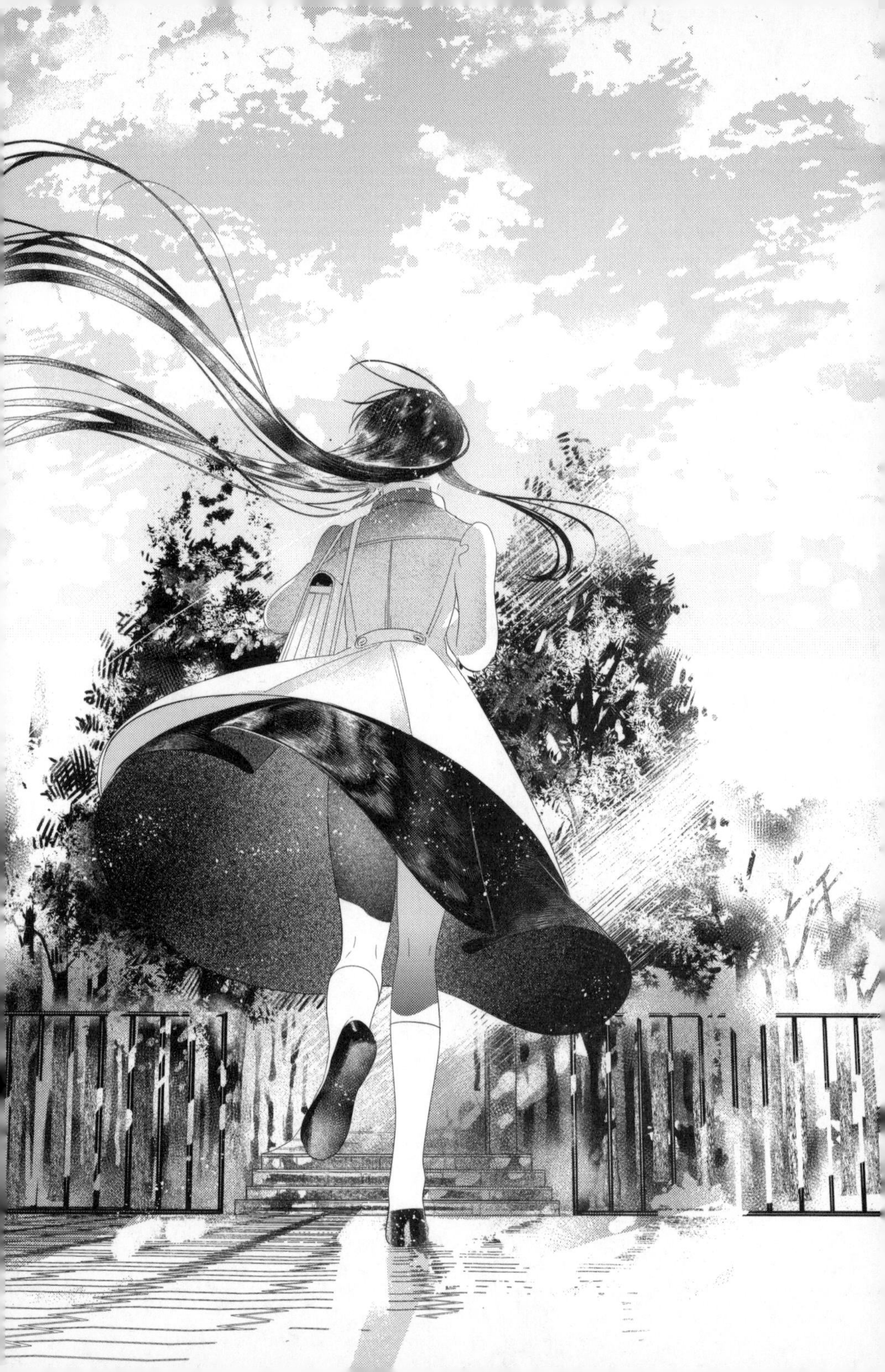

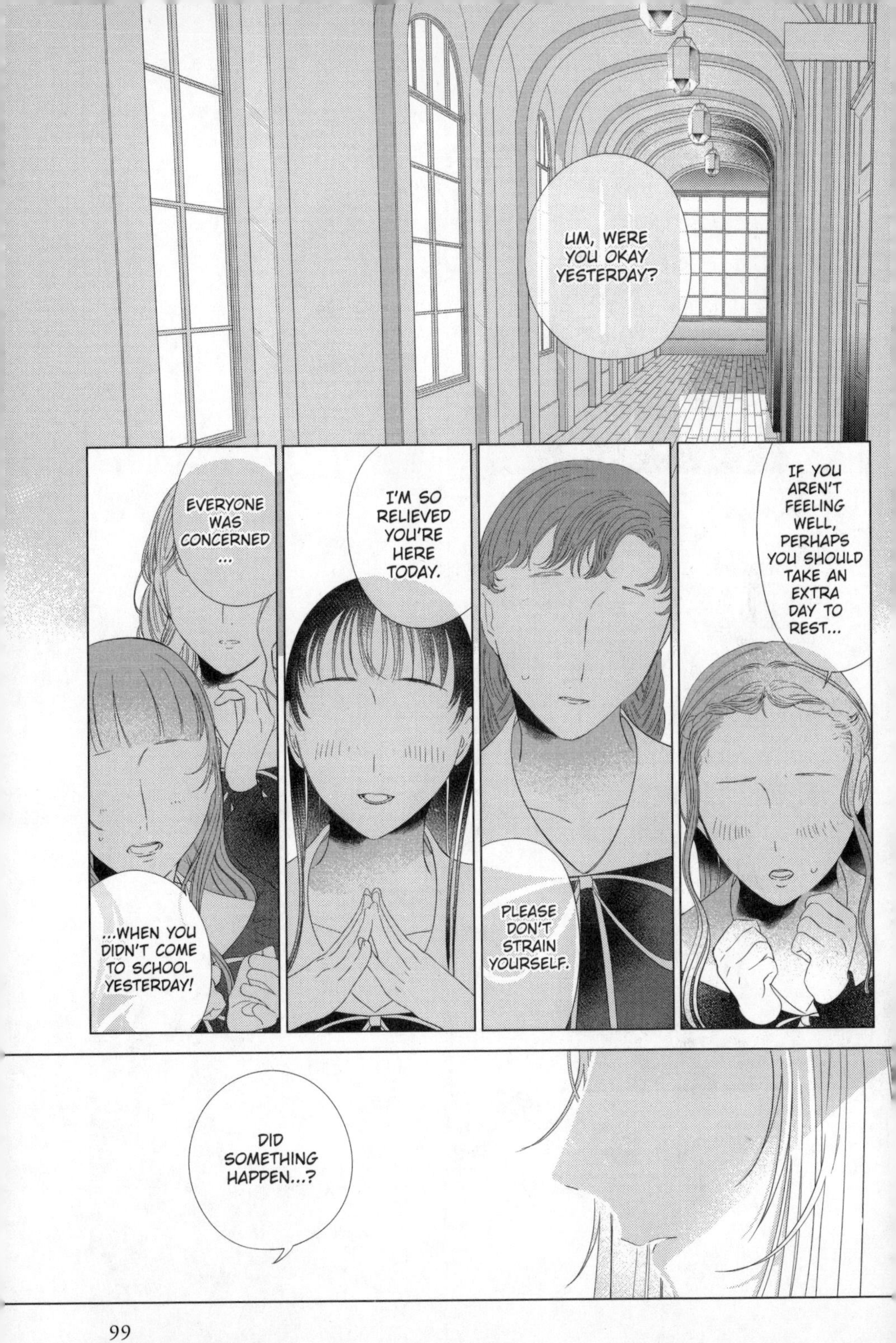
UM, WERE YOU OKAY YESTERDAY?
IF YOU AREN'T FEELING WELL, PERHAPS YOU SHOULD TAKE AN EXTRA DAY TO REST...
PLEASE DON'T STRAIN YOURSELF.
I'M SO RELIEVED YOU'RE HERE TODAY.
EVERYONE WAS CONCERNED ...
...WHEN YOU DIDN'T COME TO SCHOOL YESTERDAY!
DID SOMETHING HAPPEN...?

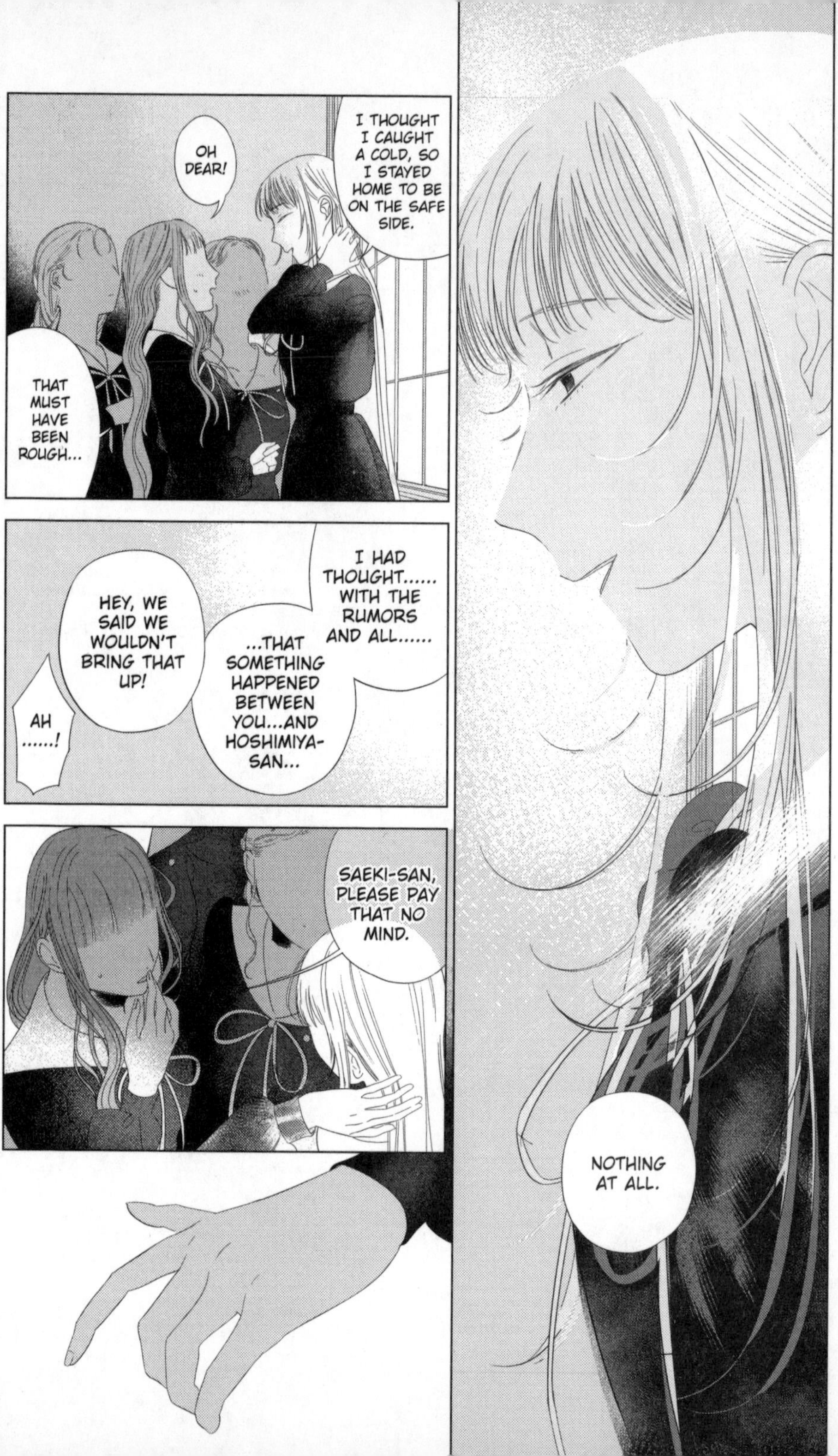
I THOUGHT I CAUGHT A COLD, SO I STAYED HOME TO BE ON THE SAFE SIDE.
OH DEAR!
THAT MUST HAVE BEEN ROUGH...
I HAD THOUGHT...... WITH THE RUMORS AND ALL......
...THAT SOMETHING HAPPENED BETWEEN YOU...AND HOSHIMIYA-SAN...
HEY, WE SAID WE WOULDN'T BRING THAT UP!
AH ......!
SAEKI-SAN, PLEASE PAY THAT NO MIND.
NOTHING AT ALL.

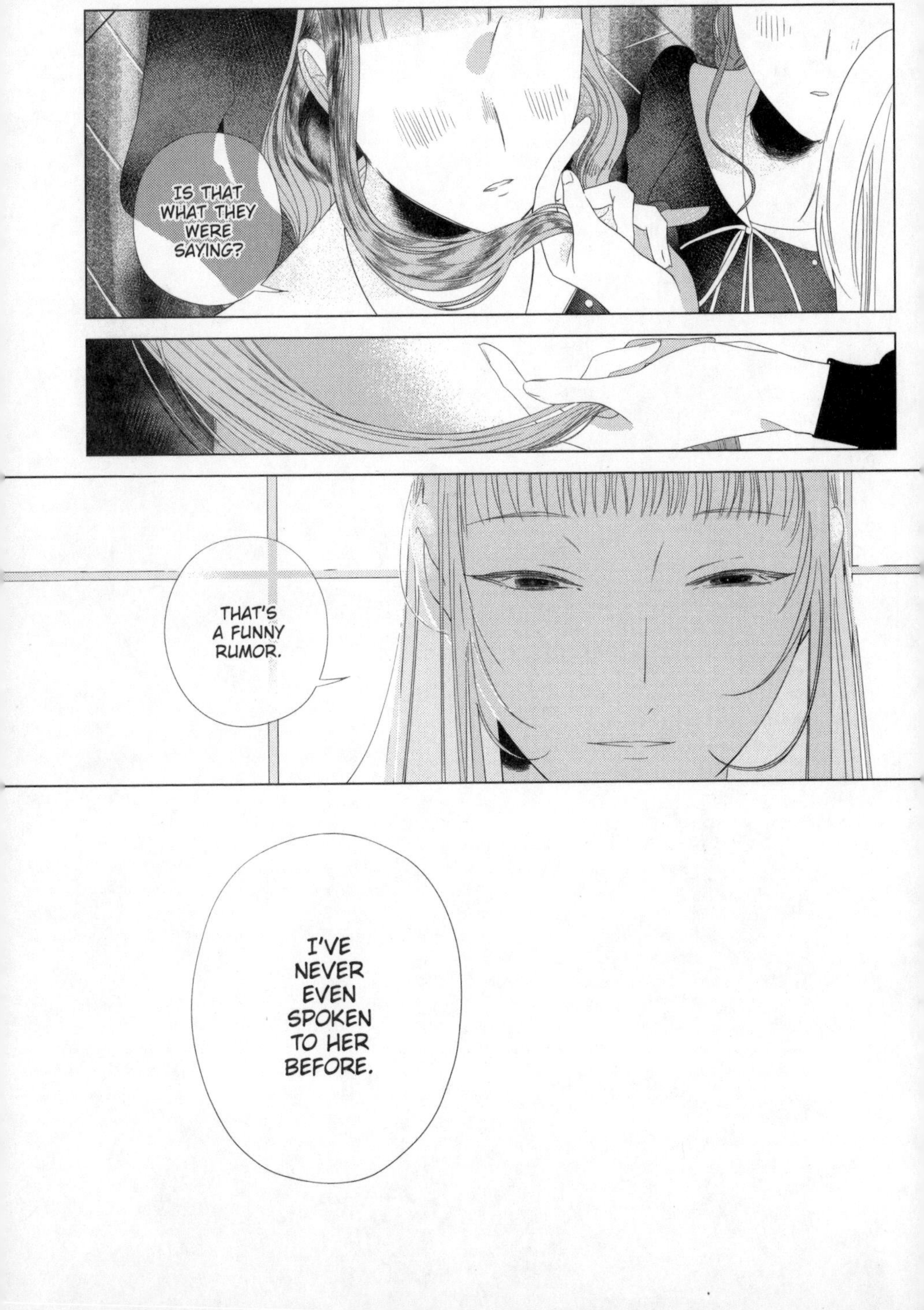
IS THAT WHAT THEY WERE SAYING?
THAT'S A FUNNY RUMOR.
I'VE NEVER EVEN SPOKEN TO HER BEFORE.

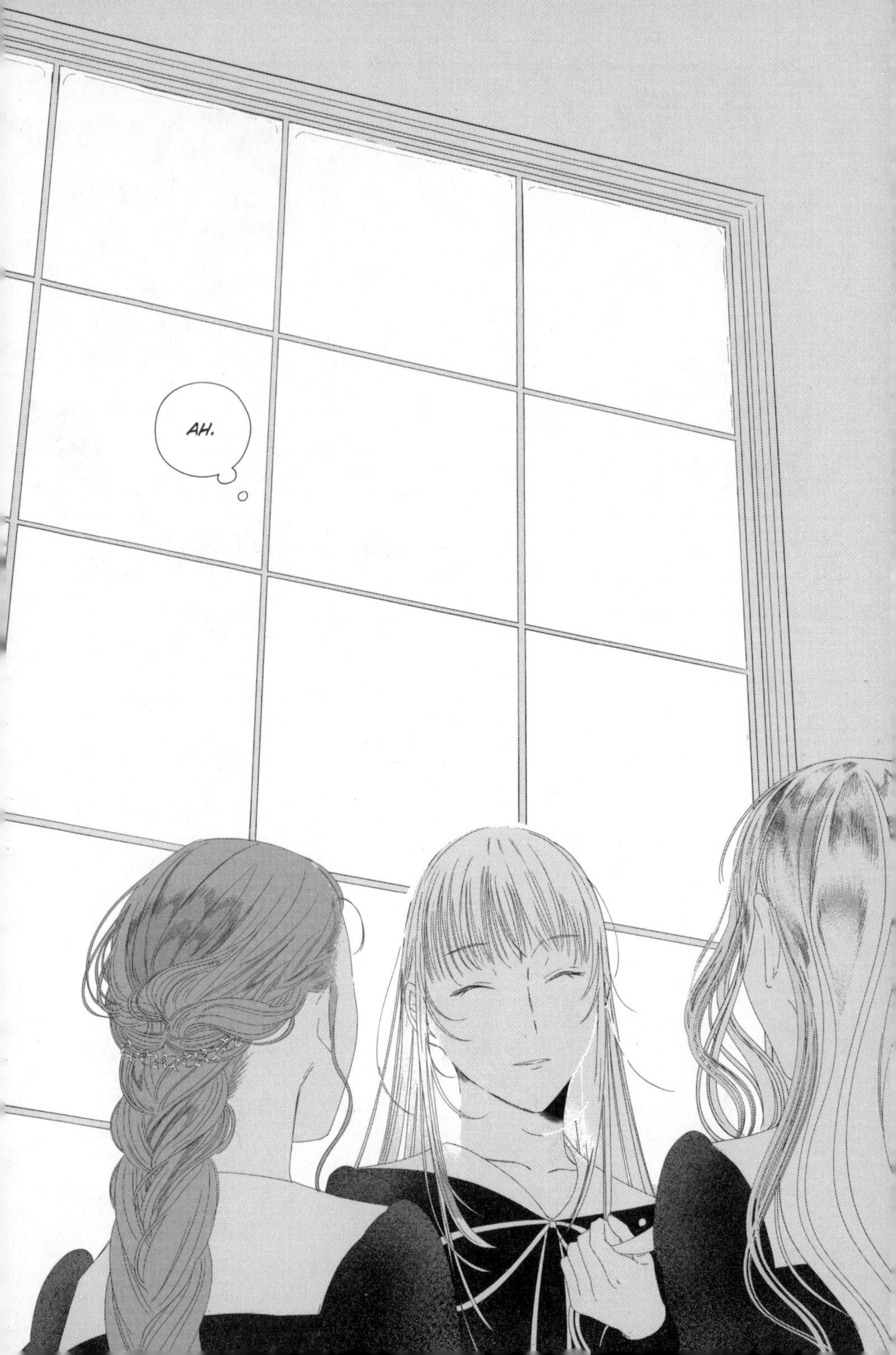
AH.

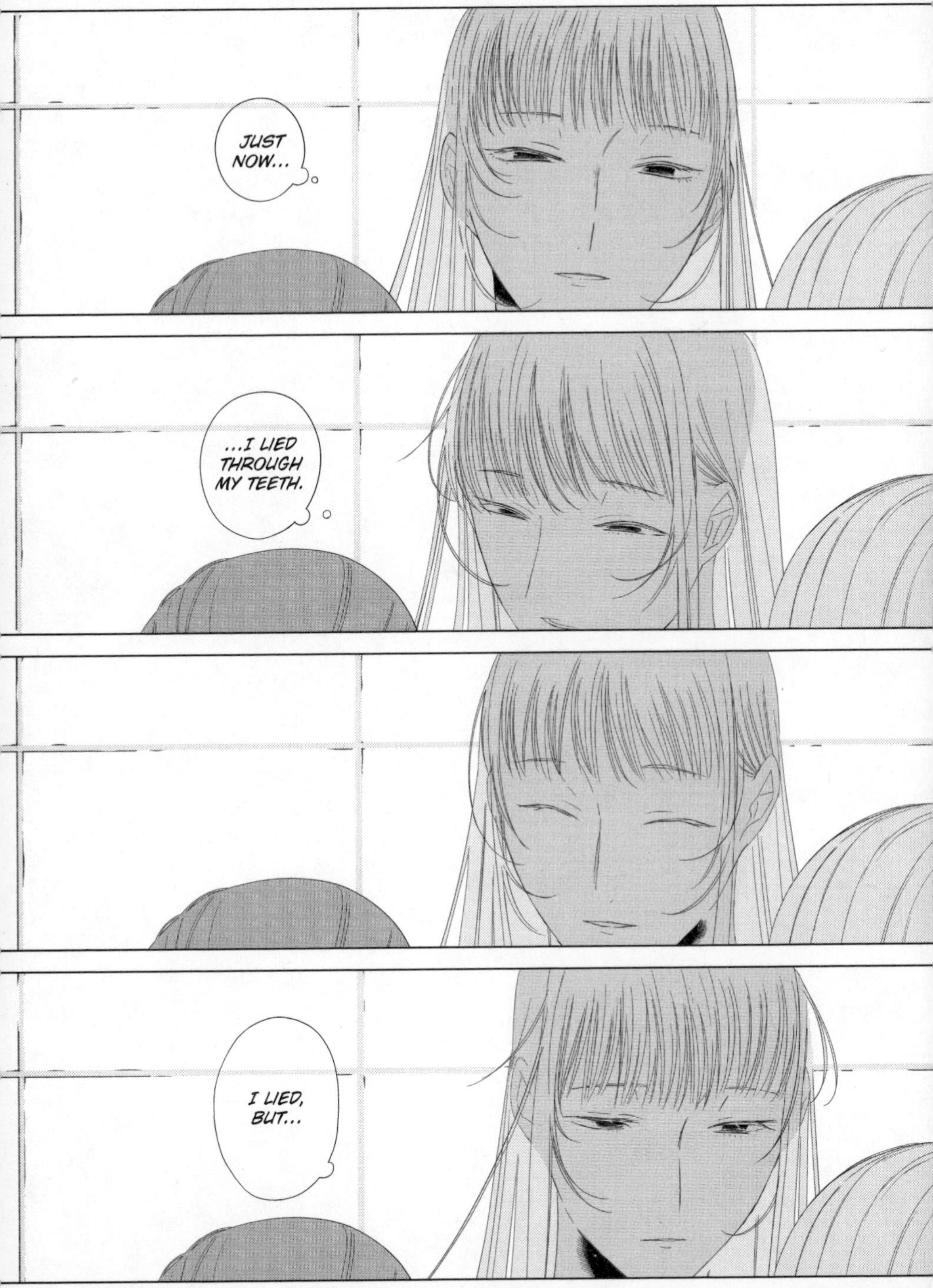
JUST NOW...
...I LIED THROUGH MY TEETH.
I LIED, BUT...

...I DON'T
FEEL A
THING...

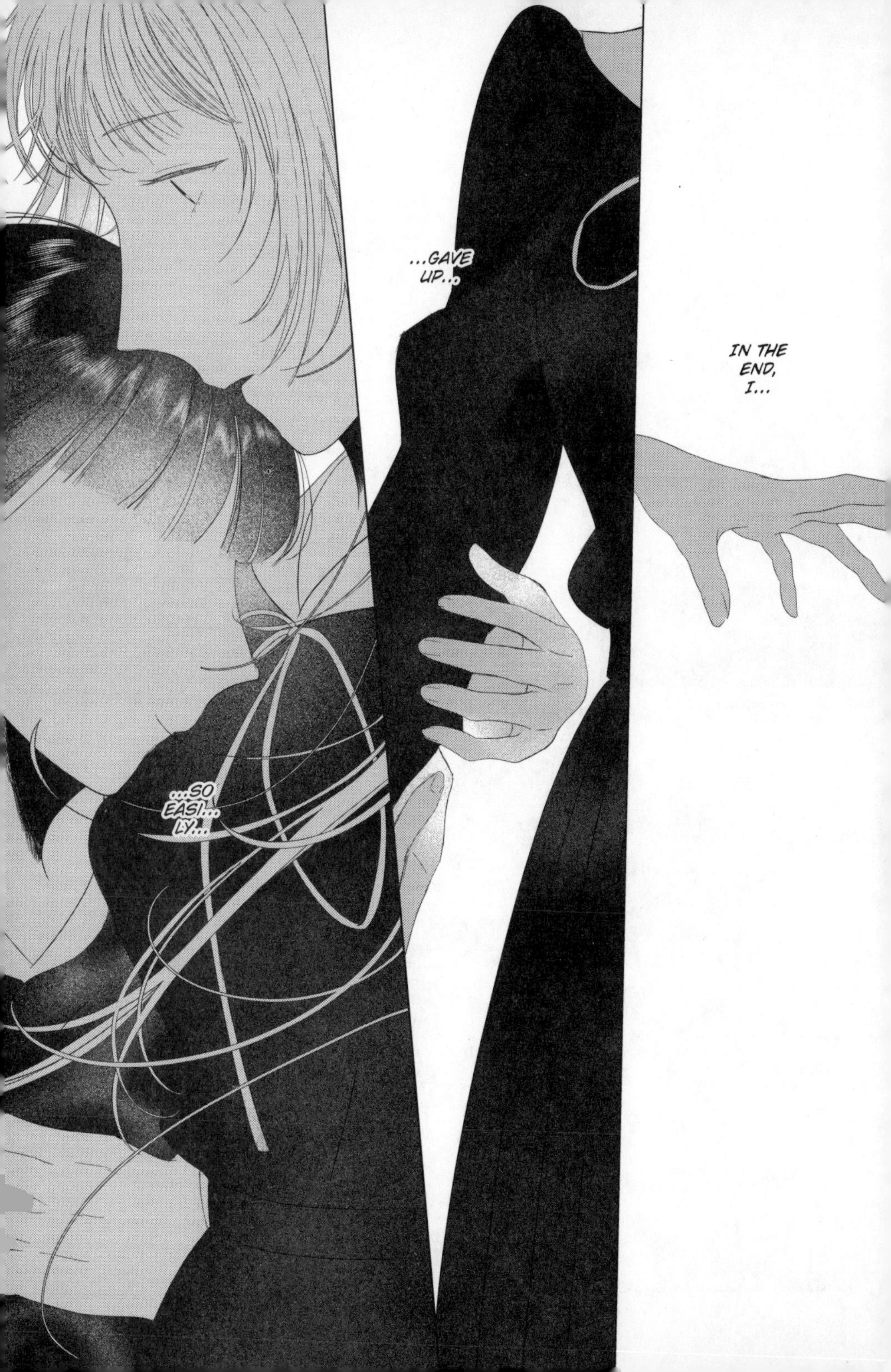
IN THE END, I...
...GAVE UP...
...SO EASI... LY...

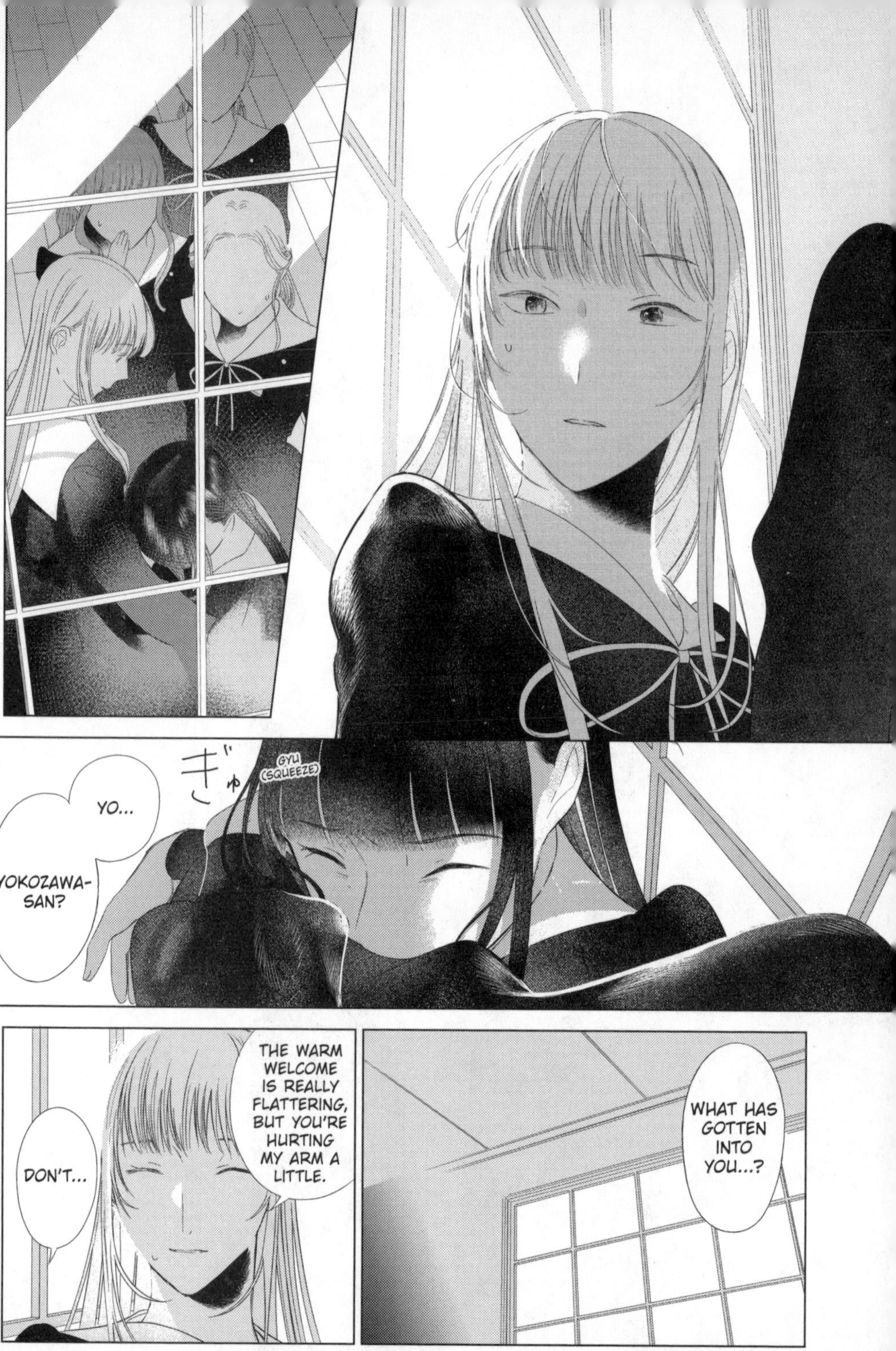
ぎゅ
GYU (SQUEEZE)
YO...
YOKOZAWA-SAN?
WHAT HAS GOTTEN INTO YOU...?
THE WARM WELCOME IS REALLY FLATTERING, BUT YOU'RE HURTING MY ARM A LITTLE.
DON'T...

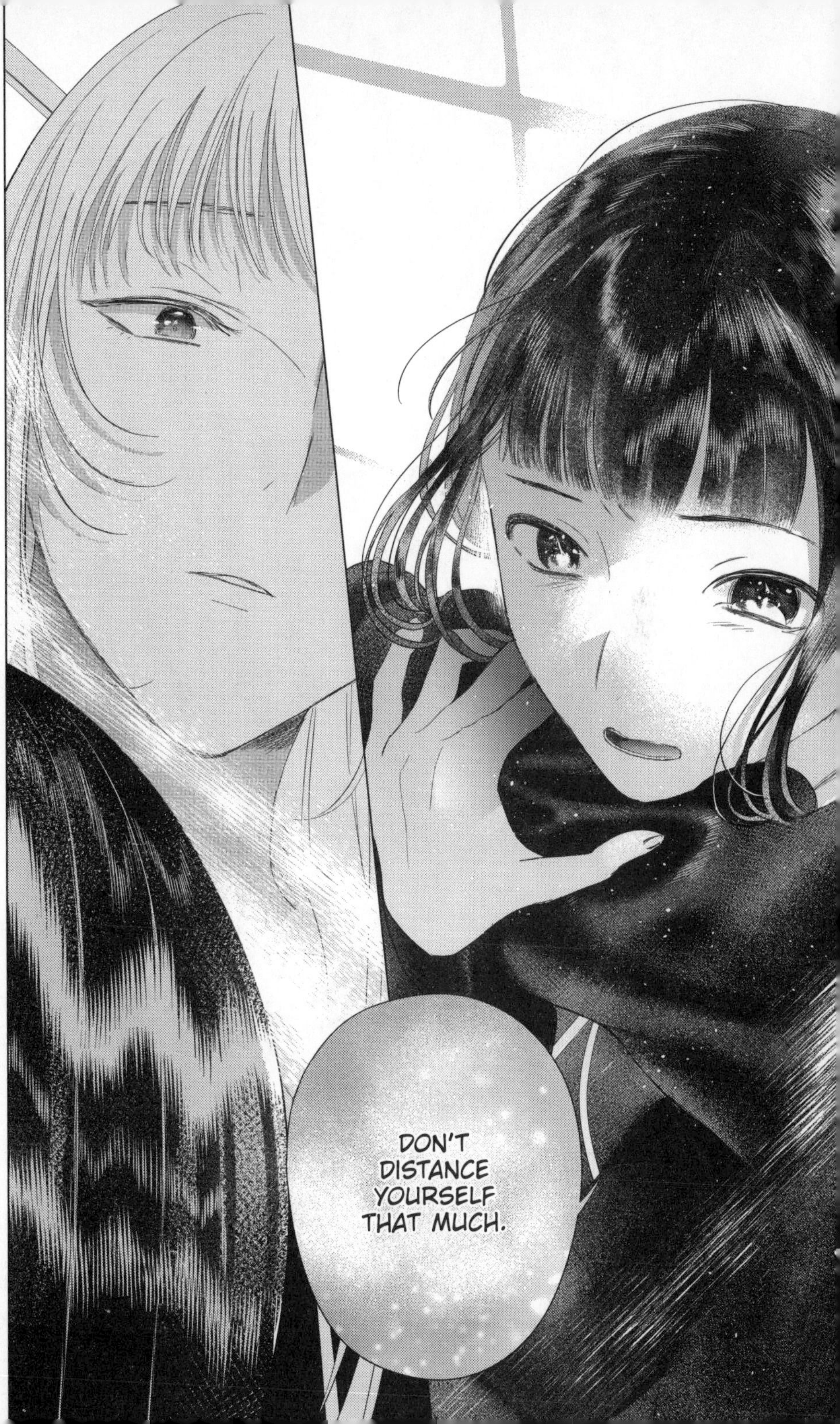
DON'T DISTANCE YOURSELF THAT MUCH.

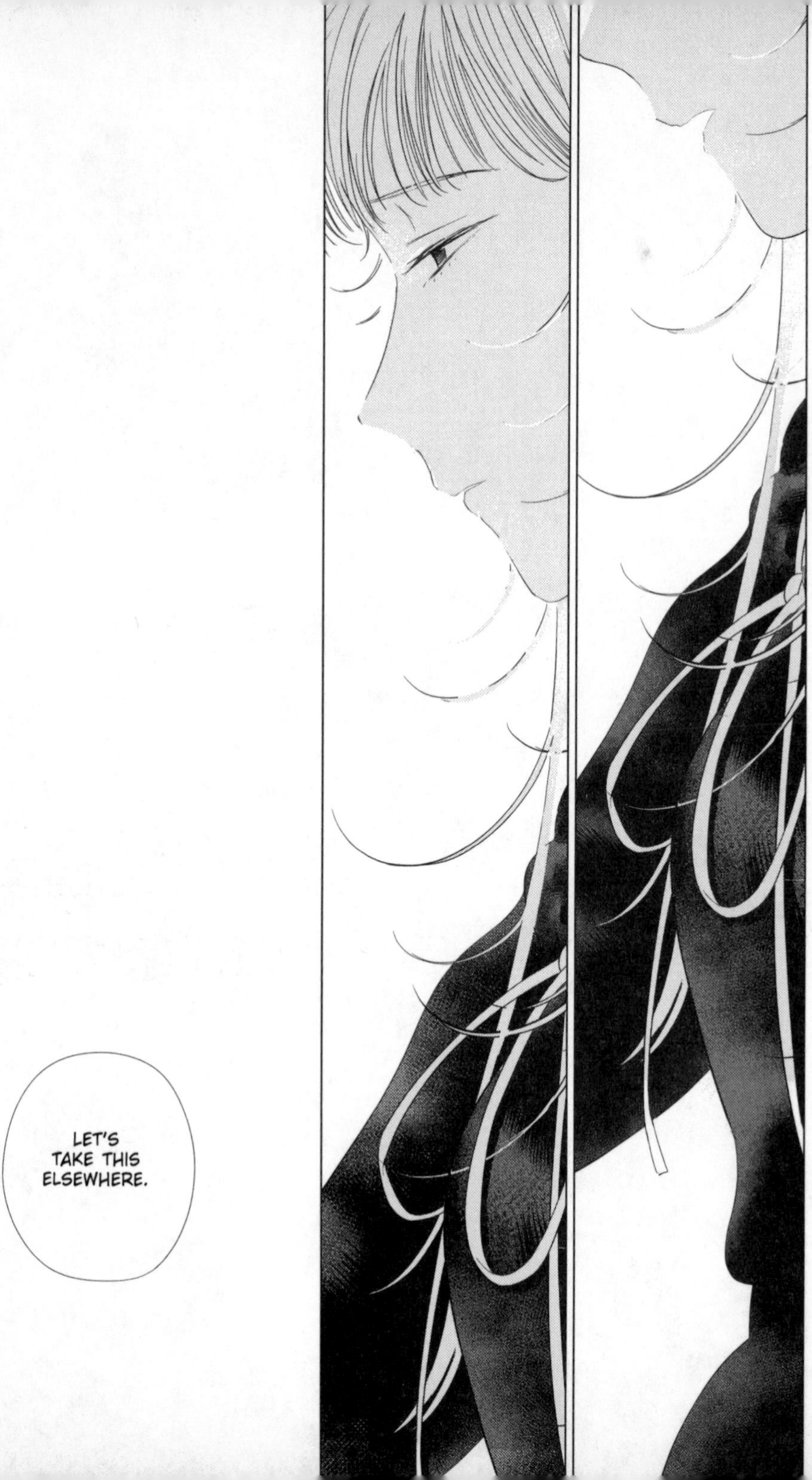
LET'S TAKE THIS ELSEWHERE.

*Cocoon
Entwined*

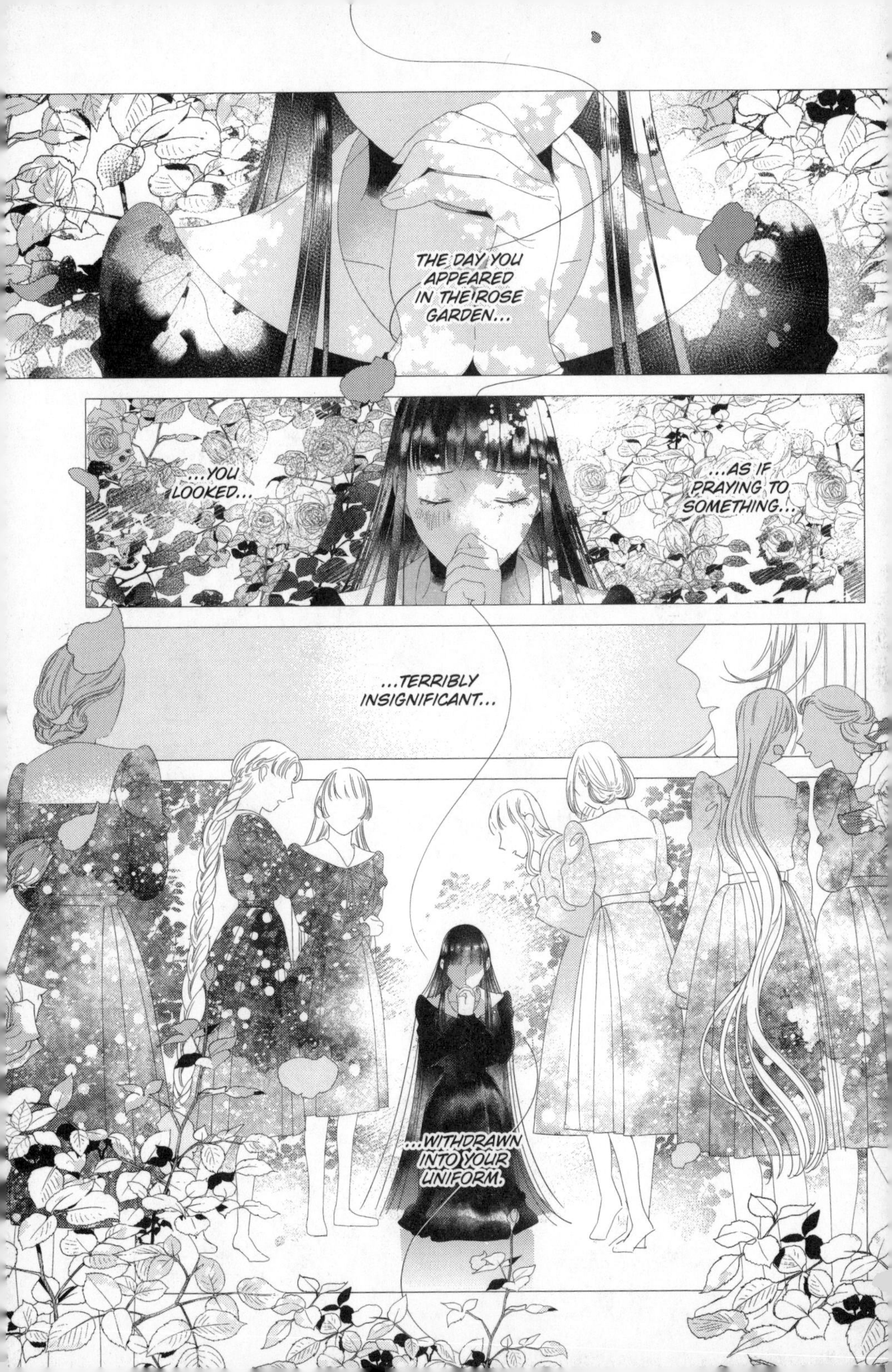
THE DAY YOU APPEARED IN THE ROSE GARDEN...
...AS IF PRAYING TO SOMETHING...
...YOU LOOKED...
...TERRIBLY INSIGNIFICANT...
...WITHDRAWN INTO YOUR UNIFORM.

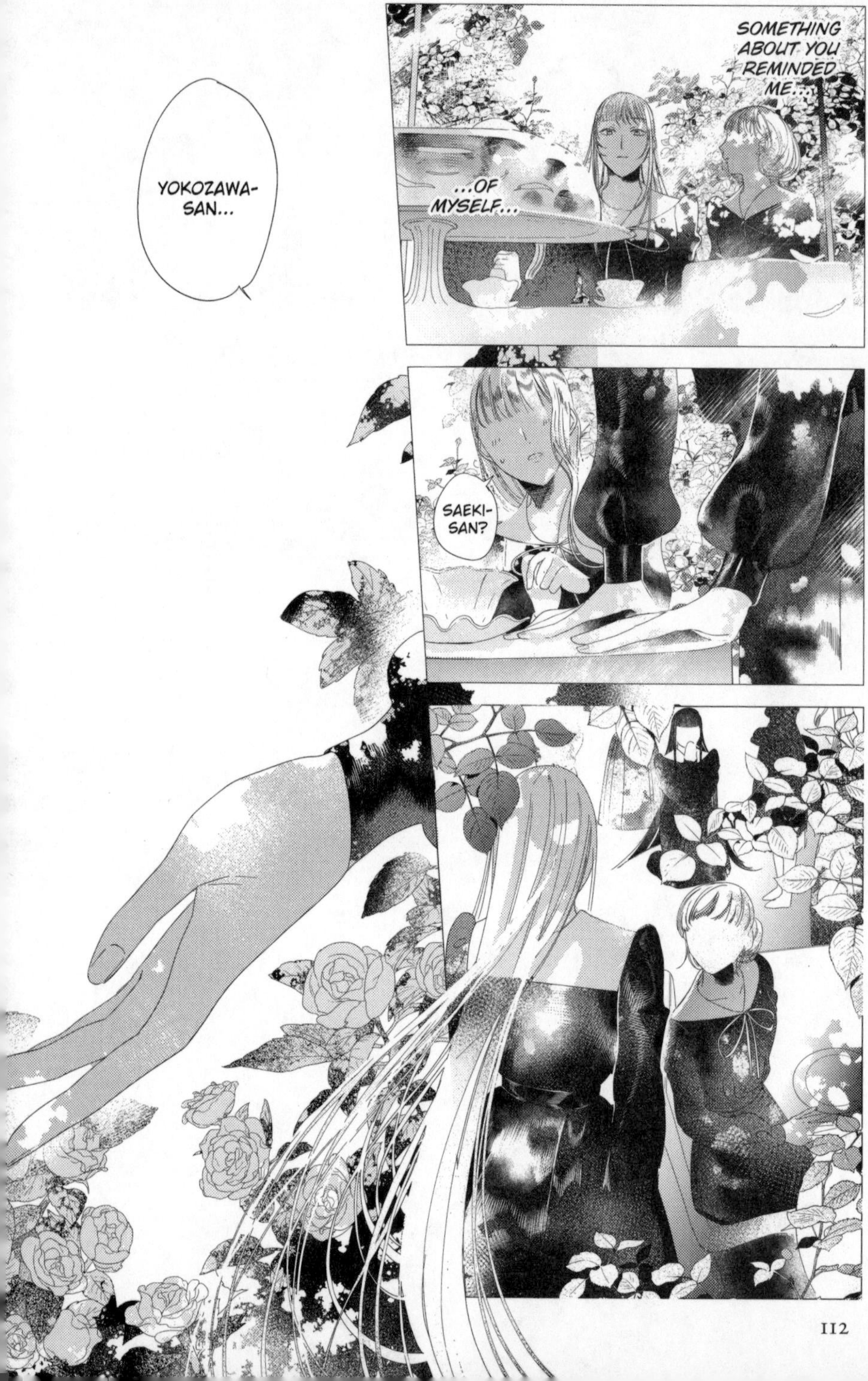
SOMETHING ABOUT YOU REMINDED ME...
...OF MYSELF...
YOKOZAWA-SAN...
SAEKI-SAN?

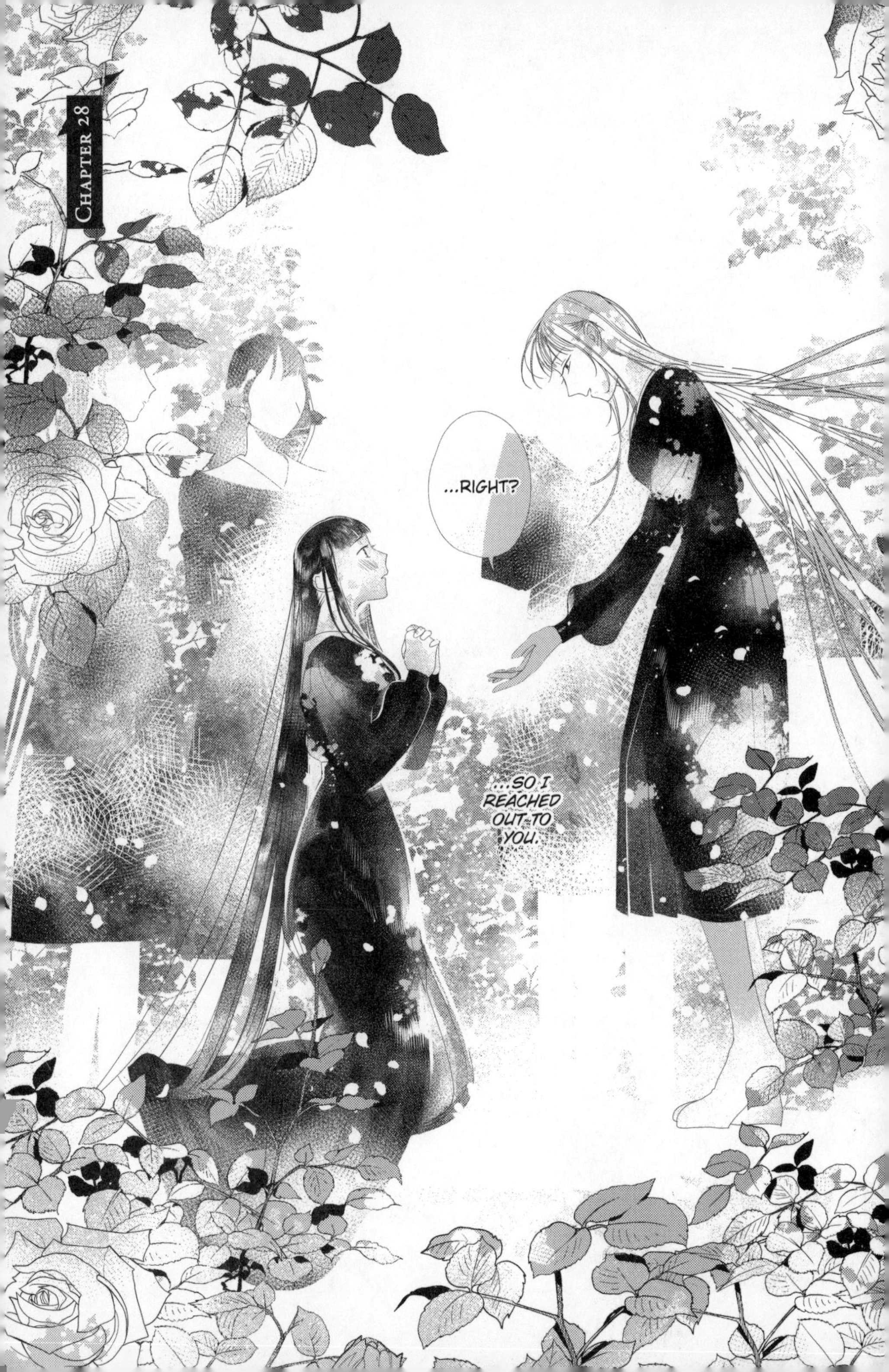
Chapter 28
...RIGHT?
...SO I REACHED OUT TO YOU.

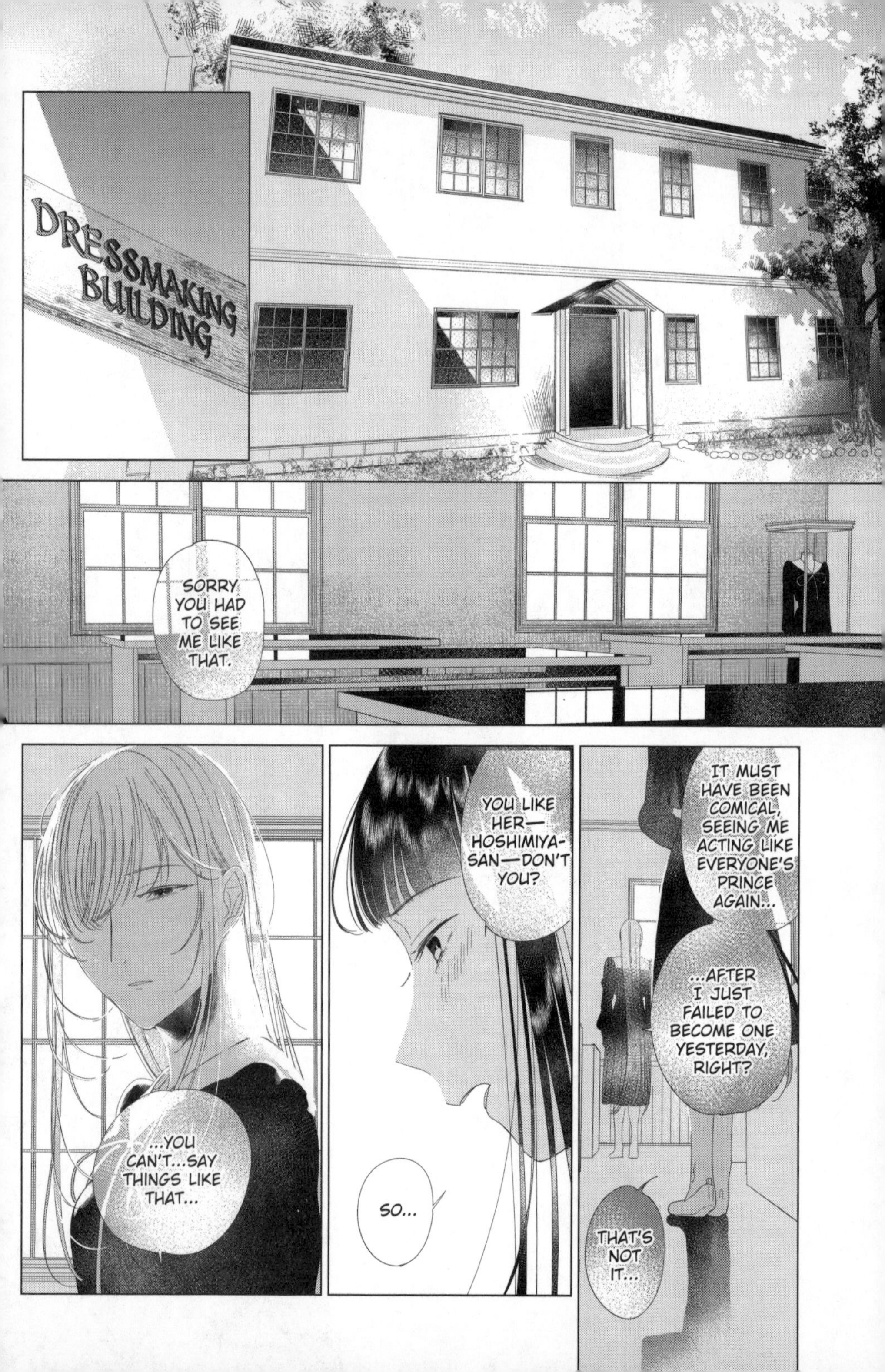
DRESSMAKING BUILDING
SORRY YOU HAD TO SEE ME LIKE THAT.
IT MUST HAVE BEEN COMICAL, SEEING ME ACTING LIKE EVERYONE'S PRINCE AGAIN...
...AFTER I JUST FAILED TO BECOME ONE YESTERDAY, RIGHT?
THAT'S NOT IT...
YOU LIKE HER—HOSHIMIYA-SAN—DON'T YOU?
SO...
...YOU CAN'T...SAY THINGS LIKE THAT...

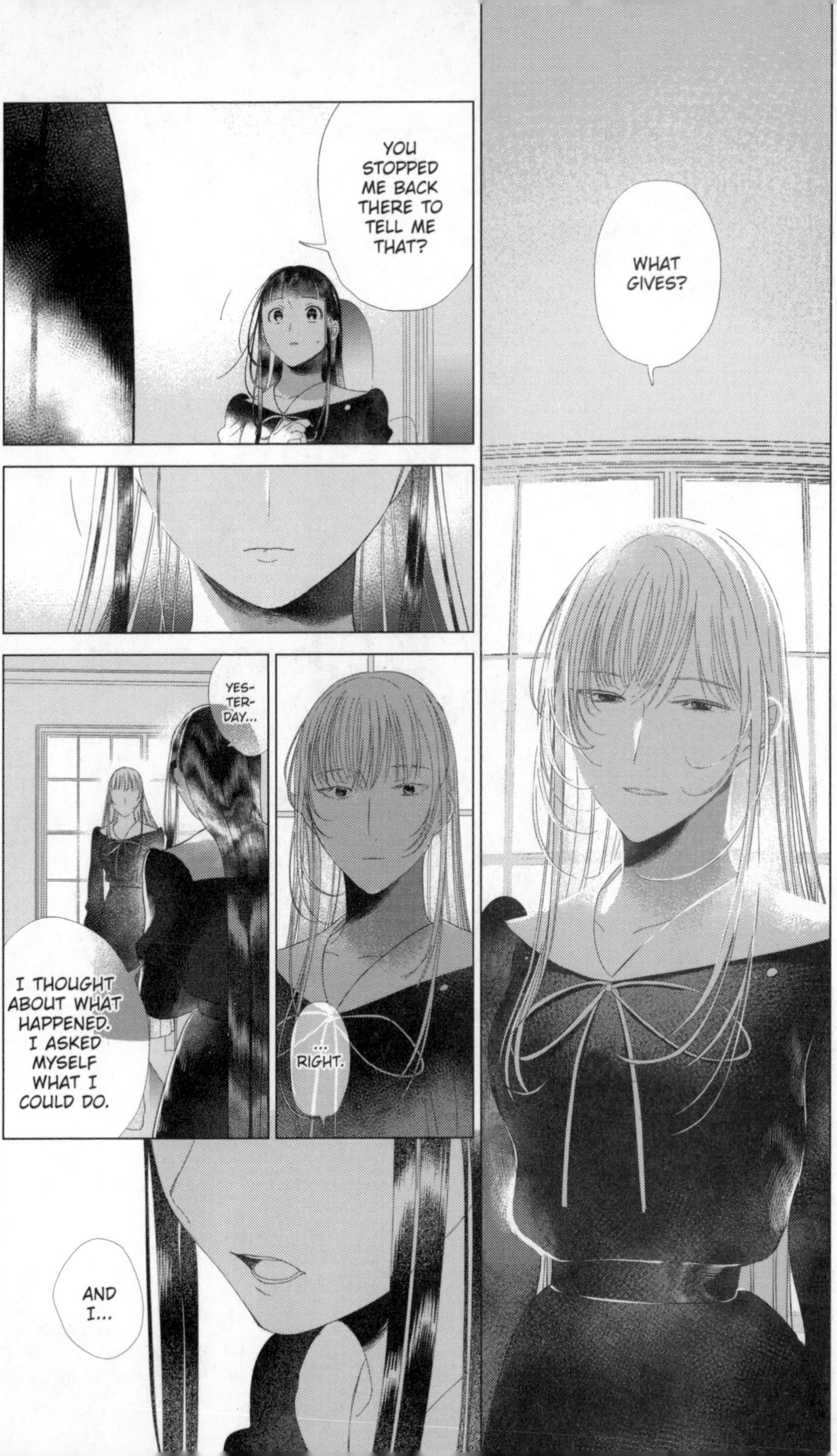
WHAT GIVES?
YOU STOPPED ME BACK THERE TO TELL ME THAT?
...RIGHT.
YES-TER-DAY...
I THOUGHT ABOUT WHAT HAPPENED. I ASKED MYSELF WHAT I COULD DO.
AND I...

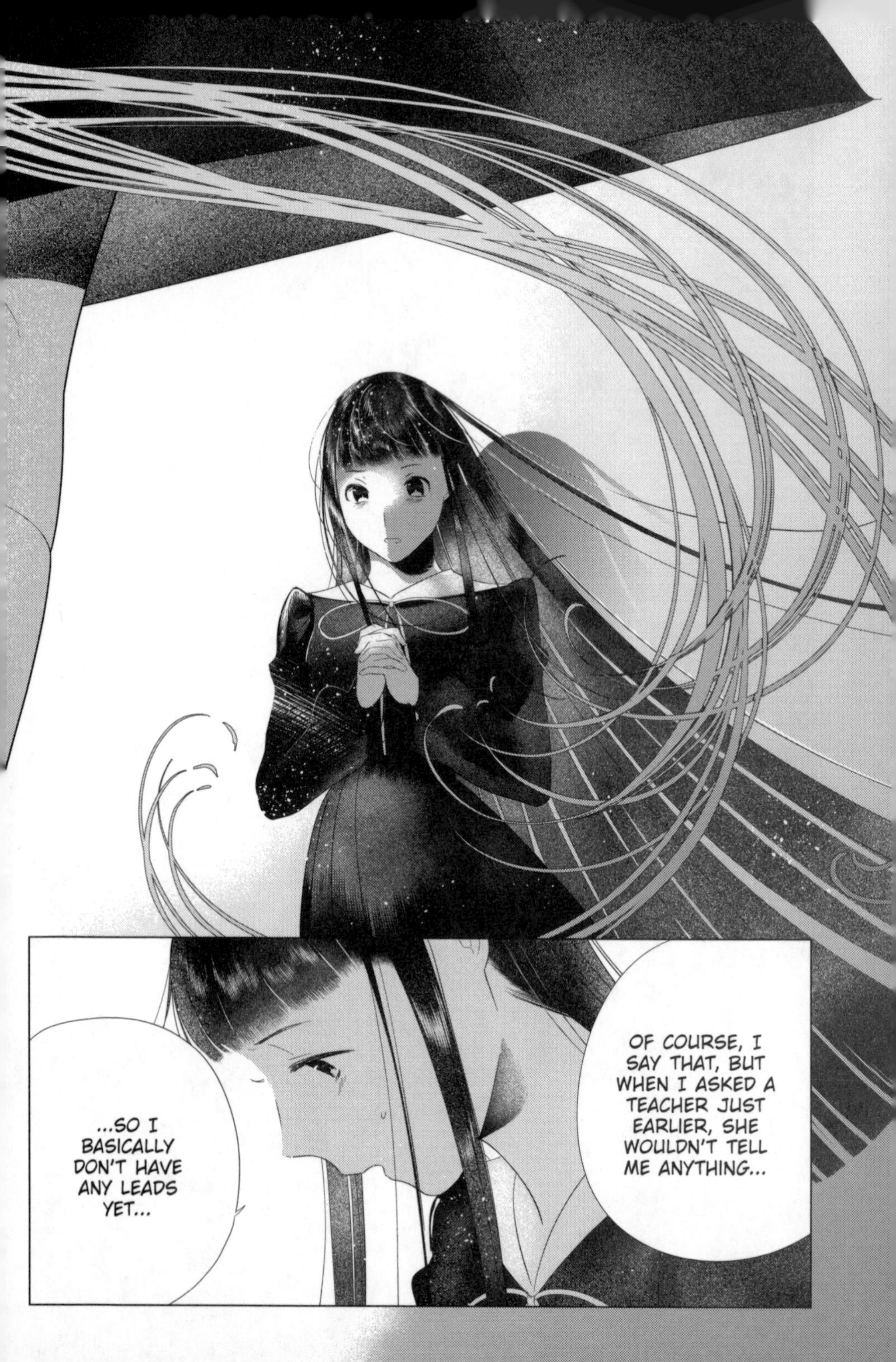
OF COURSE, I SAY THAT, BUT WHEN I ASKED A TEACHER JUST EARLIER, SHE WOULDN'T TELL ME ANYTHING...
...SO I BASICALLY DON'T HAVE ANY LEADS YET...

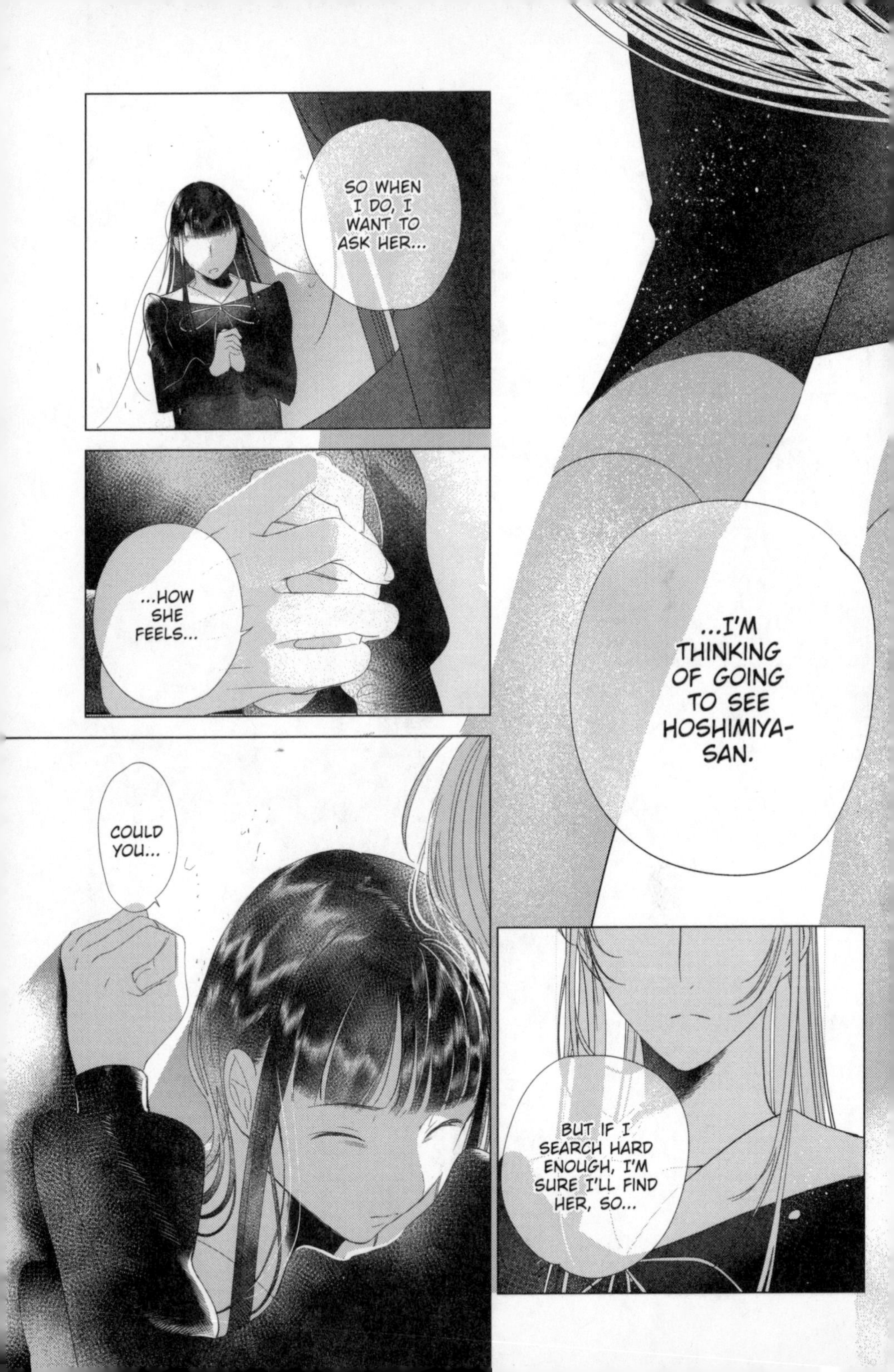
...I'M THINKING OF GOING TO SEE HOSHIMIYA-SAN.
BUT IF I SEARCH HARD ENOUGH, I'M SURE I'LL FIND HER, SO...
SO WHEN I DO, I WANT TO ASK HER...
...HOW SHE FEELS...
COULD YOU...

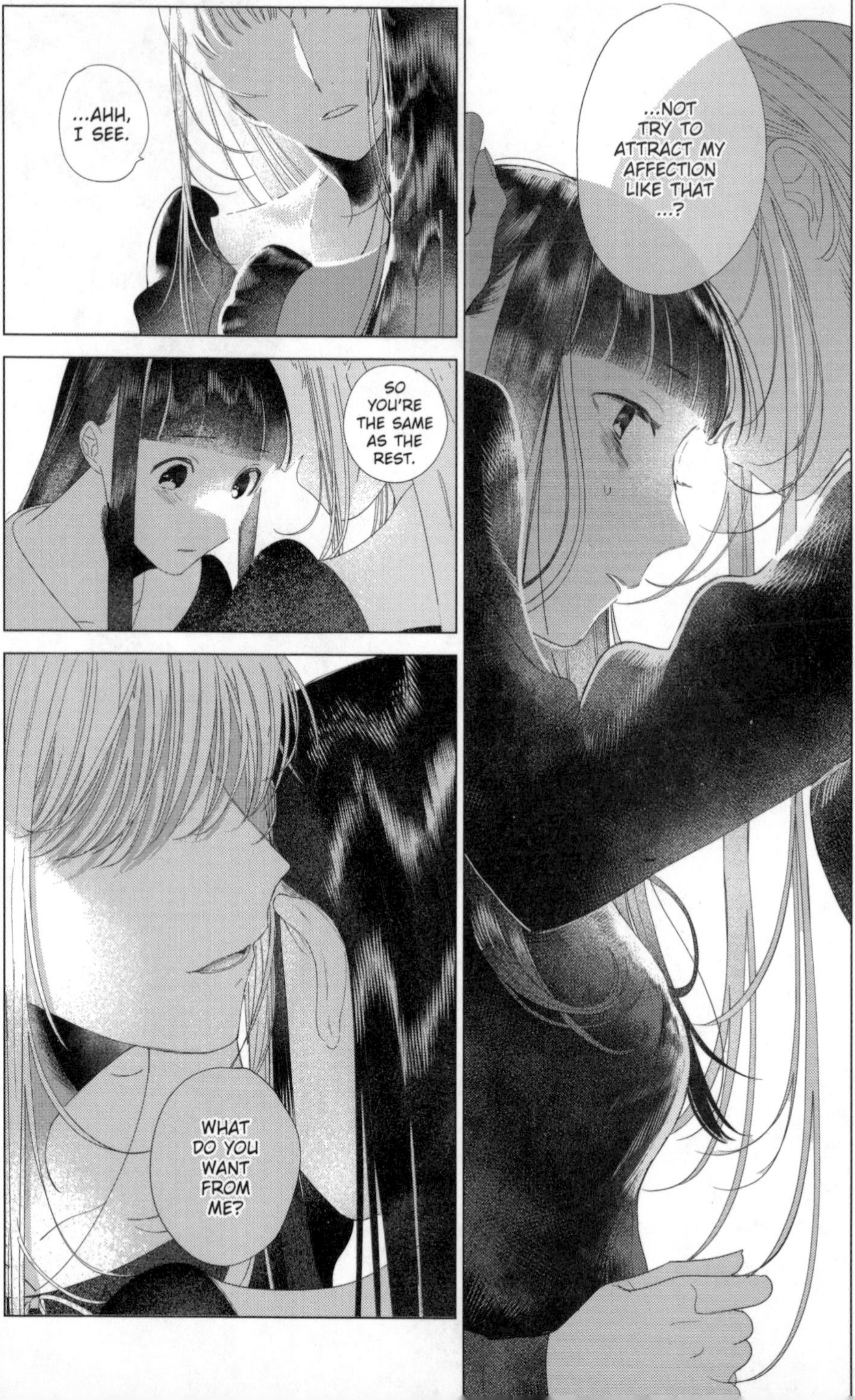
...NOT TRY TO ATTRACT MY AFFECTION LIKE THAT ...?
...AHH, I SEE.
SO YOU'RE THE SAME AS THE REST.
WHAT DO YOU WANT FROM ME?

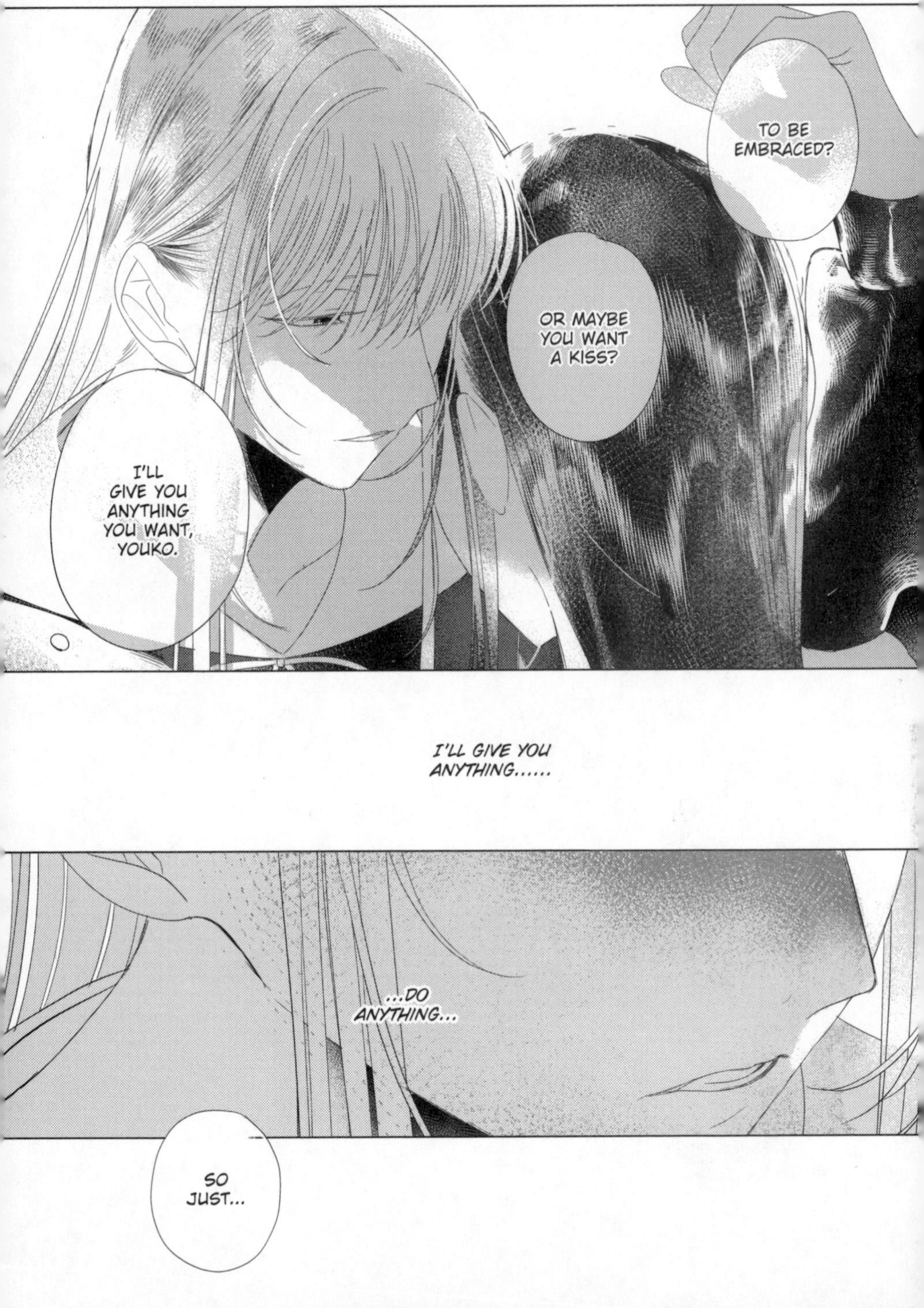
TO BE EMBRACED?
OR MAYBE YOU WANT A KISS?
I'LL GIVE YOU ANYTHING YOU WANT, YOUKO.
I'LL GIVE YOU ANYTHING......
...DO ANYTHING...
SO JUST...

...READ THE
ROOM......

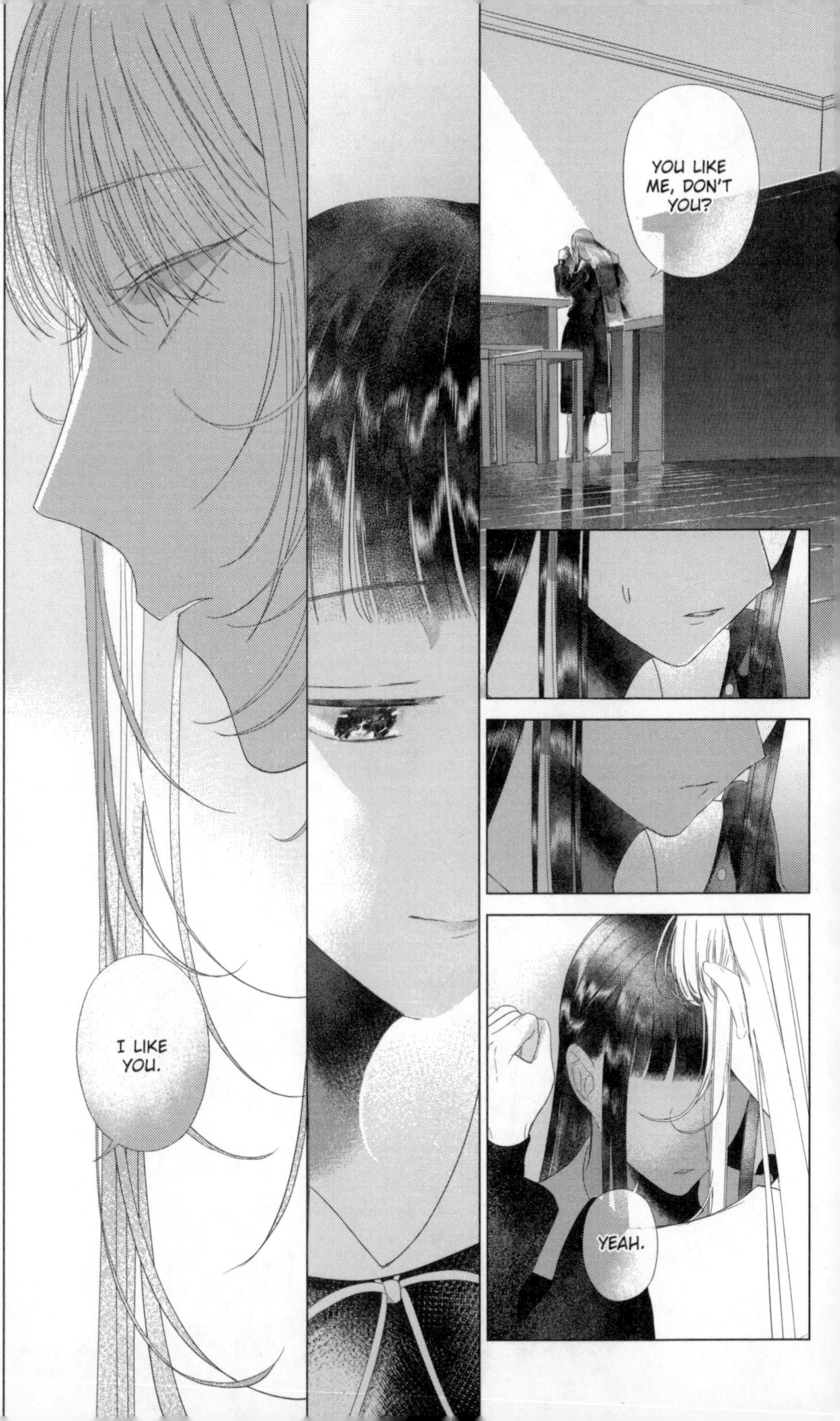
YOU LIKE ME, DON'T YOU?
YEAH.
I LIKE YOU.

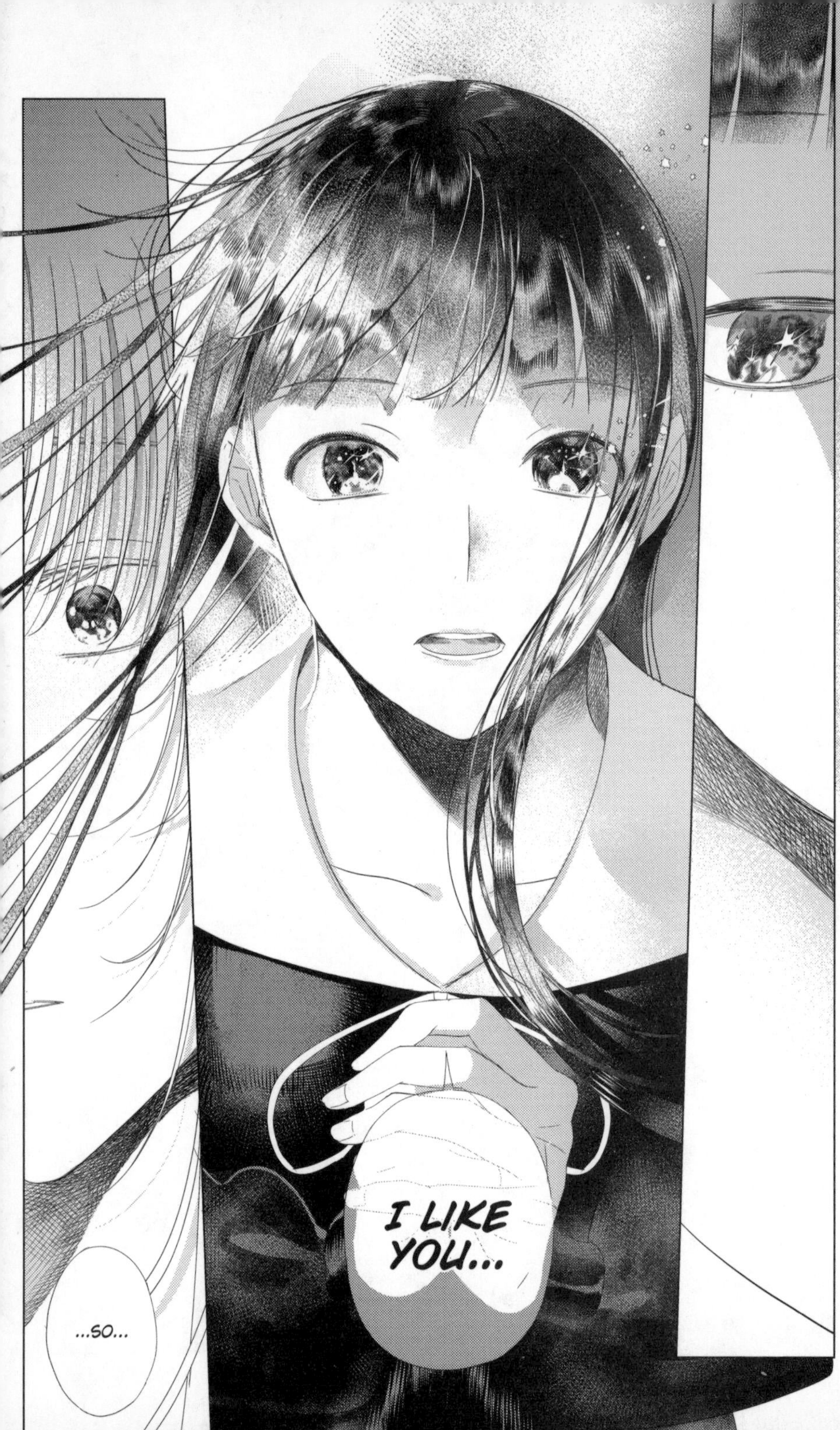
I LIKE YOU...
...SO...

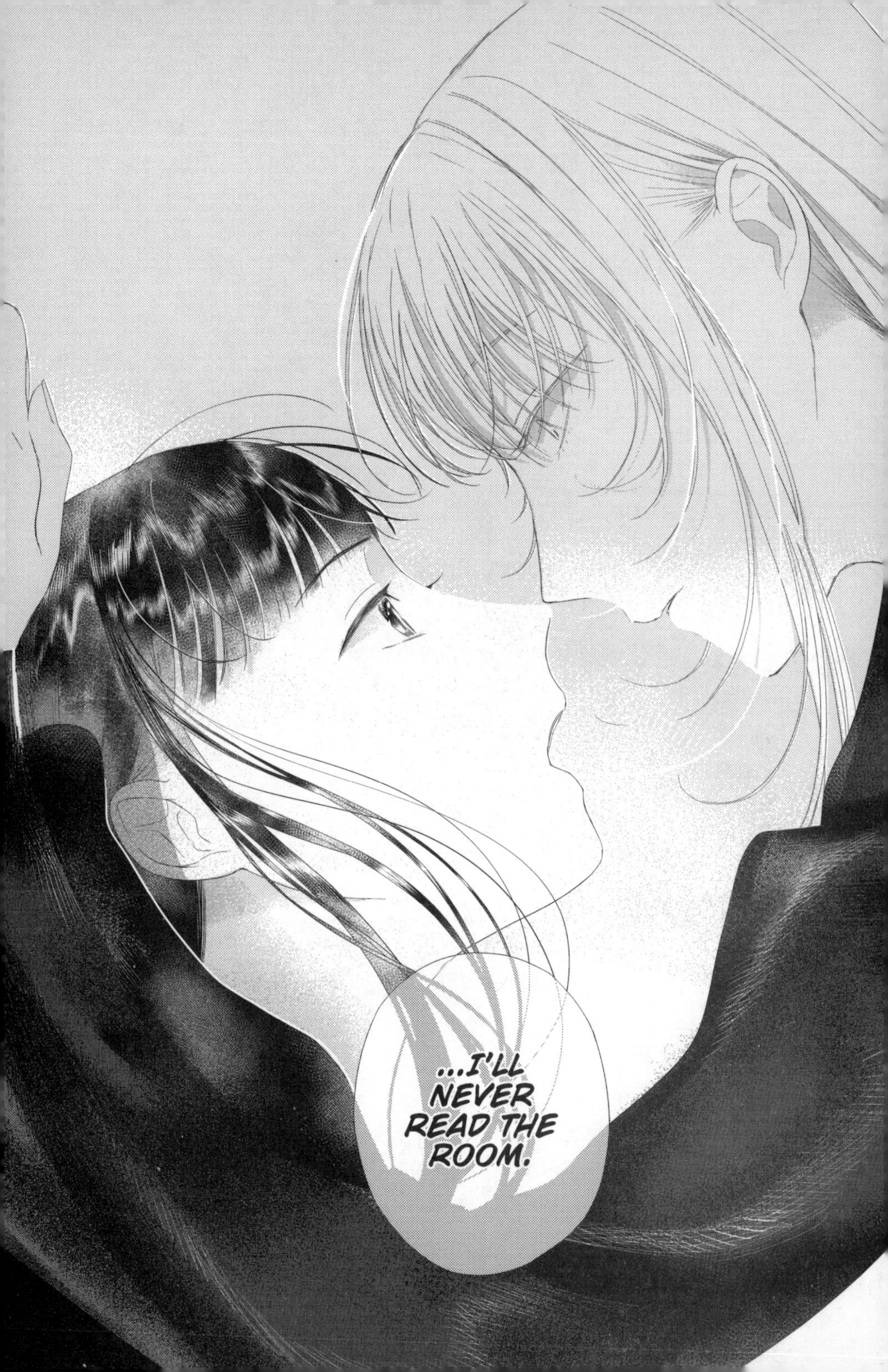
...I'LL NEVER READ THE ROOM.

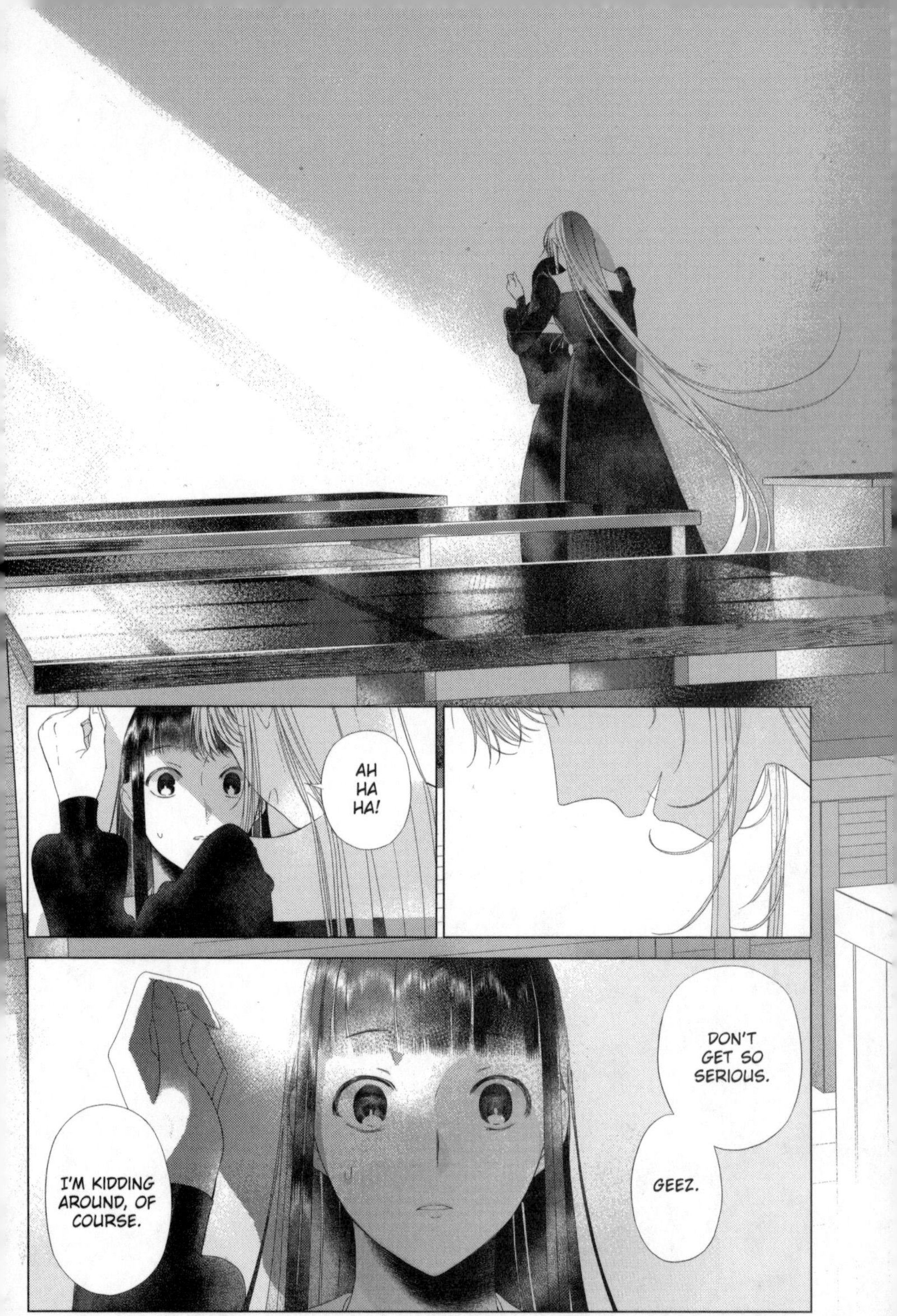
AH HA HA!
DON'T GET SO SERIOUS.
GEEZ.
I'M KIDDING AROUND, OF COURSE.

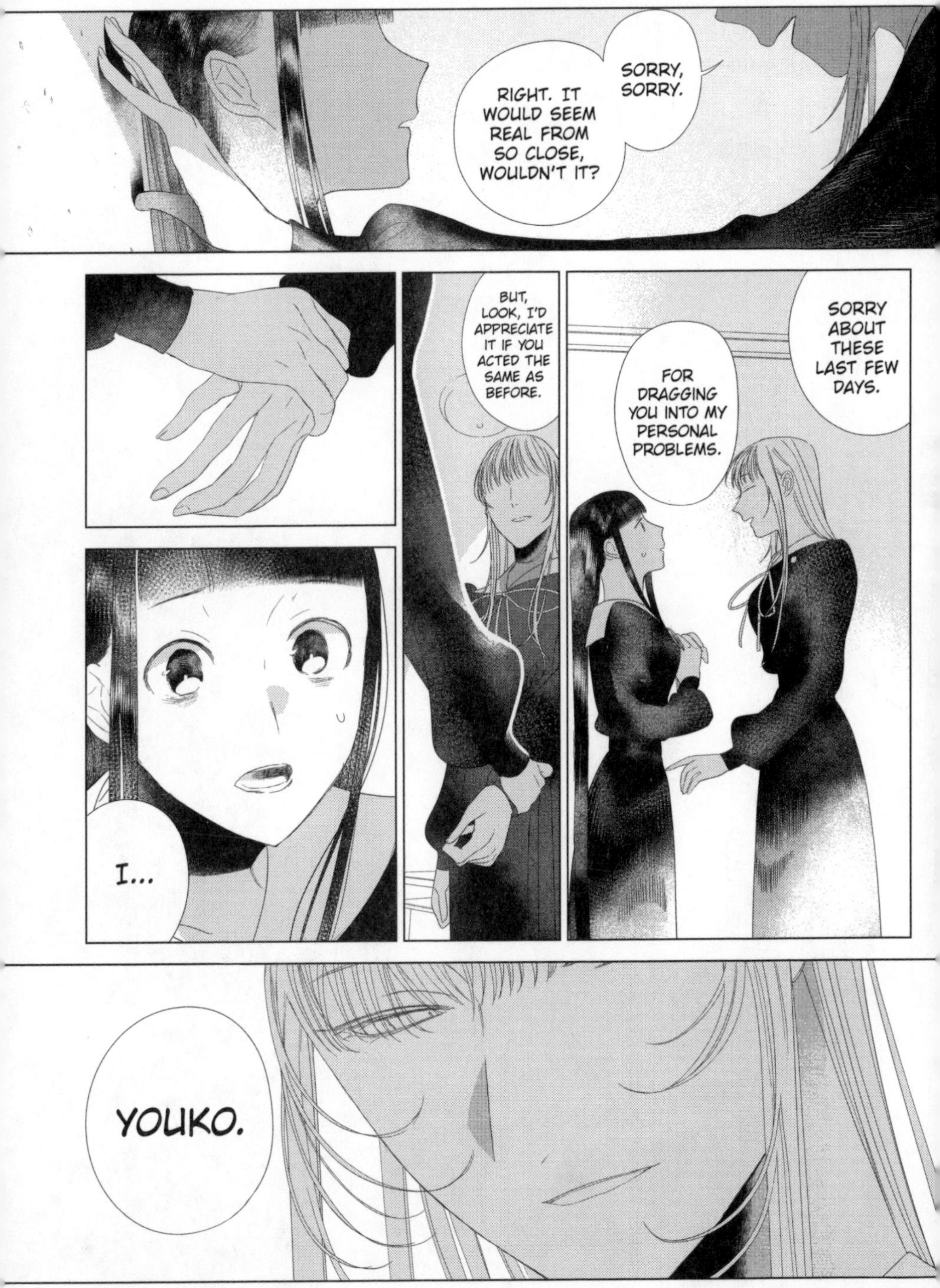
SORRY, SORRY.
RIGHT. IT WOULD SEEM REAL FROM SO CLOSE, WOULDN'T IT?
SORRY ABOUT THESE LAST FEW DAYS.
FOR DRAGGING YOU INTO MY PERSONAL PROBLEMS.
BUT, LOOK, I'D APPRECIATE IT IF YOU ACTED THE SAME AS BEFORE.
I...
YOUKO.

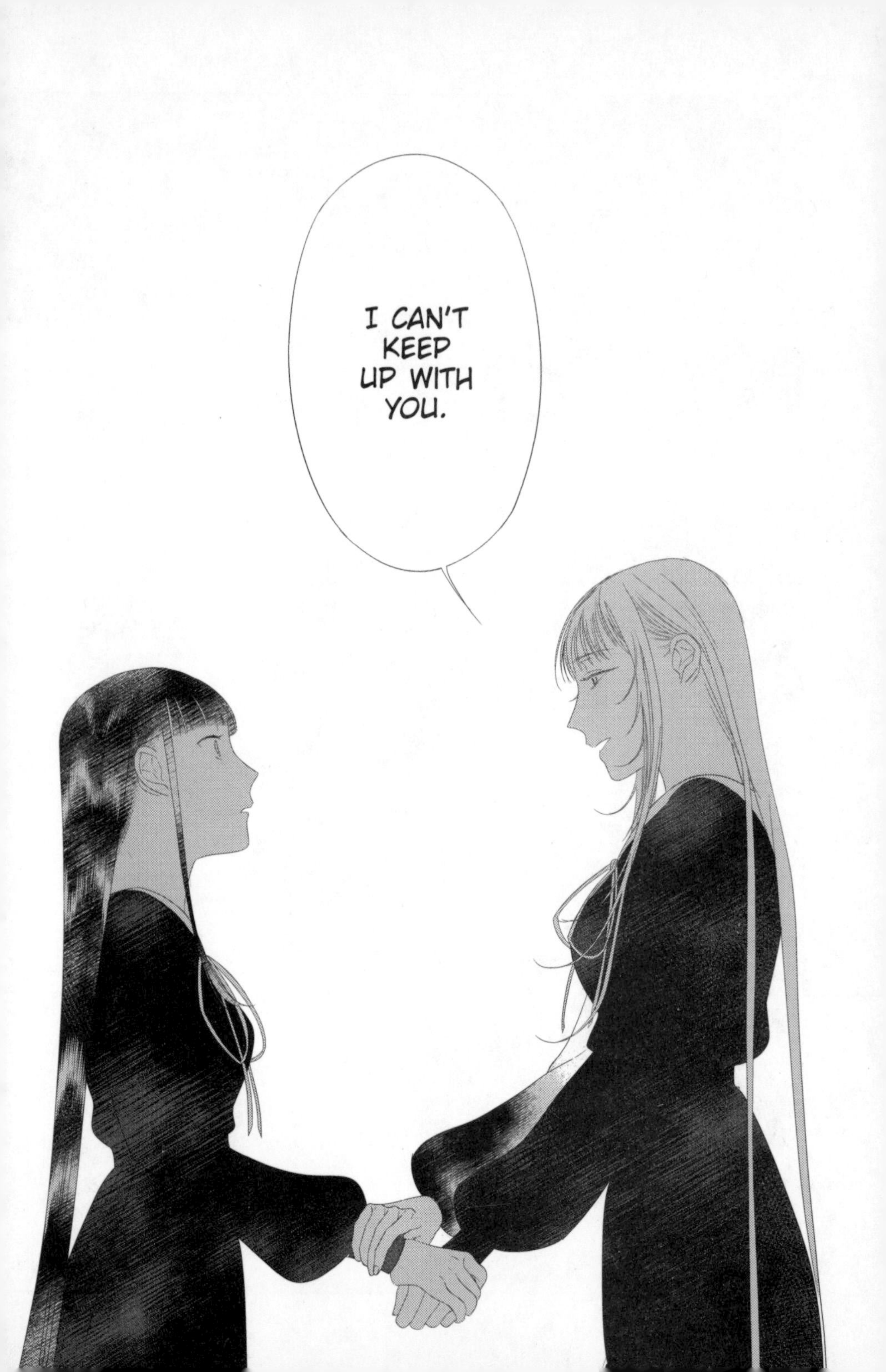
I CAN'T KEEP UP WITH YOU.

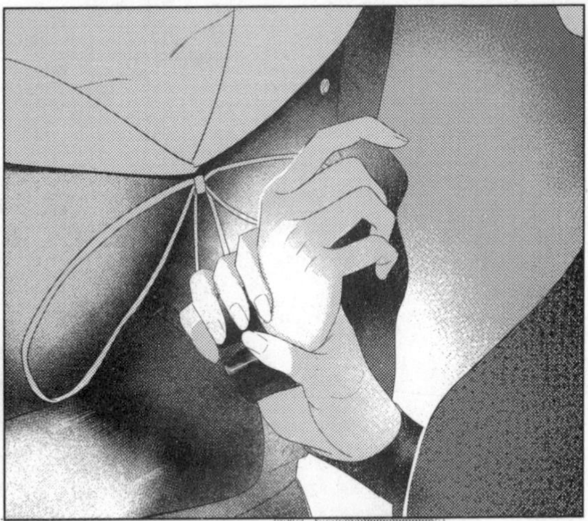
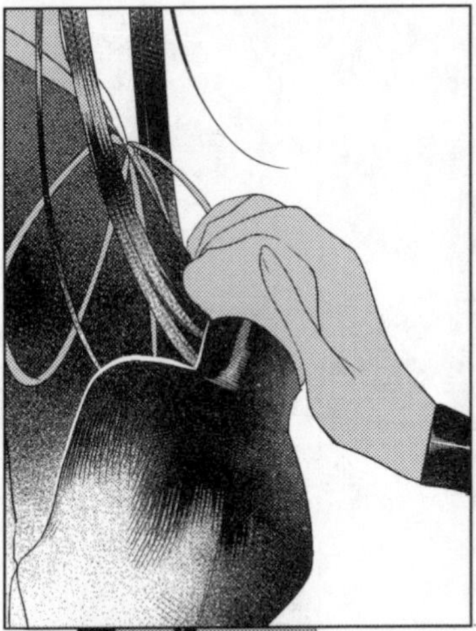
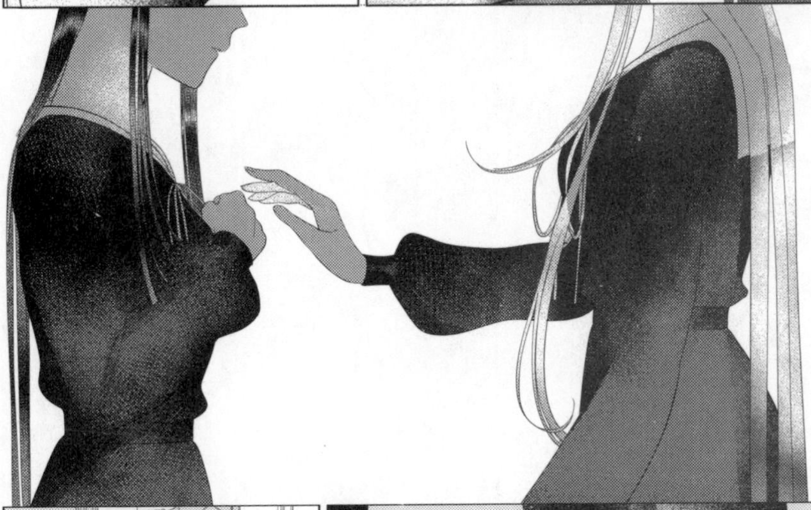
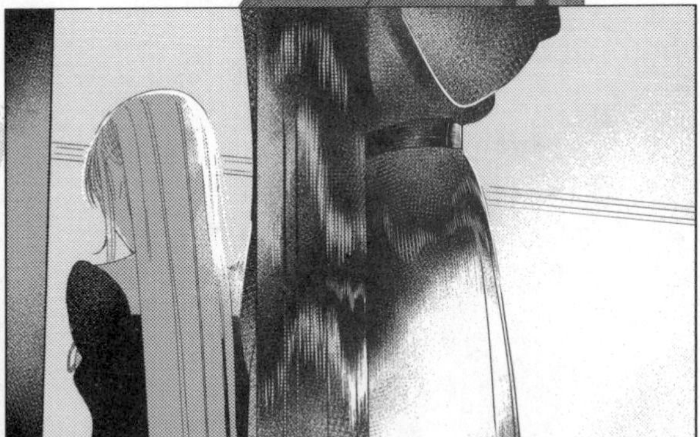
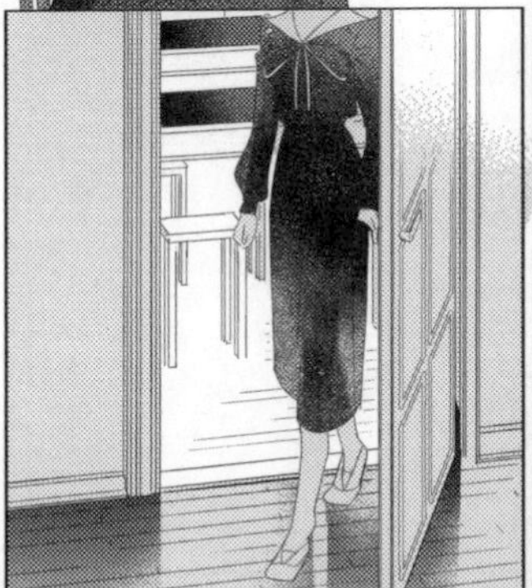

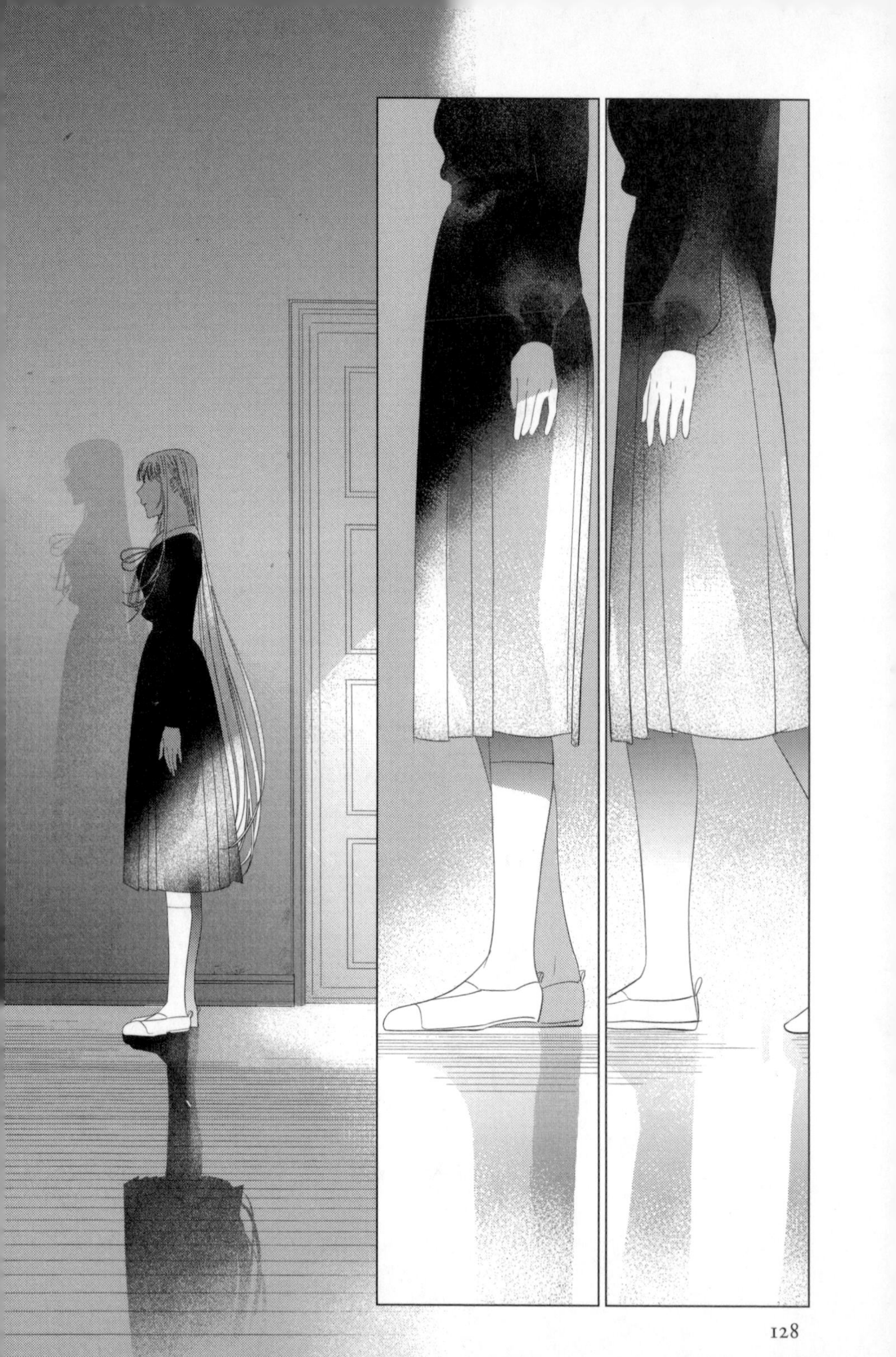

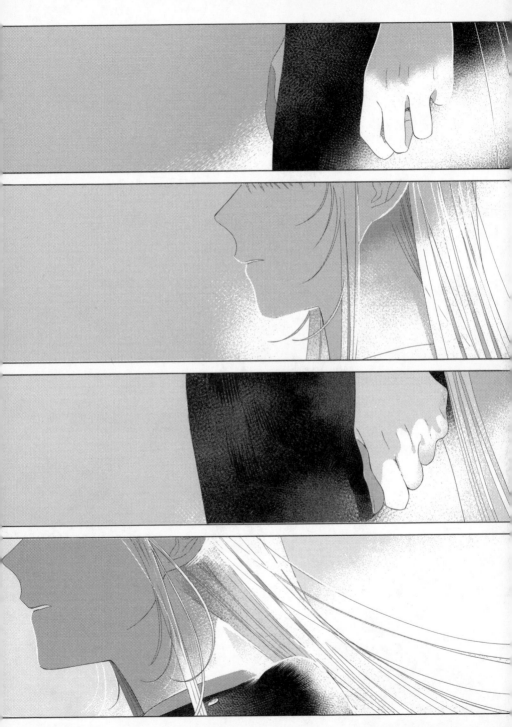

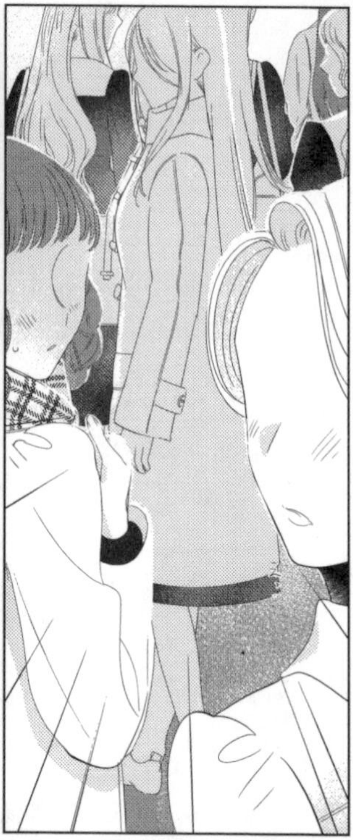
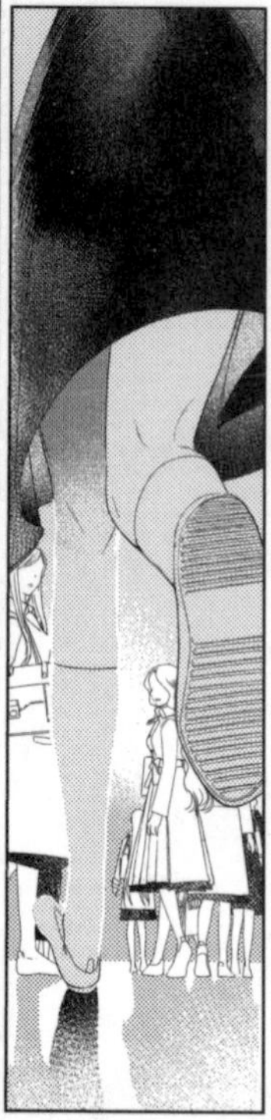
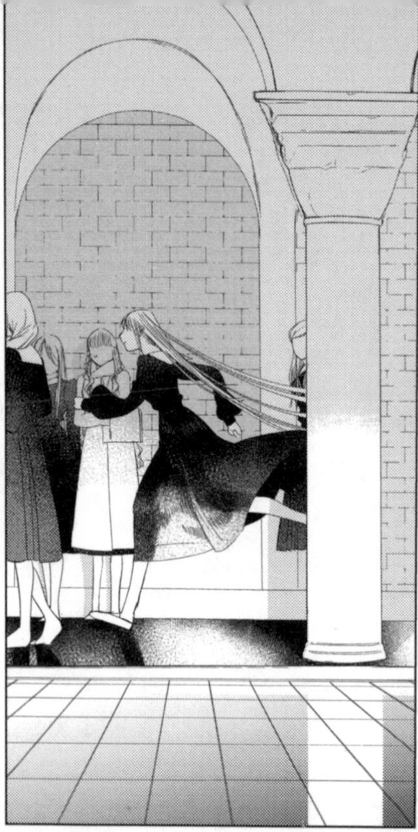
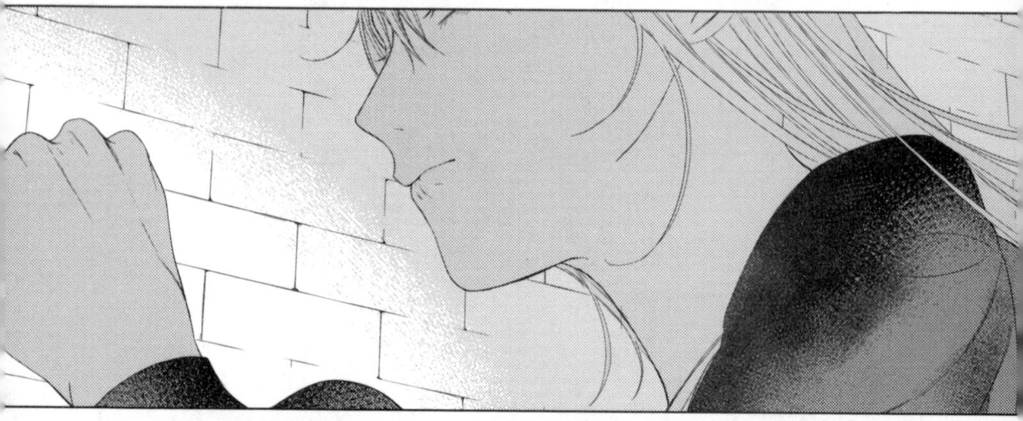
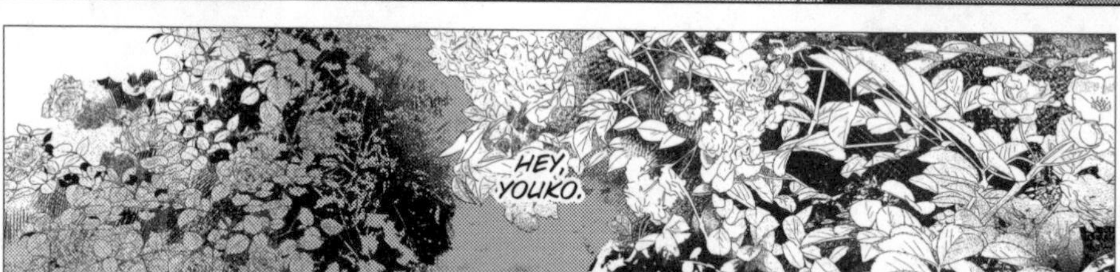
HEY, YOUKO.

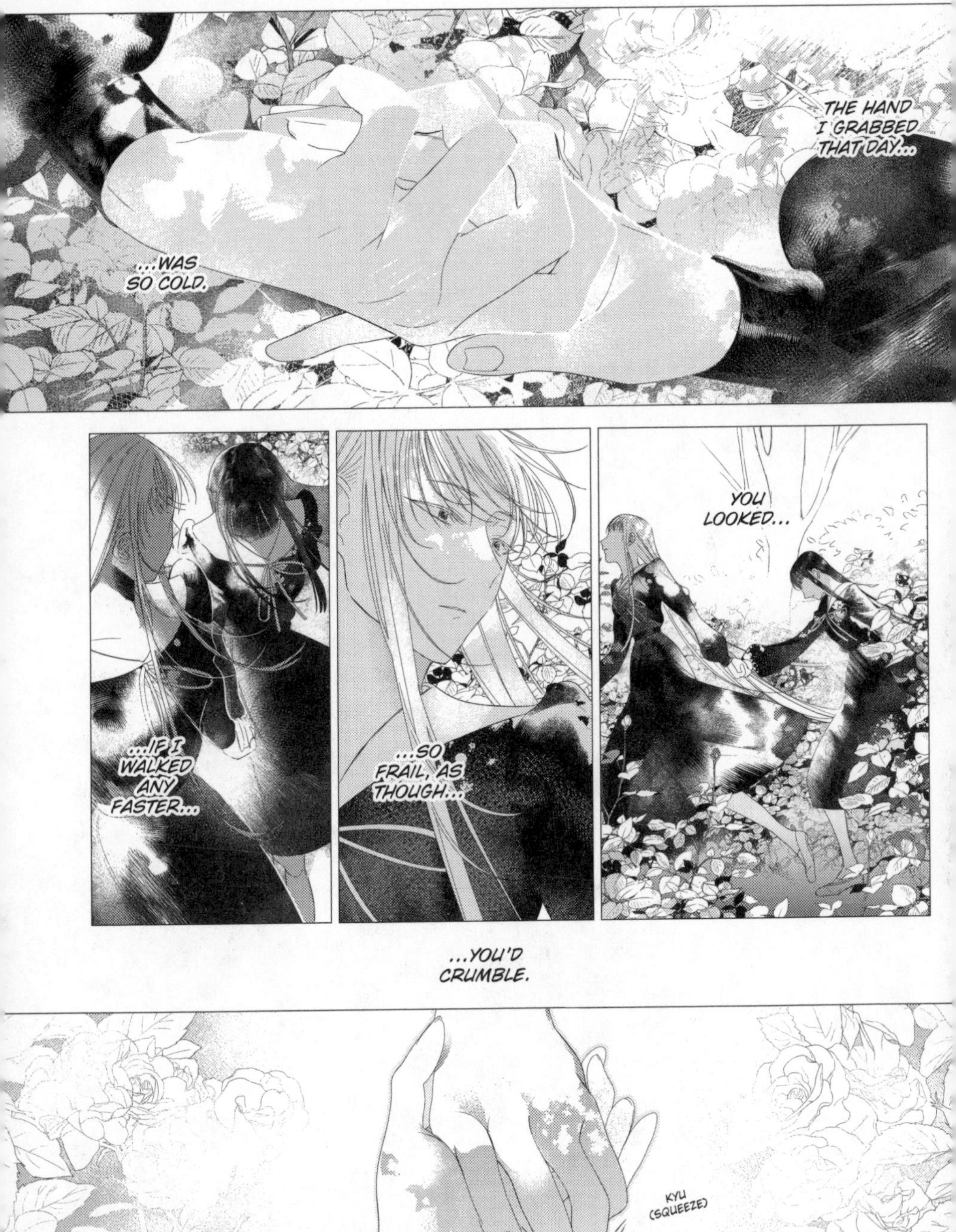
THE HAND I GRABBED THAT DAY...
...WAS SO COLD.
YOU LOOKED...
...SO FRAIL, AS THOUGH...
...IF I WALKED ANY FASTER...
...YOU'D CRUMBLE.
KYU (SQUEEZE)
きゅ

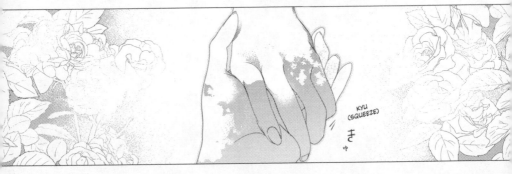

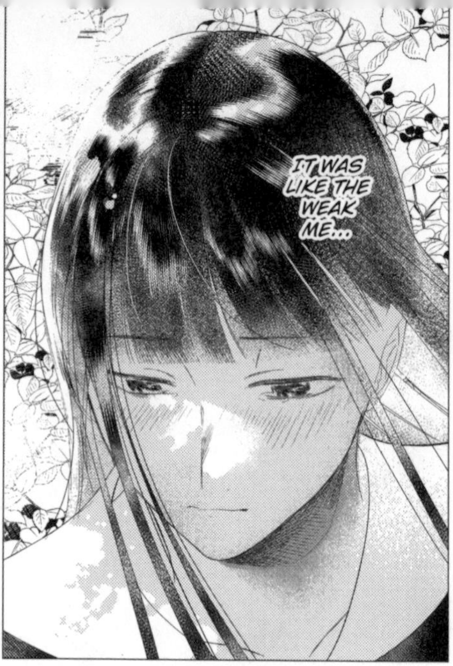
IT WAS LIKE THE WEAK ME...

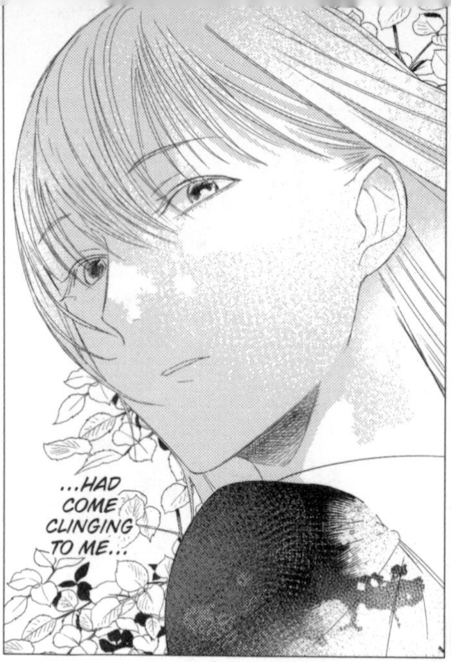
...HAD COME CLINGING TO ME...

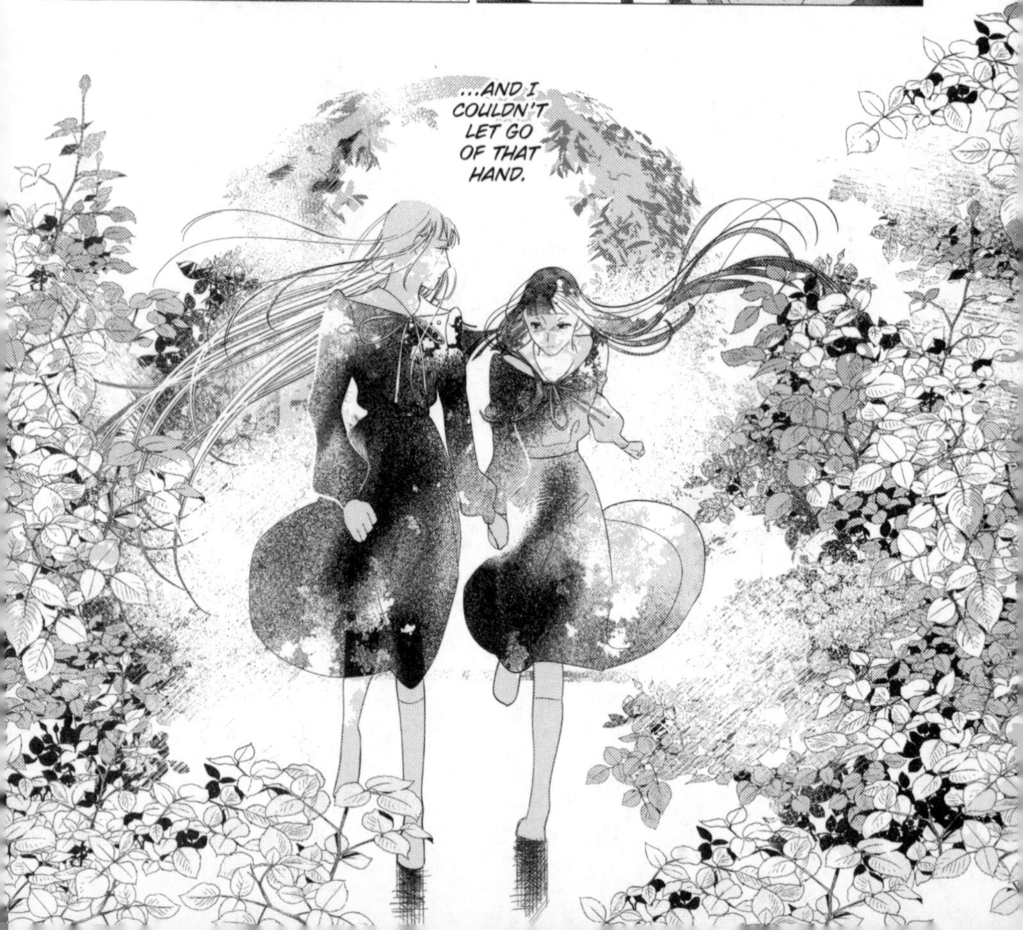
...AND I COULDN'T LET GO OF THAT HAND.

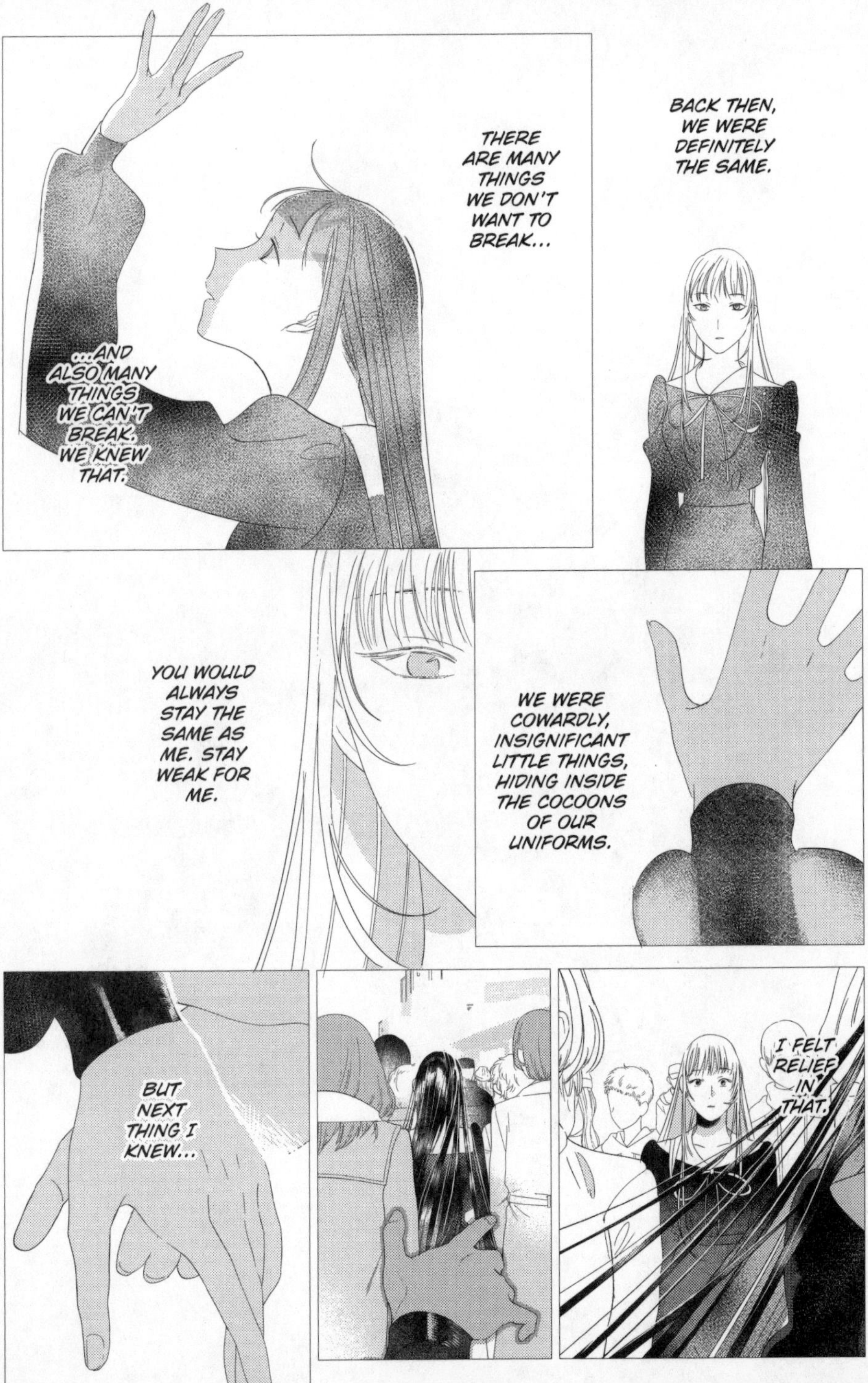
BACK THEN, WE WERE DEFINITELY THE SAME.
THERE ARE MANY THINGS WE DON'T WANT TO BREAK...
...AND ALSO MANY THINGS WE CAN'T BREAK. WE KNEW THAT.
WE WERE COWARDLY, INSIGNIFICANT LITTLE THINGS, HIDING INSIDE THE COCOONS OF OUR UNIFORMS.
YOU WOULD ALWAYS STAY THE SAME AS ME. STAY WEAK FOR ME.
I FELT RELIEF IN THAT.
BUT NEXT THING I KNEW...

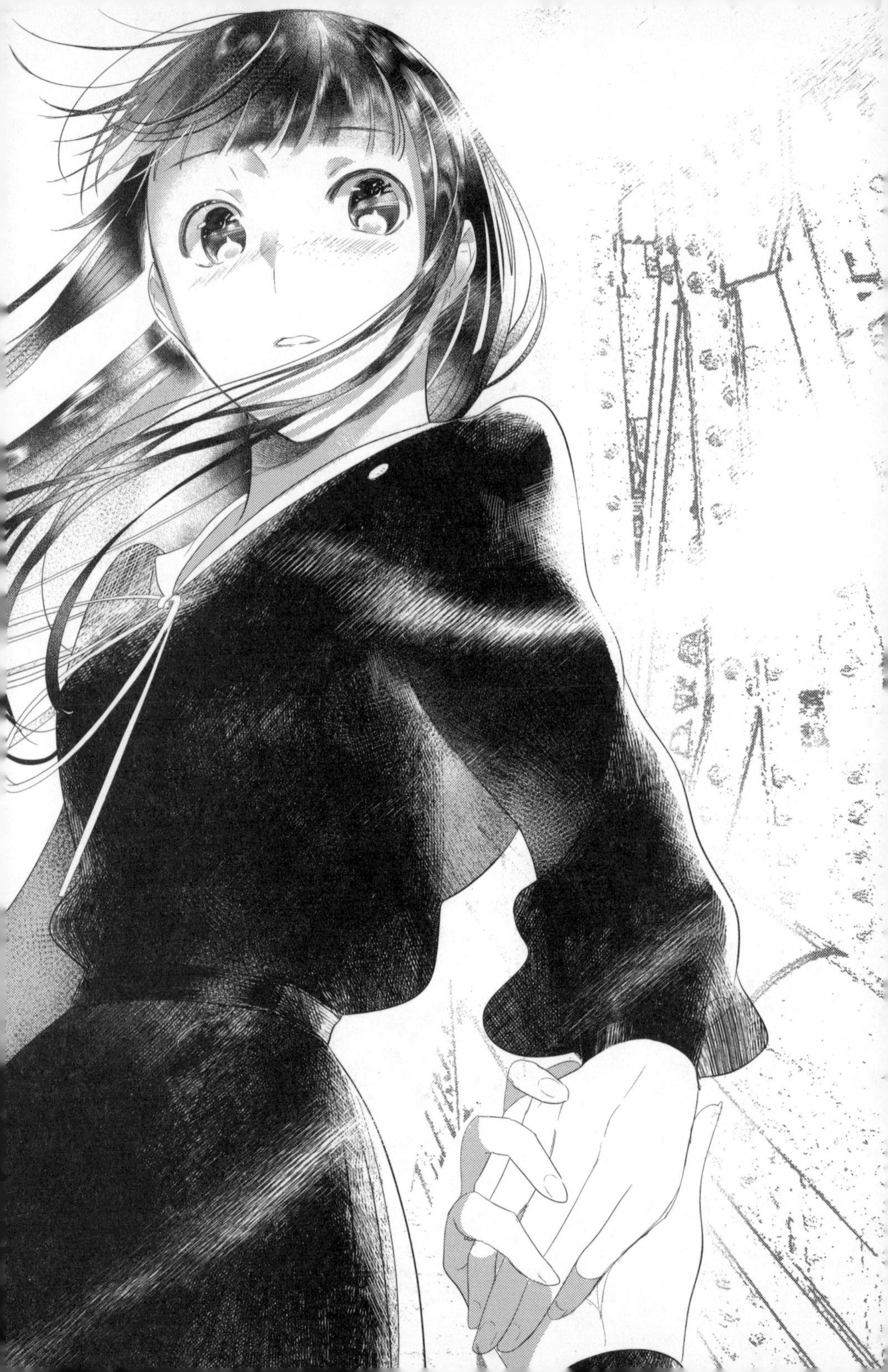

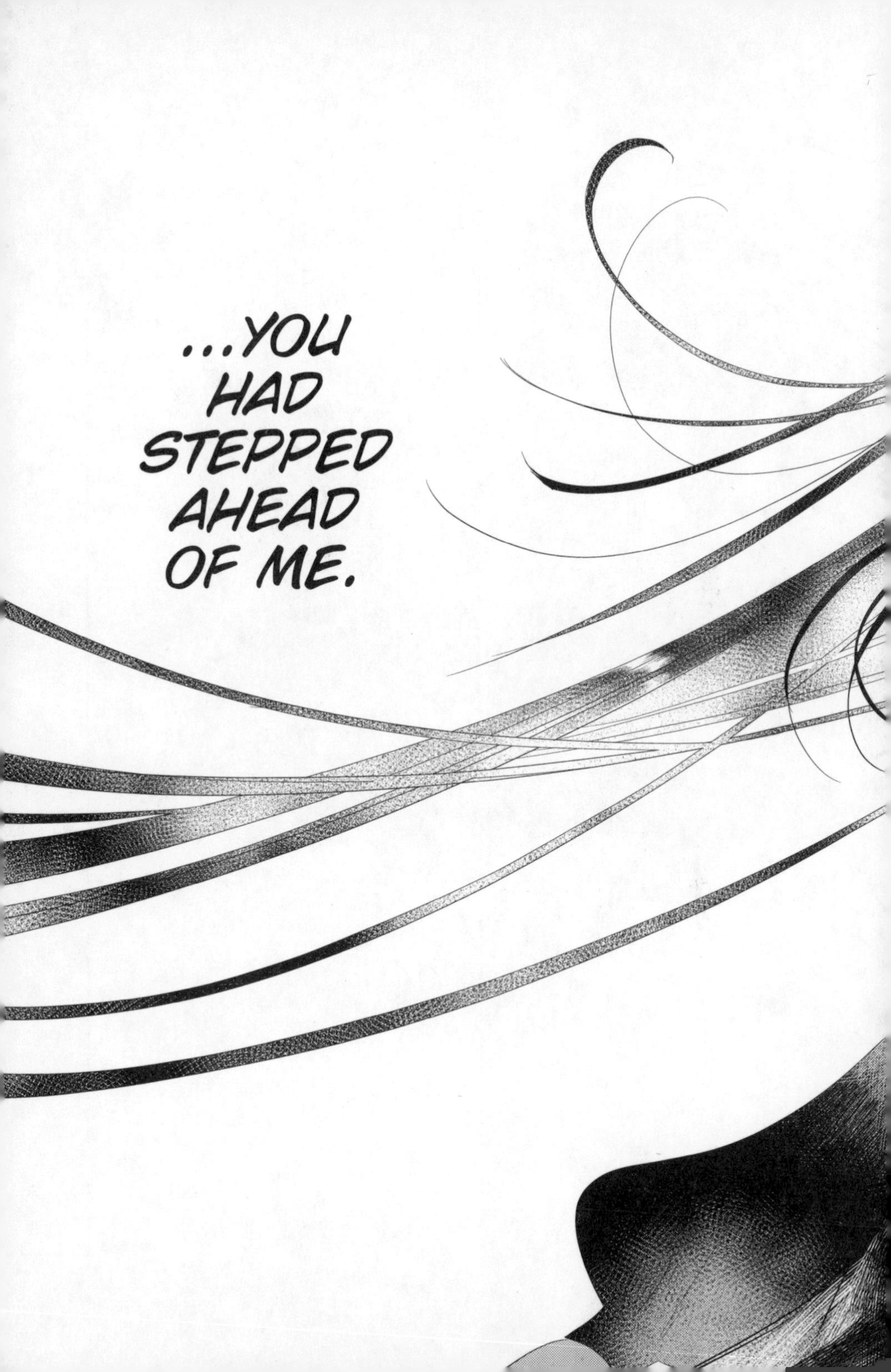
...YOU HAD STEPPED AHEAD OF ME.

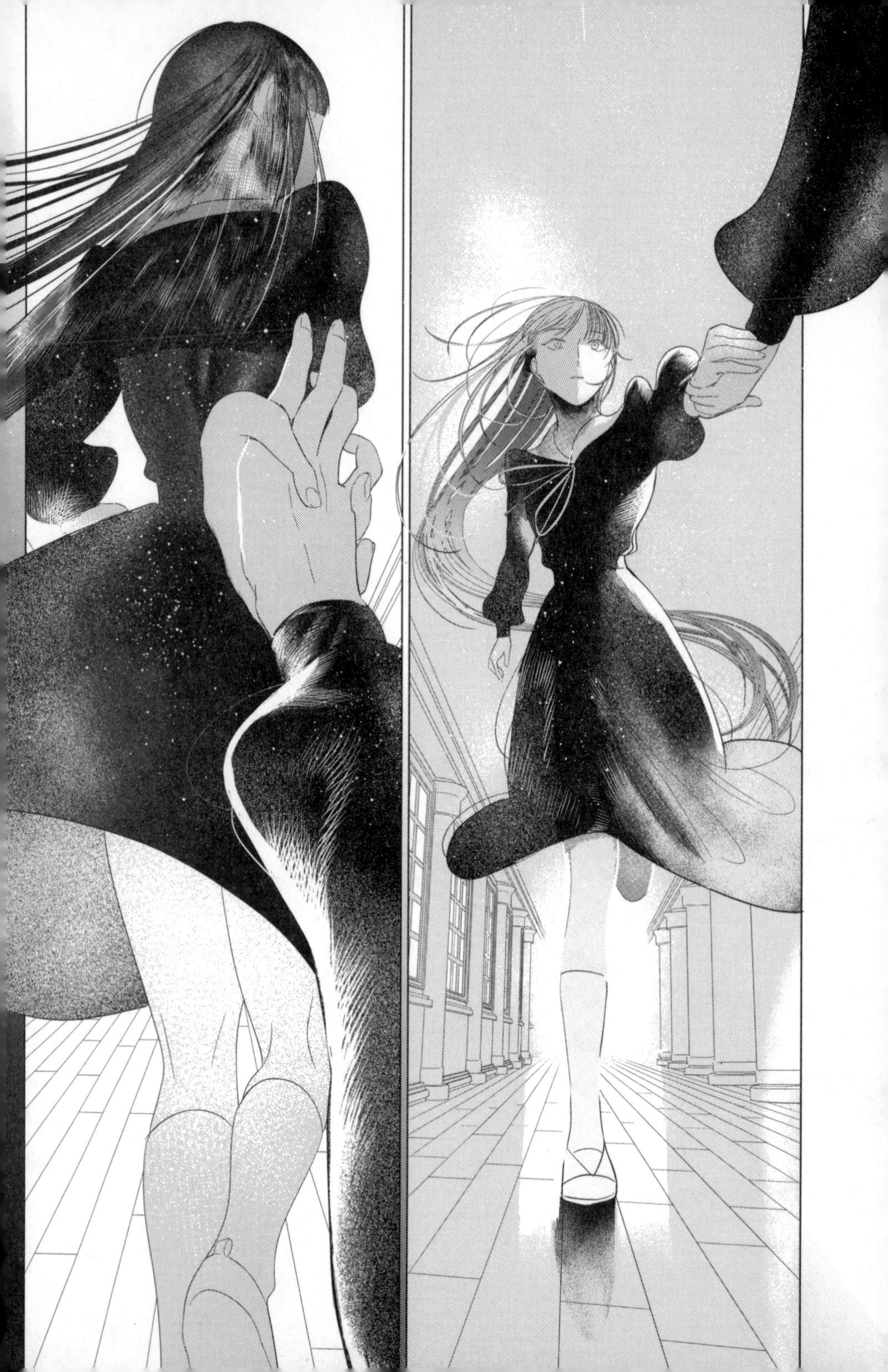

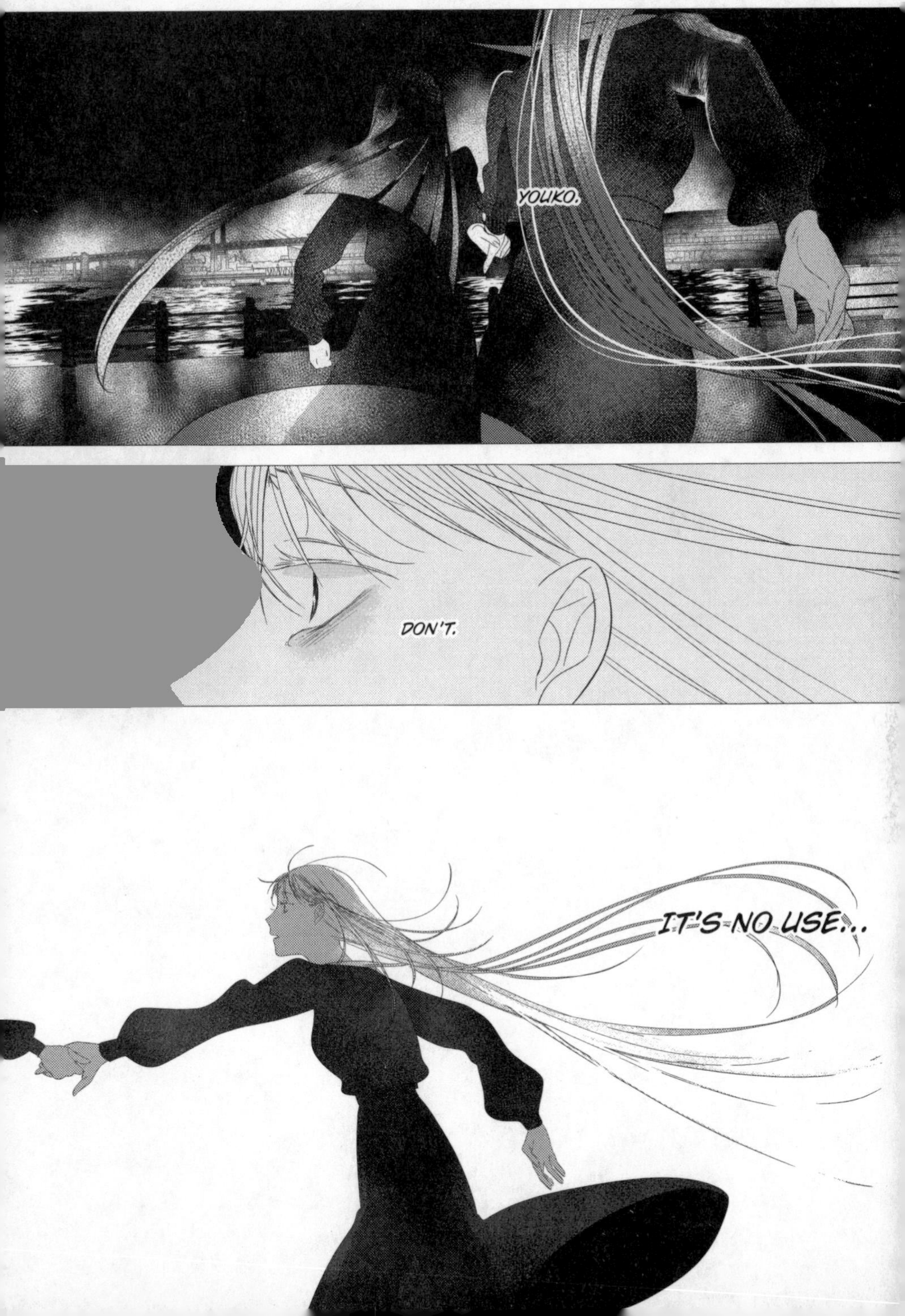
YOUKO.
DON'T.
IT'S NO USE...

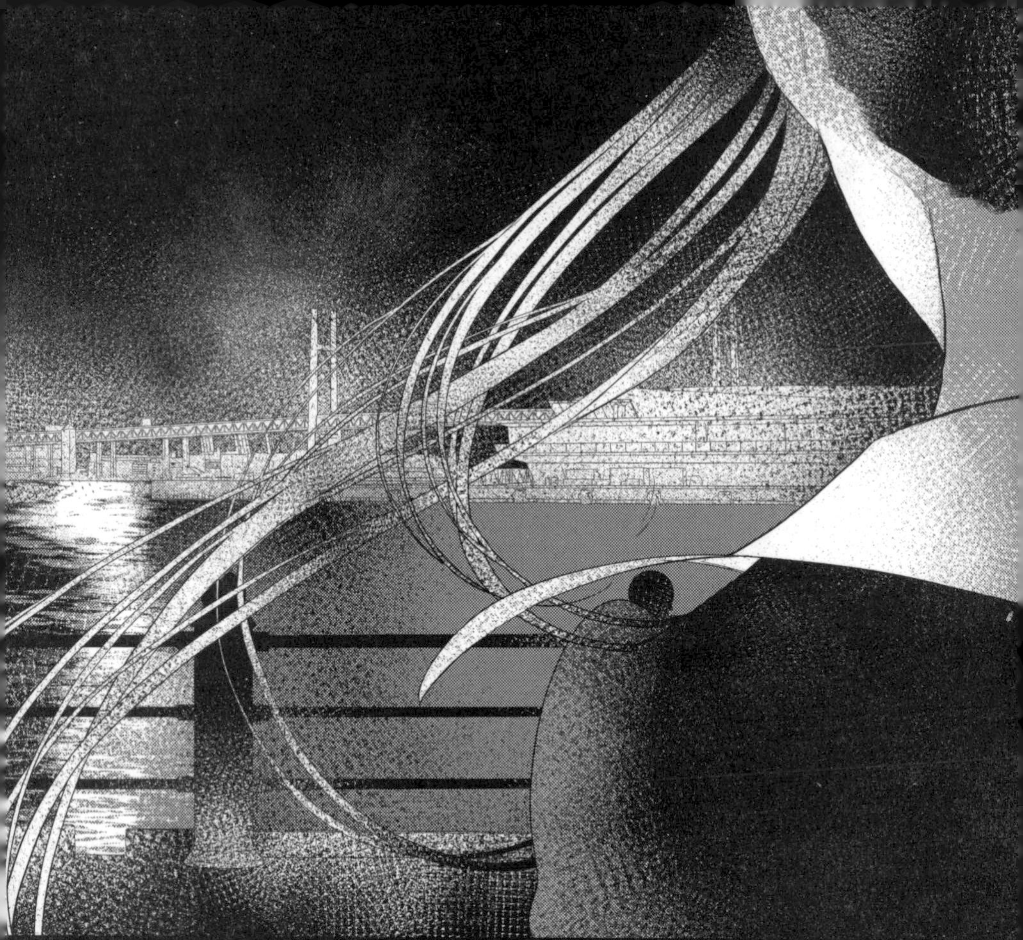

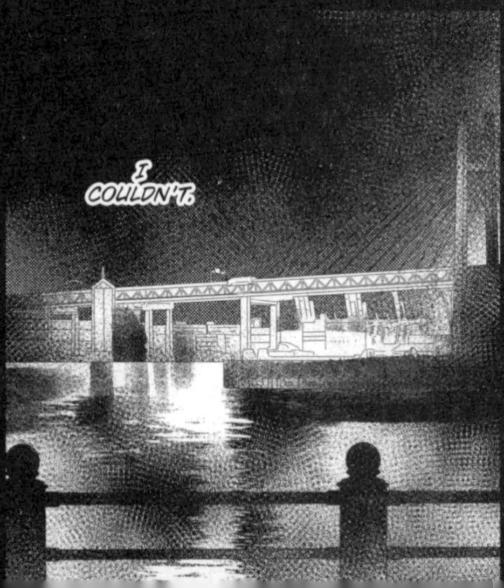
I COULDN'T.

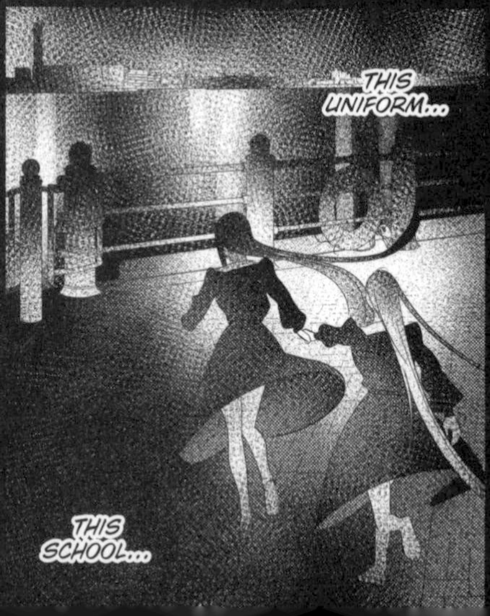
THIS UNIFORM...
THIS SCHOOL...

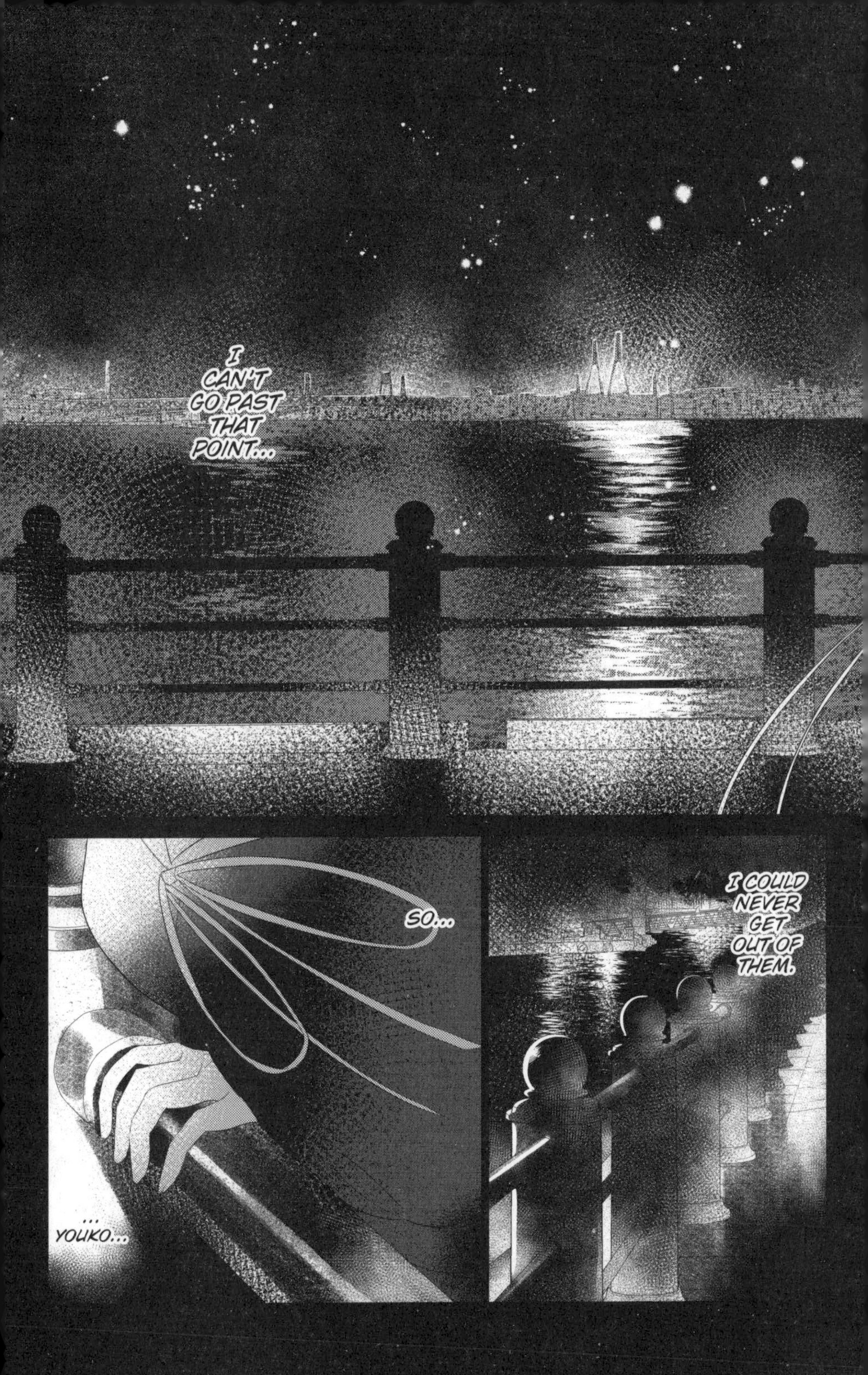
I CAN'T GO PAST THAT POINT...
I COULD NEVER GET OUT OF THEM.
SO...
...YOUKO...

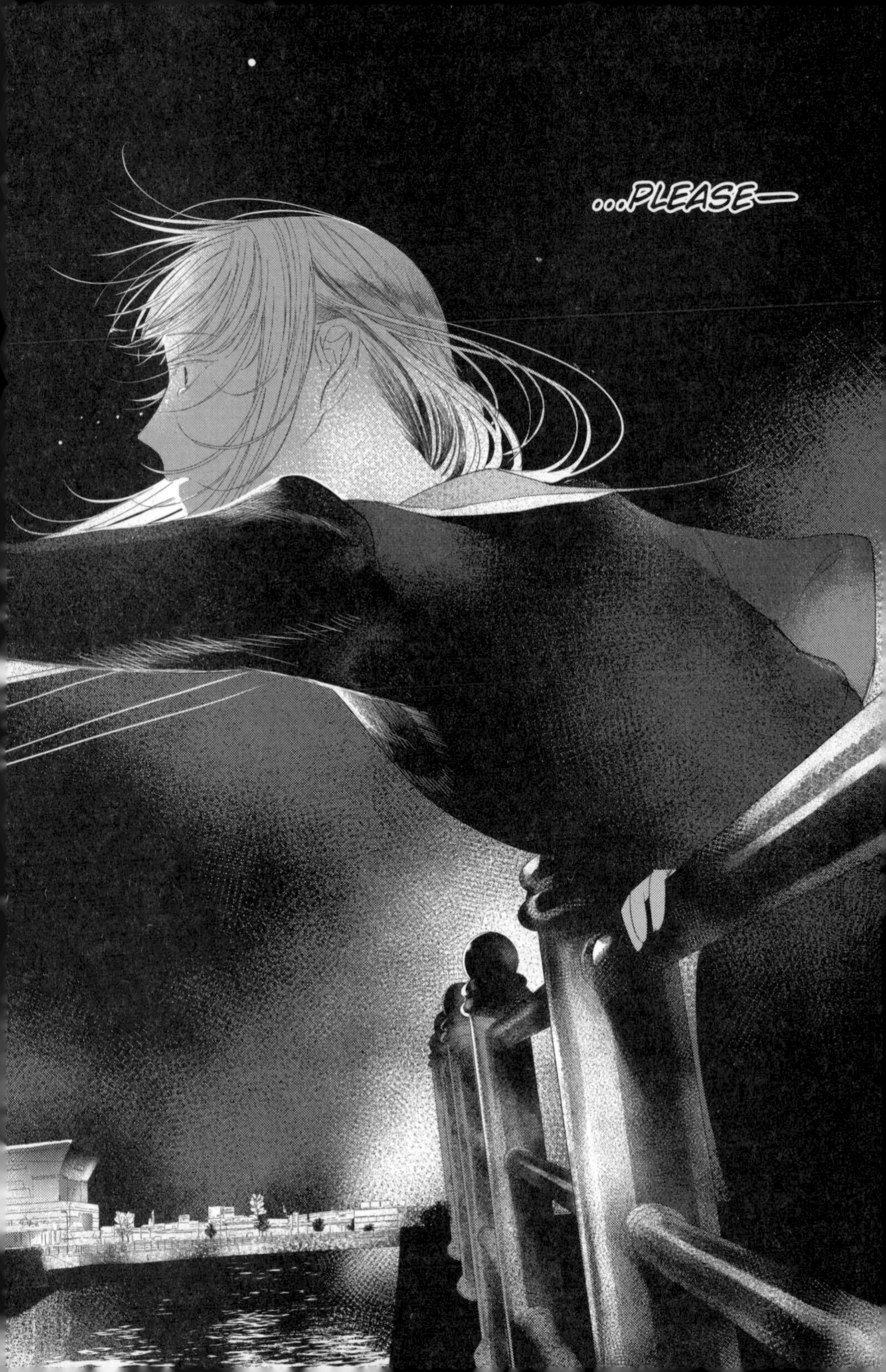
...PLEASE—

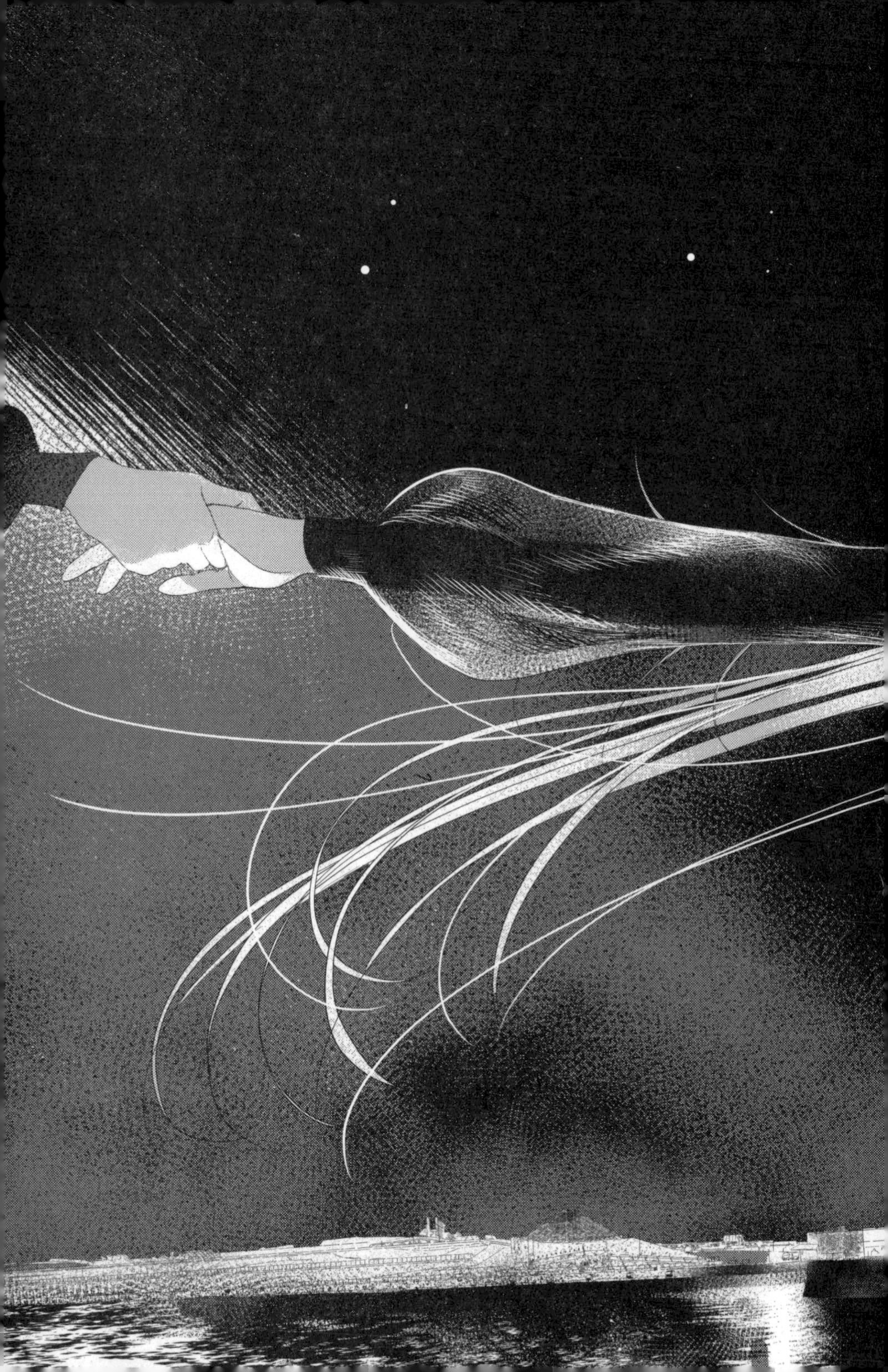

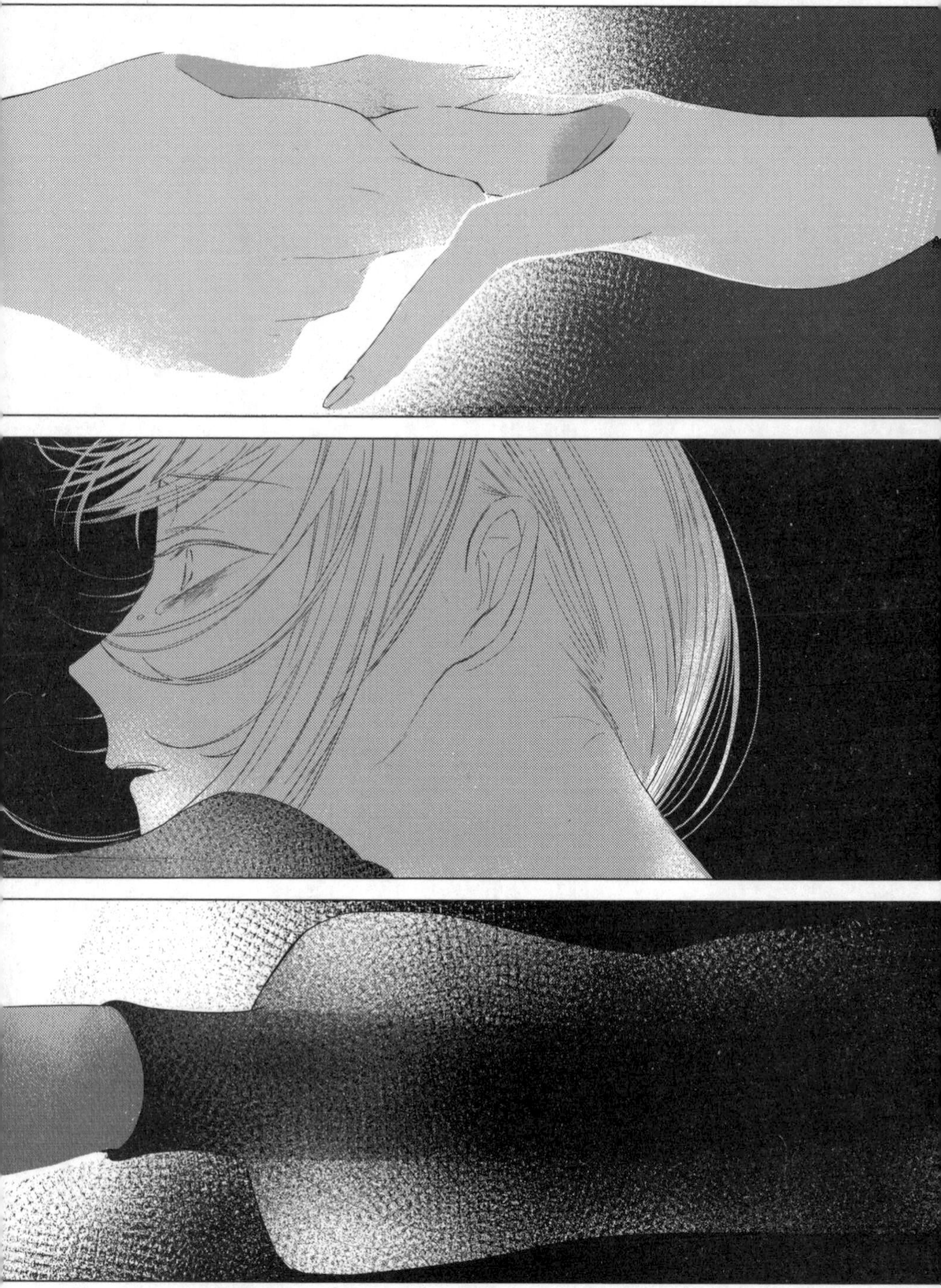

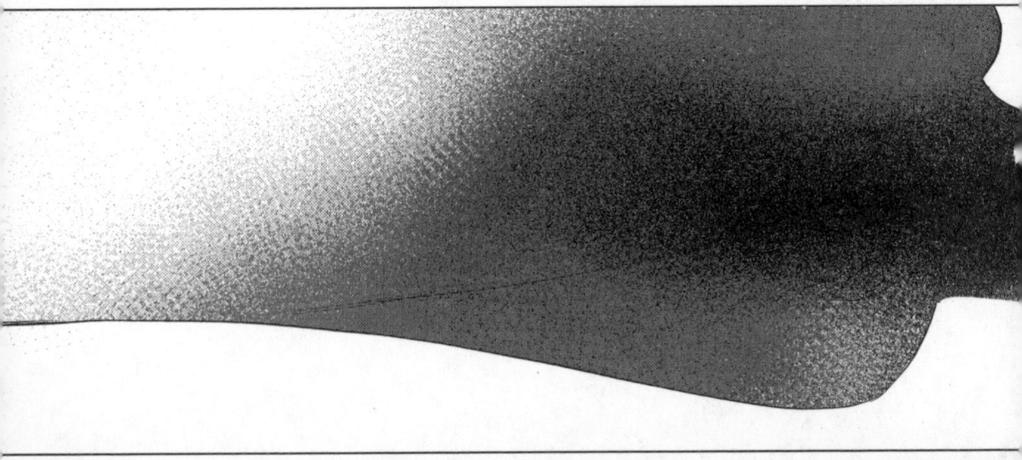
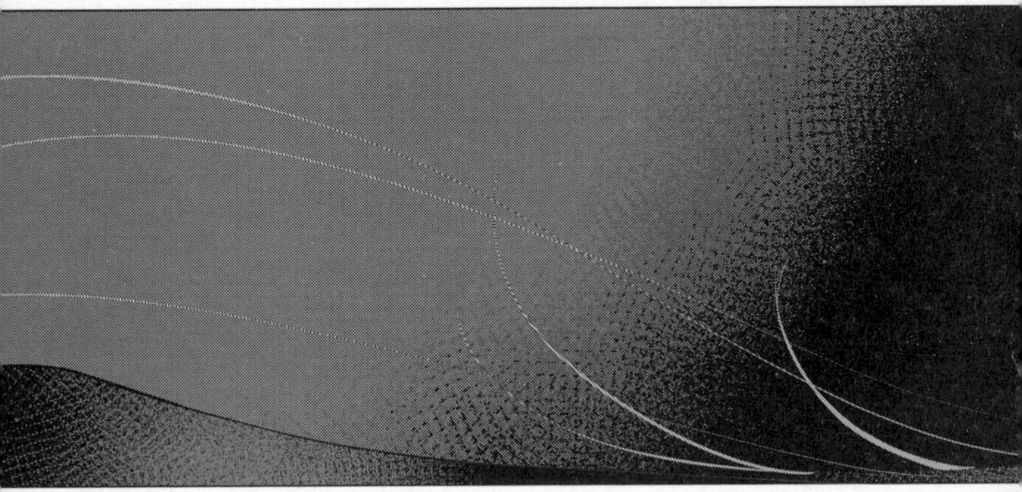
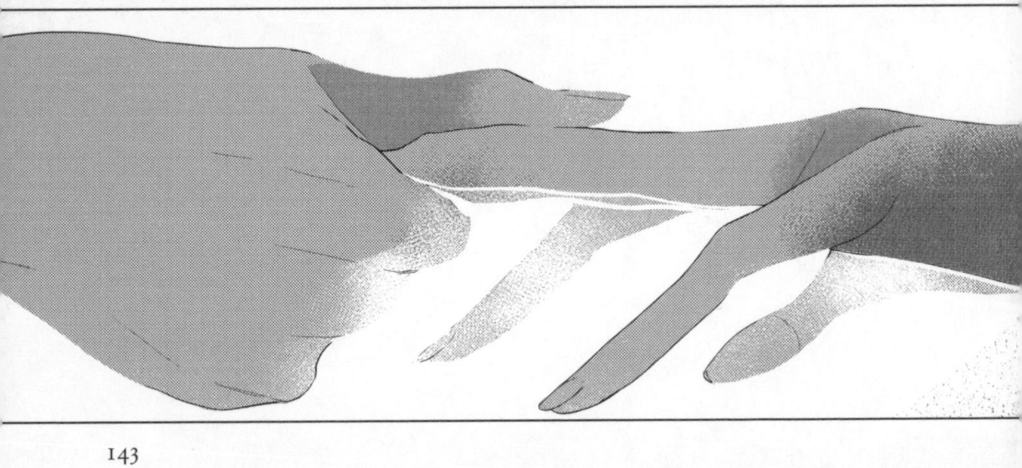

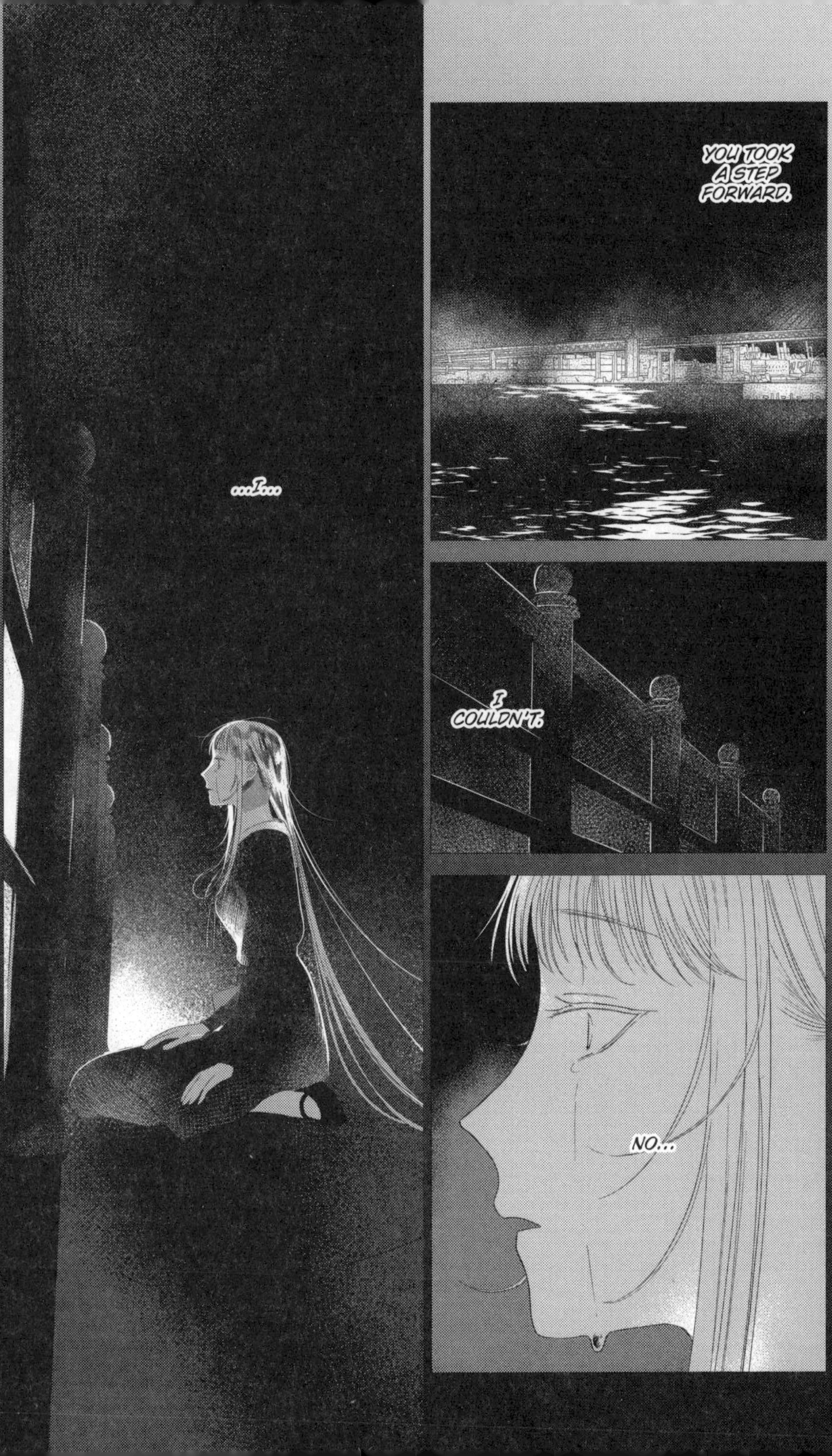
YOU TOOK A STEP FORWARD.
I COULDN'T.
NO...
...I...

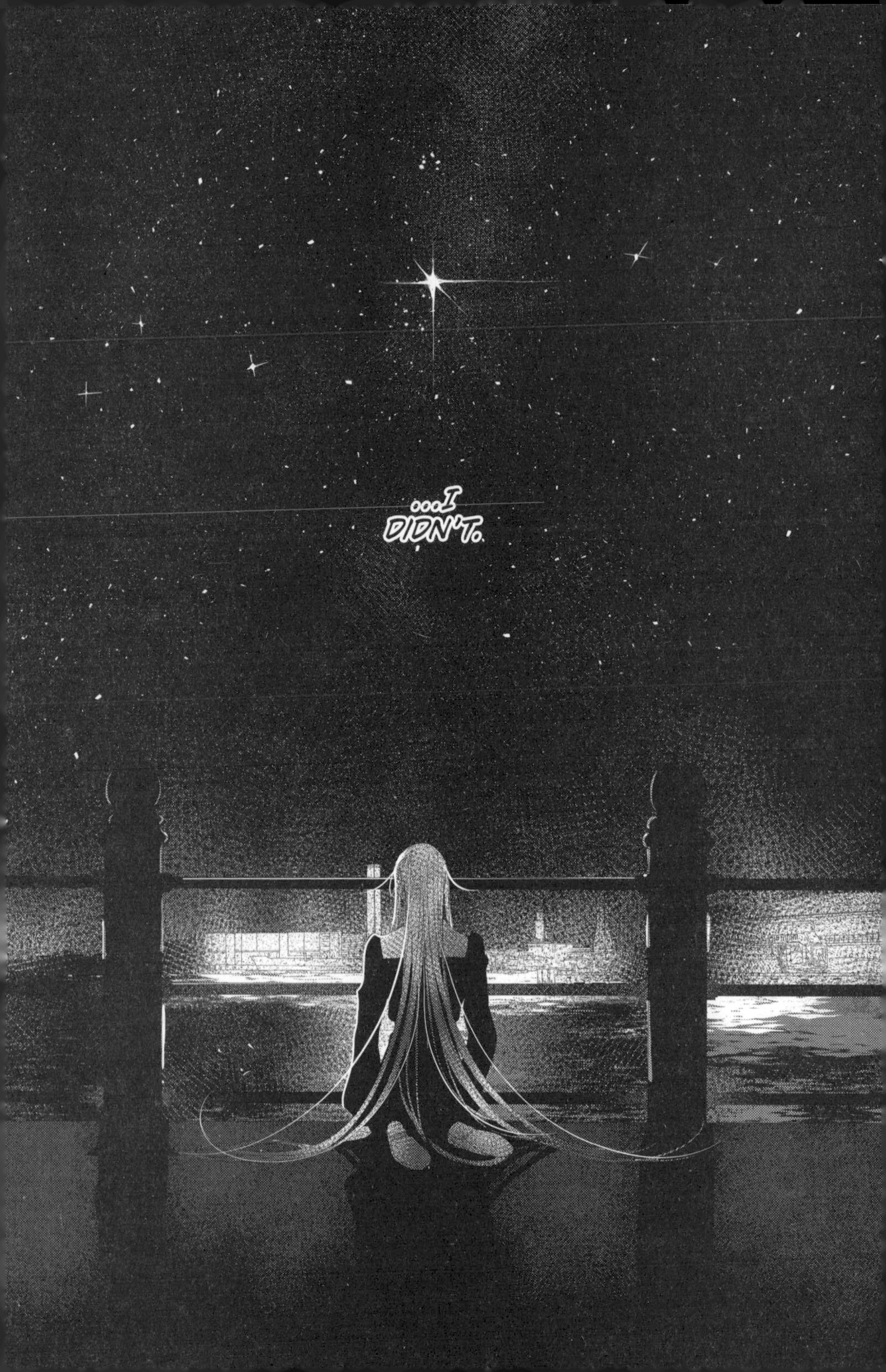
...I DIDN'T.

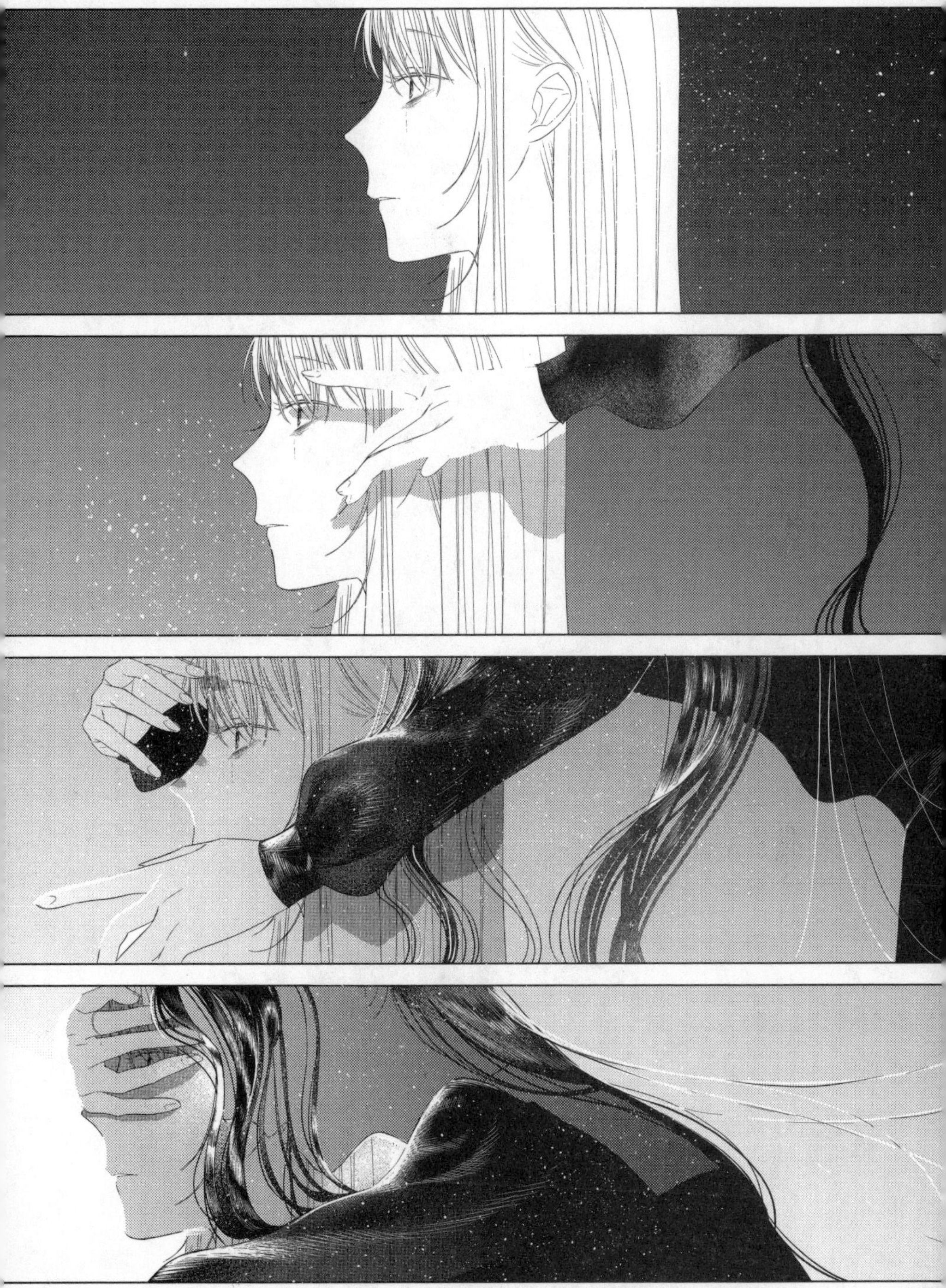

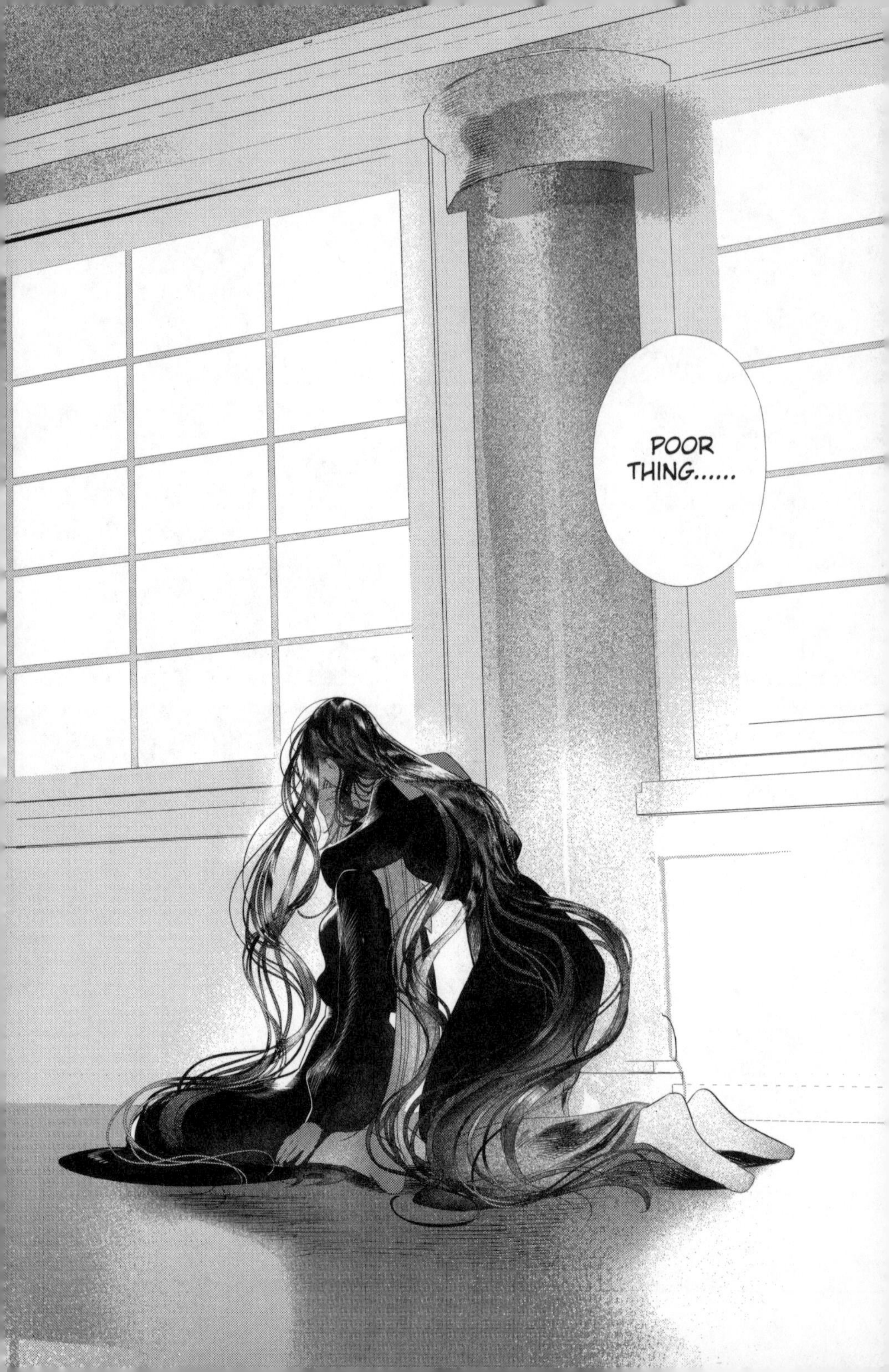
POOR THING......

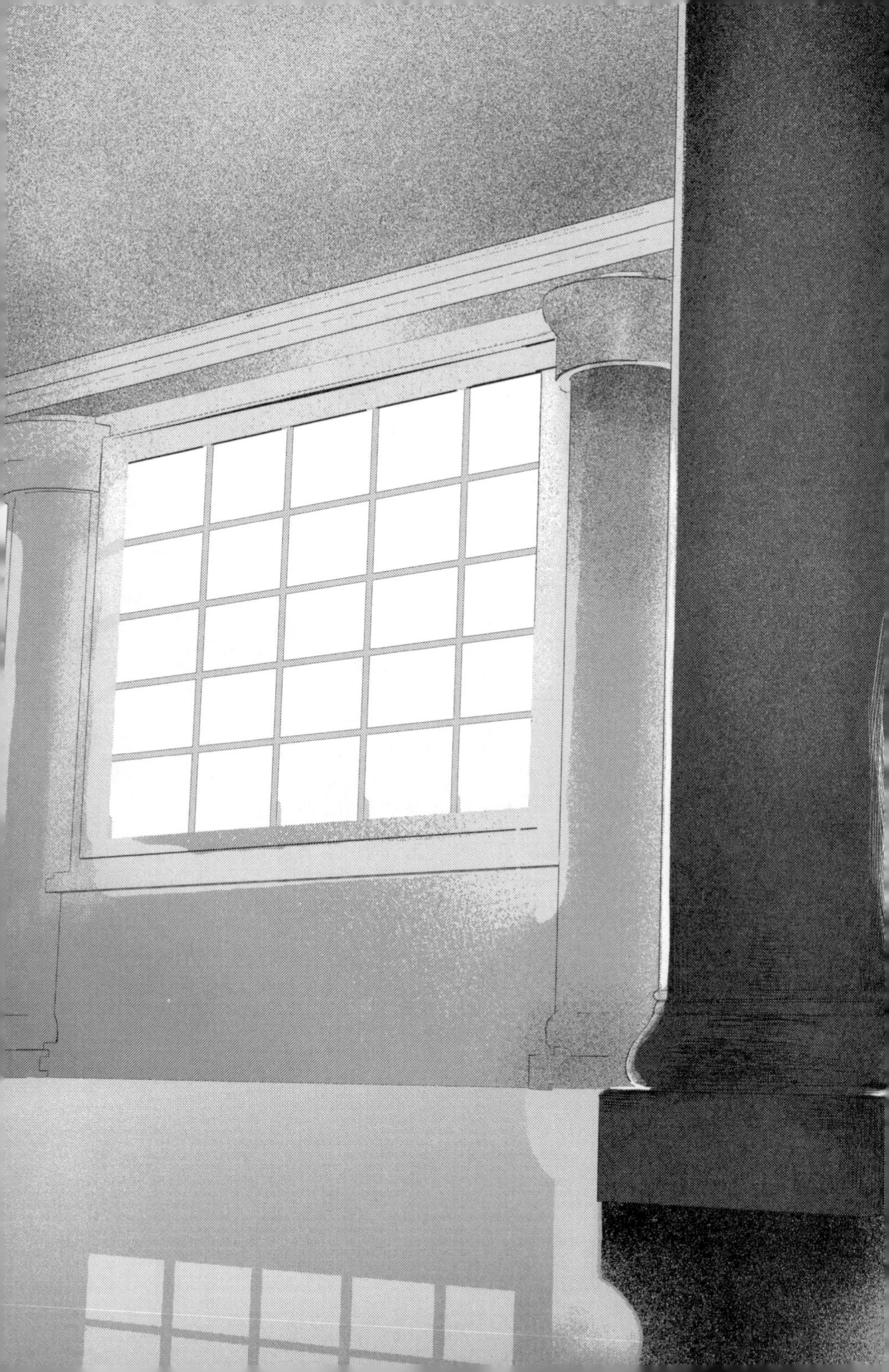

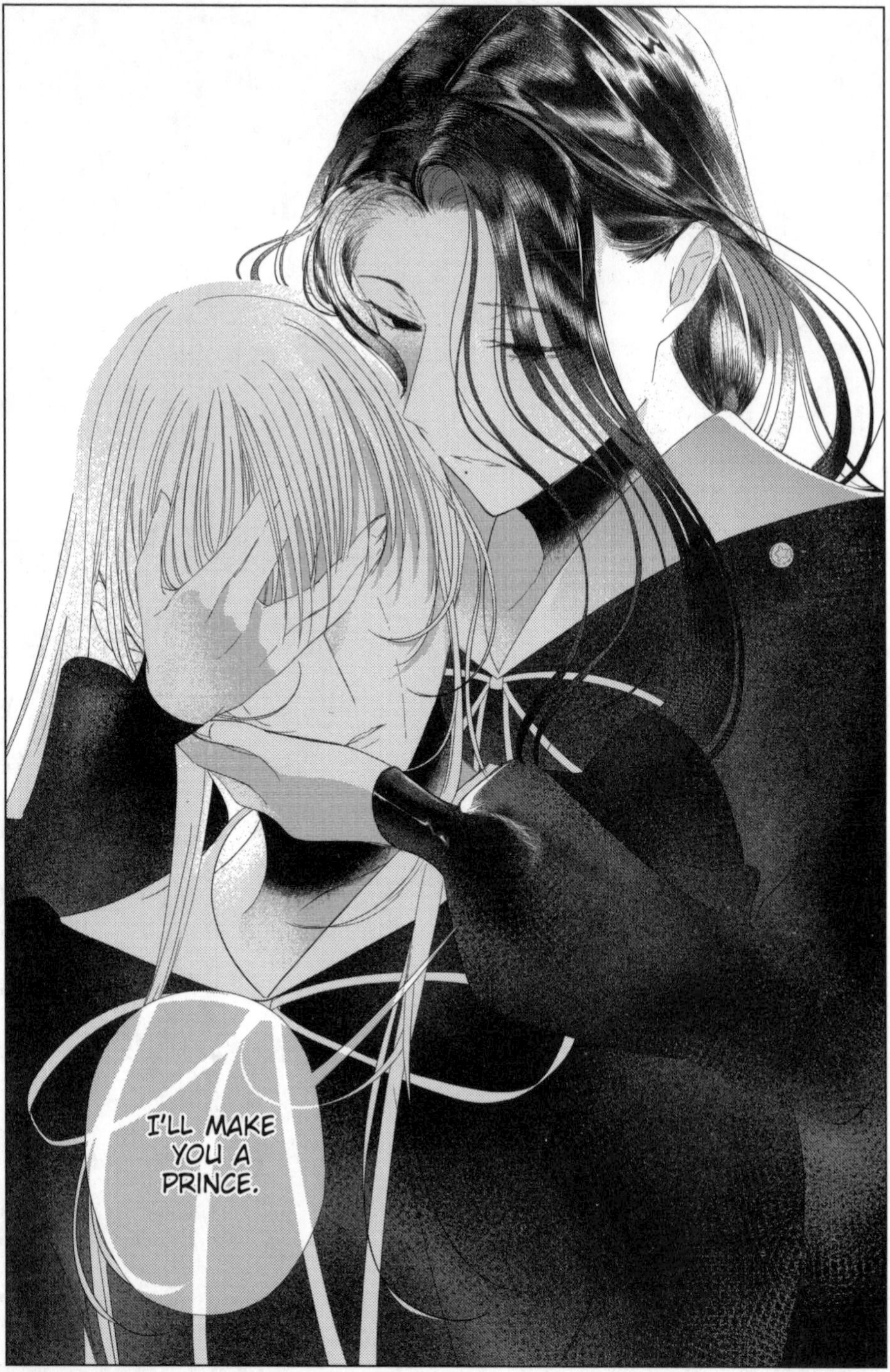
I'LL MAKE YOU A PRINCE.

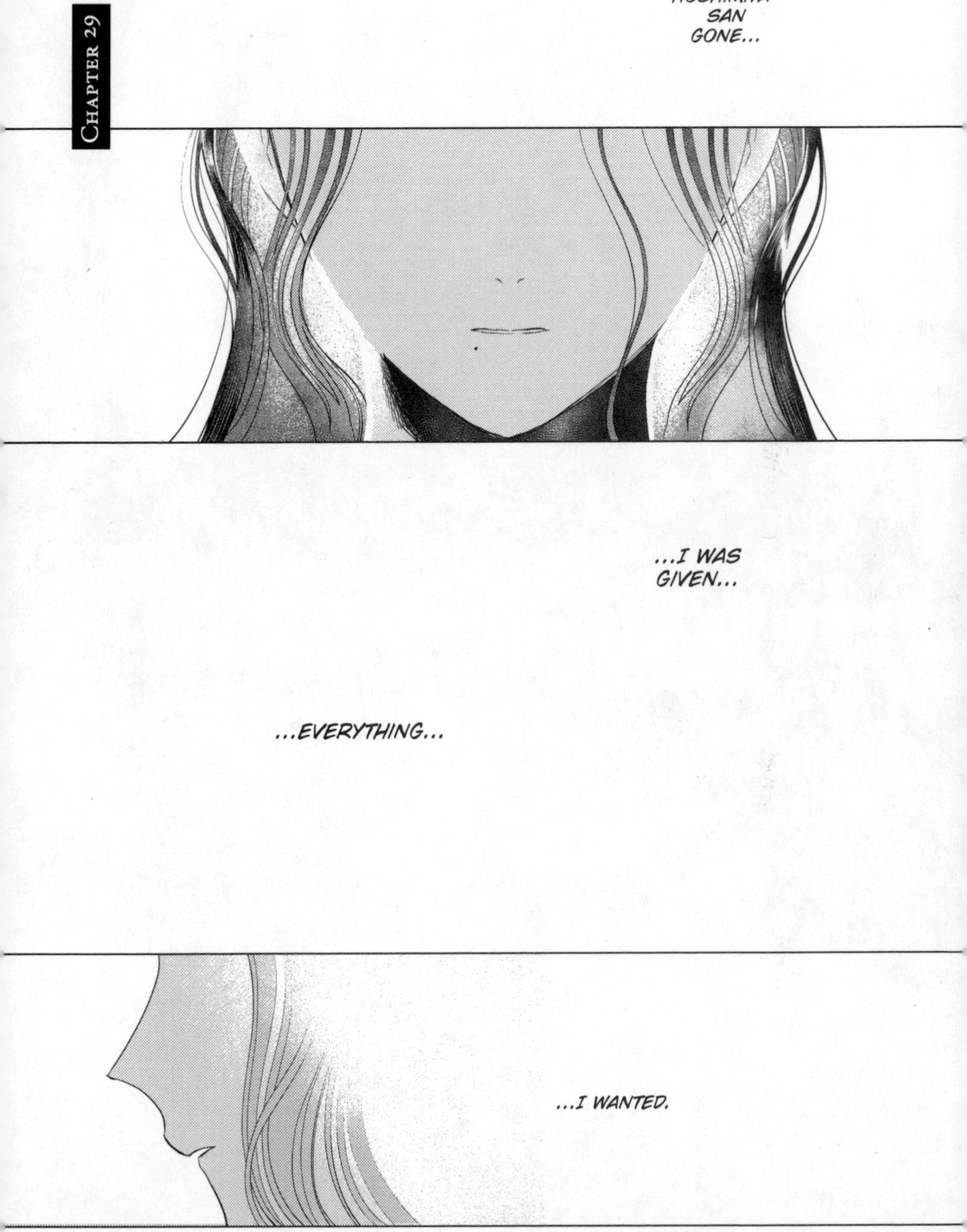
Chapter 29
WITH HOSHIMIYA-SAN GONE...
...I WAS GIVEN...
...EVERYTHING...
...I WANTED.

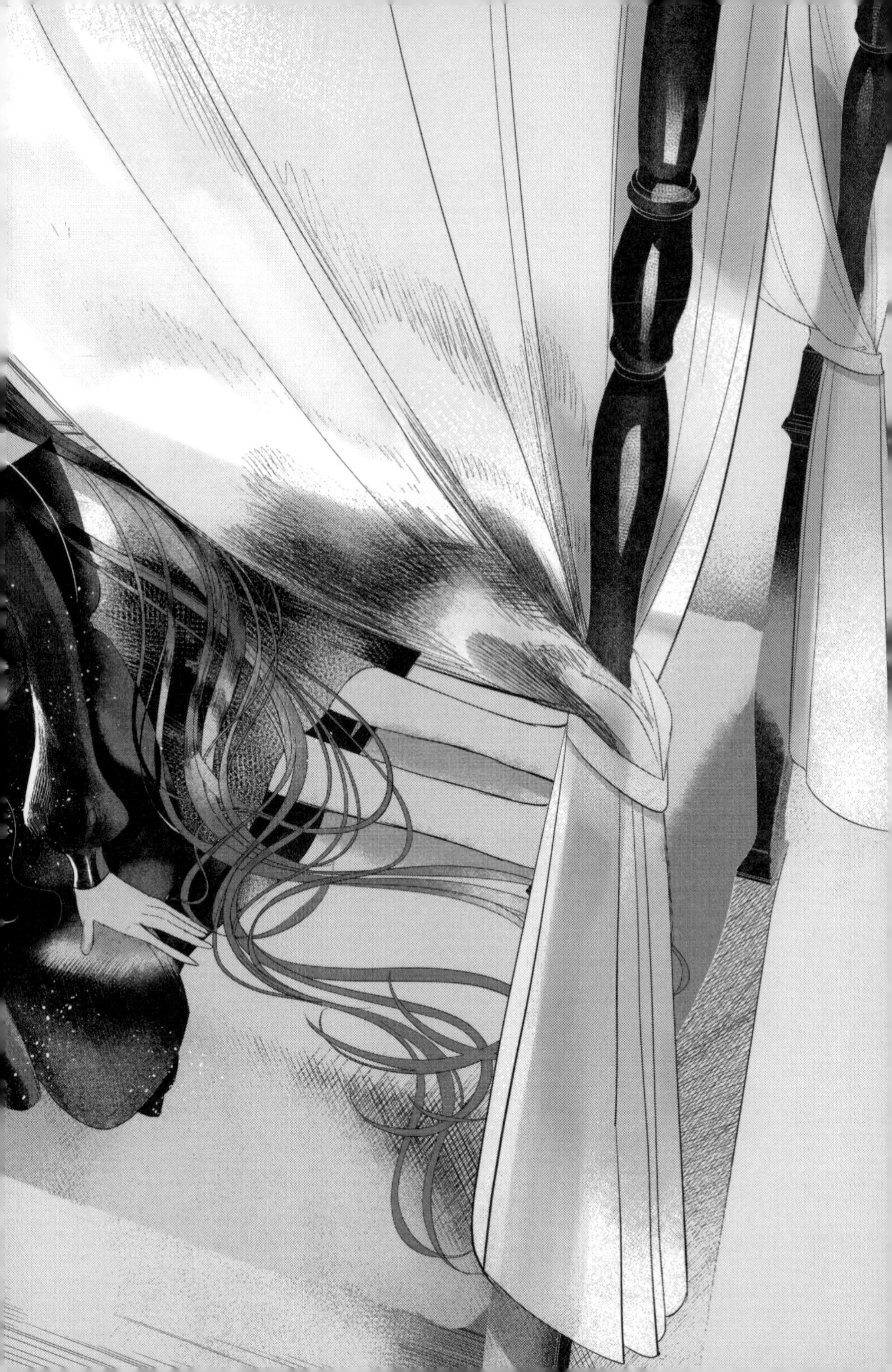

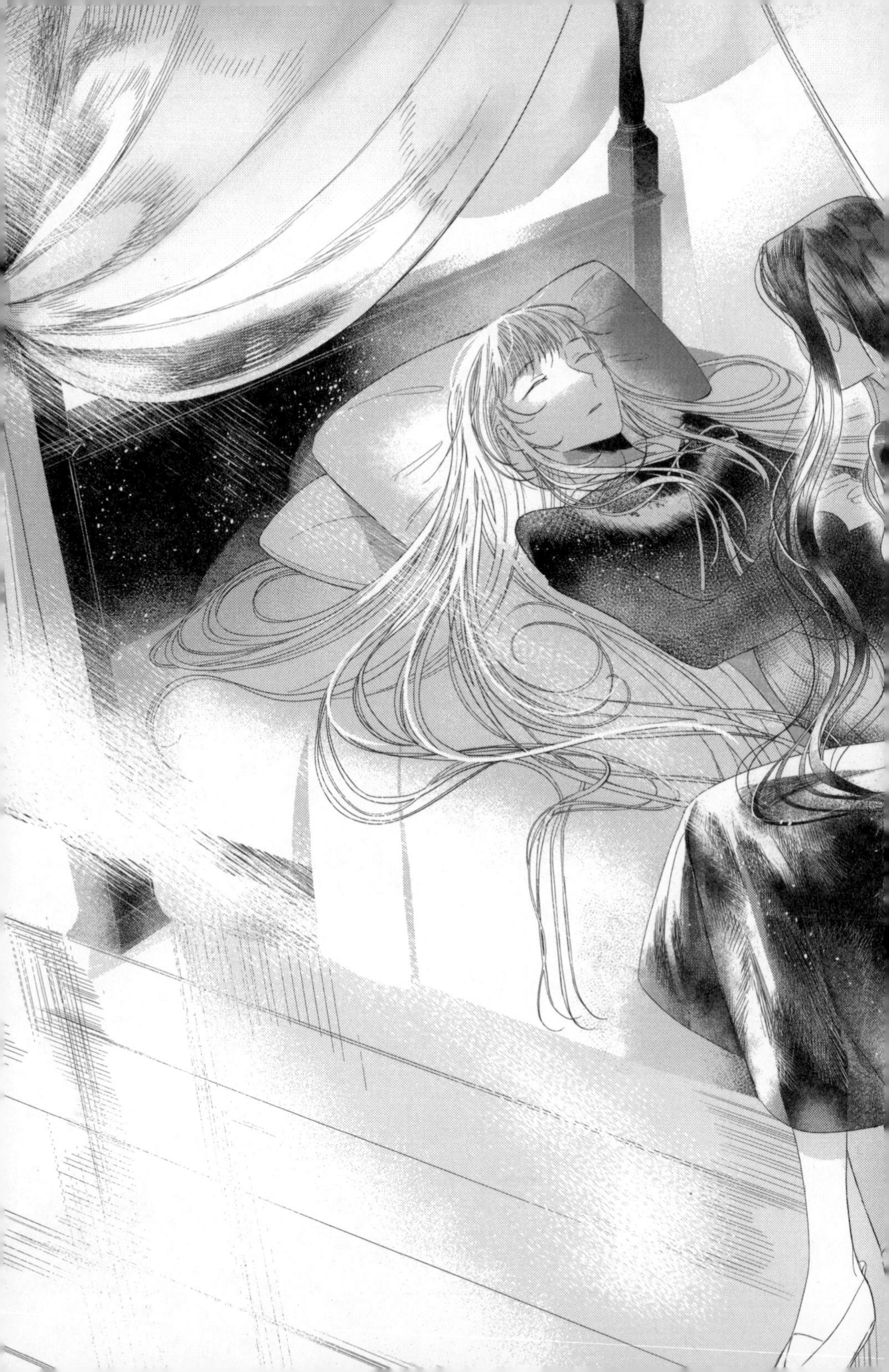

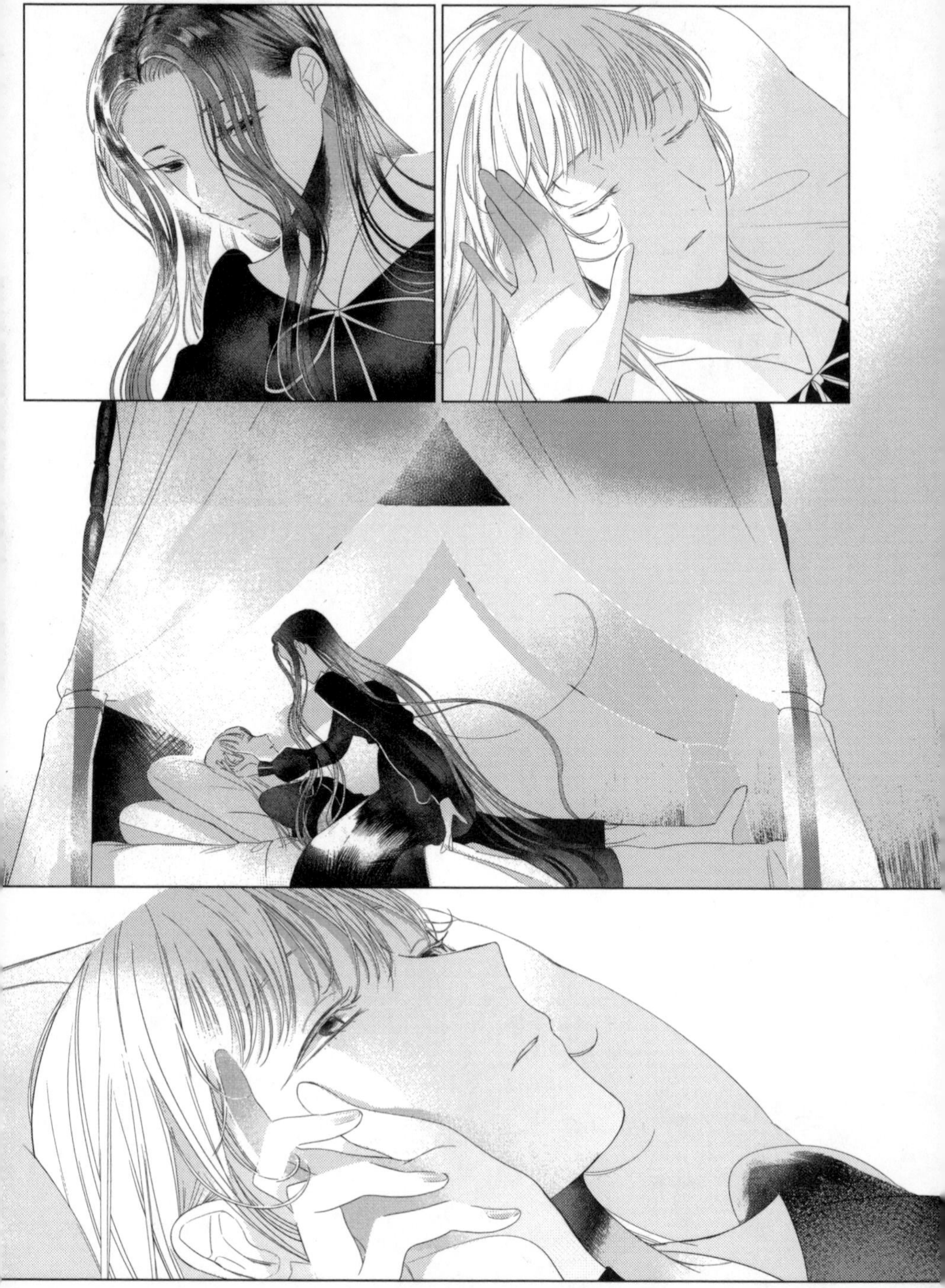

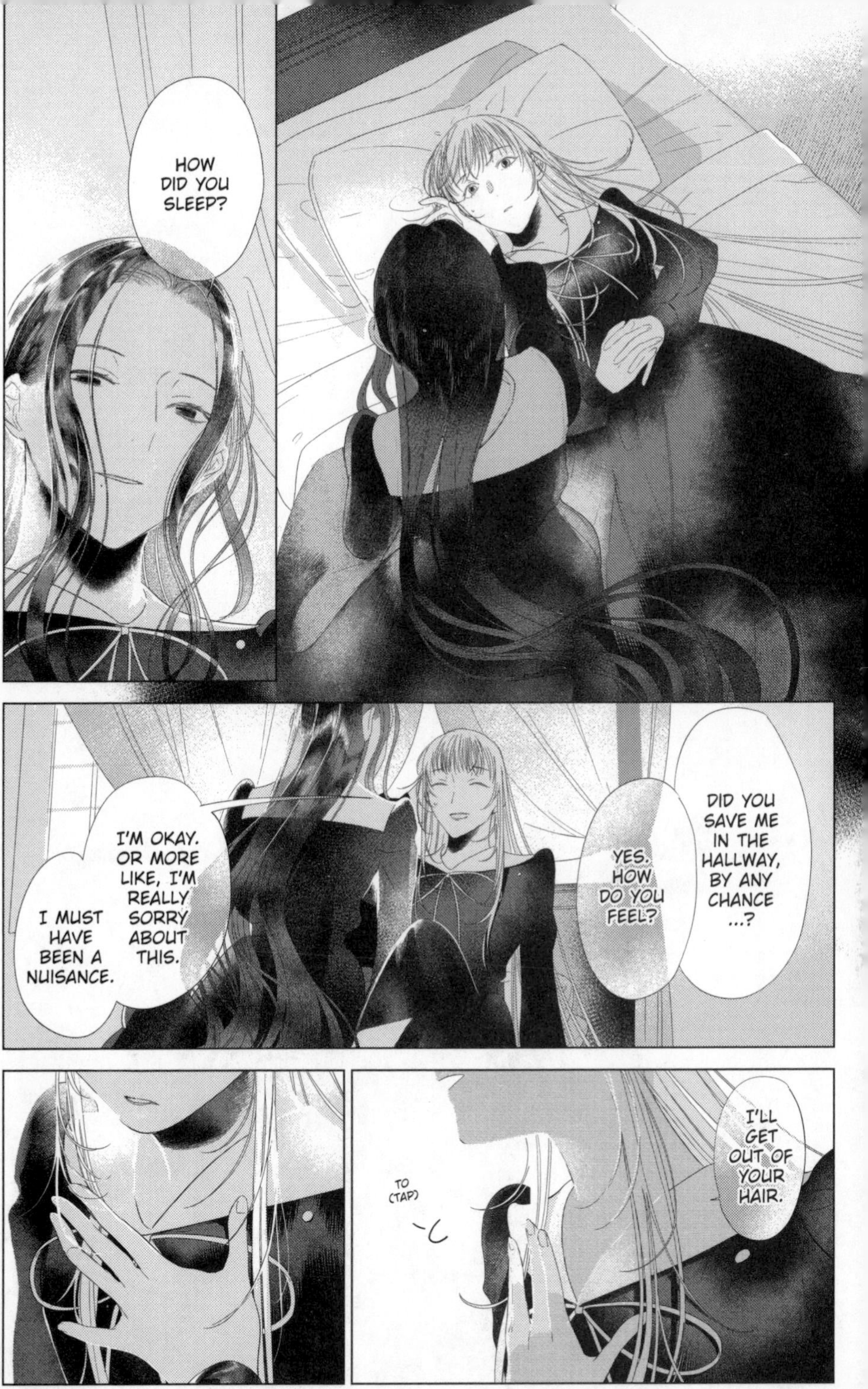
HOW DID YOU SLEEP?
DID YOU SAVE ME IN THE HALLWAY, BY ANY CHANCE ...?
YES. HOW DO YOU FEEL?
I'M OKAY. OR MORE LIKE, I'M REALLY SORRY ABOUT THIS.
I MUST HAVE BEEN A NUISANCE.
I'LL GET OUT OF YOUR HAIR.
TO (TAP)

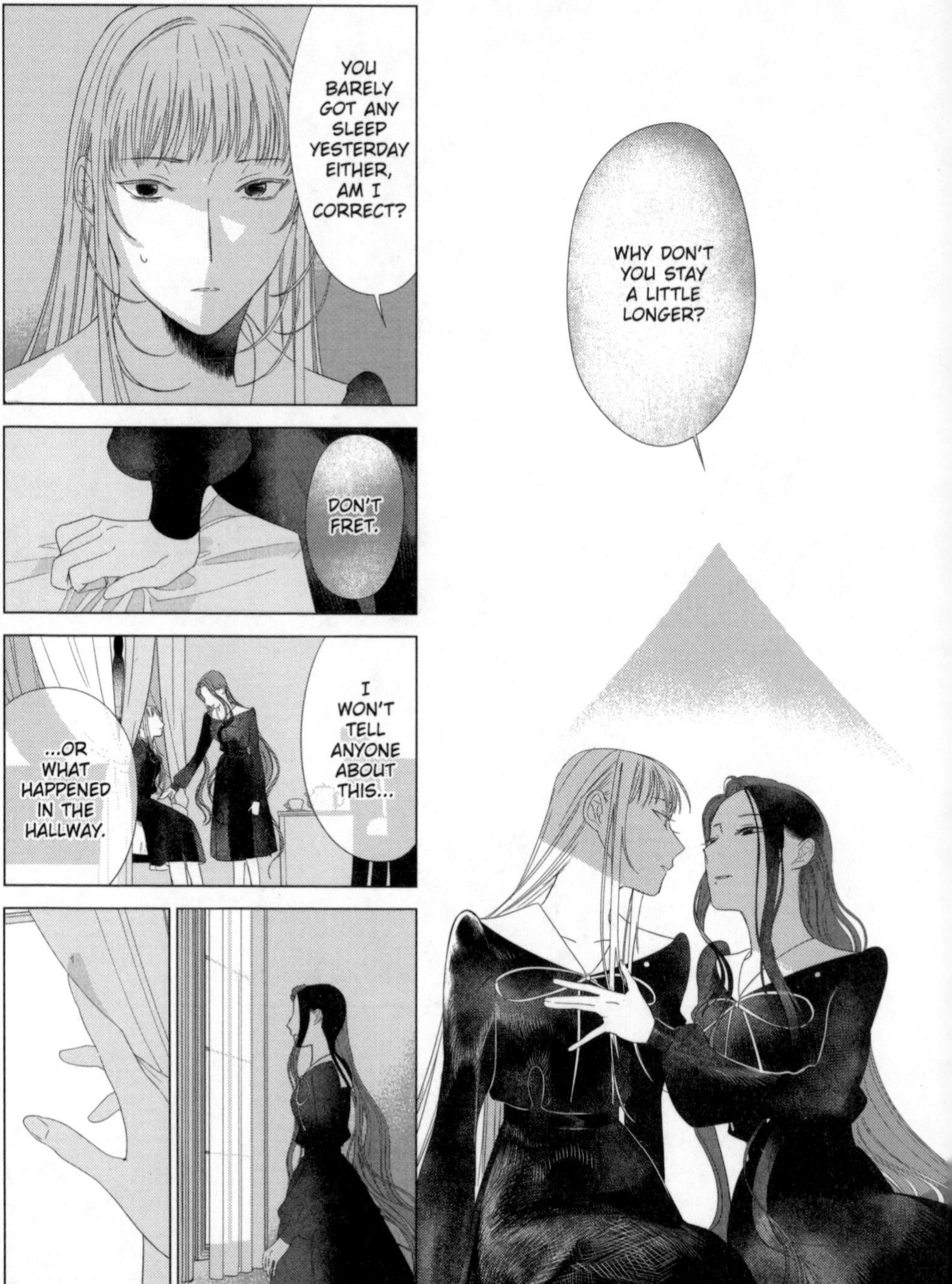
WHY DON'T YOU STAY A LITTLE LONGER?
YOU BARELY GOT ANY SLEEP YESTERDAY EITHER, AM I CORRECT?
DON'T FRET.
I WON'T TELL ANYONE ABOUT THIS...
...OR WHAT HAPPENED IN THE HALLWAY.

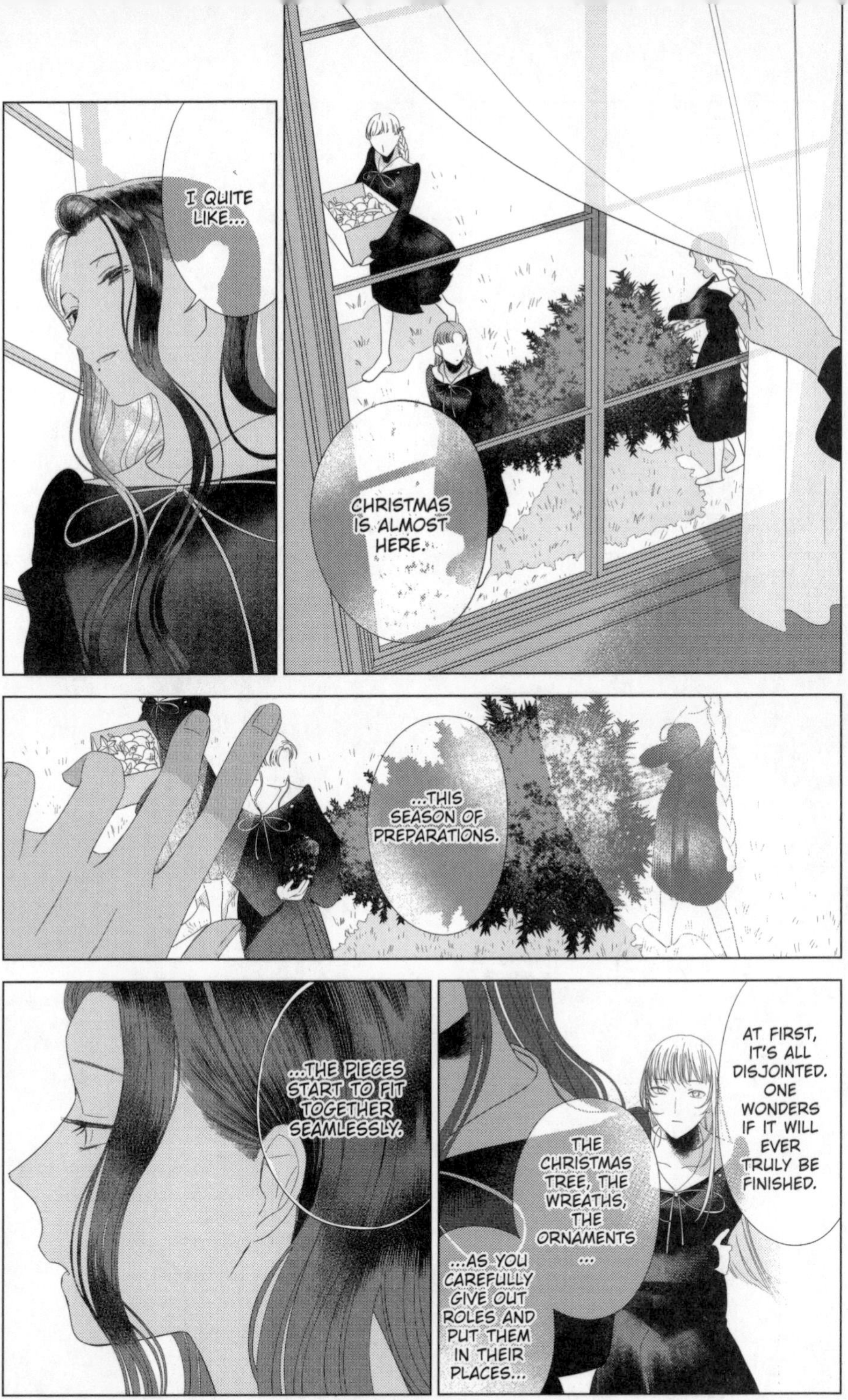
CHRISTMAS IS ALMOST HERE.
I QUITE LIKE...
...THIS SEASON OF PREPARATIONS.
AT FIRST, IT'S ALL DISJOINTED. ONE WONDERS IF IT WILL EVER TRULY BE FINISHED.
THE CHRISTMAS TREE, THE WREATHS, THE ORNAMENTS...
...AS YOU CAREFULLY GIVE OUT ROLES AND PUT THEM IN THEIR PLACES...
...THE PIECES START TO FIT TOGETHER SEAMLESSLY.

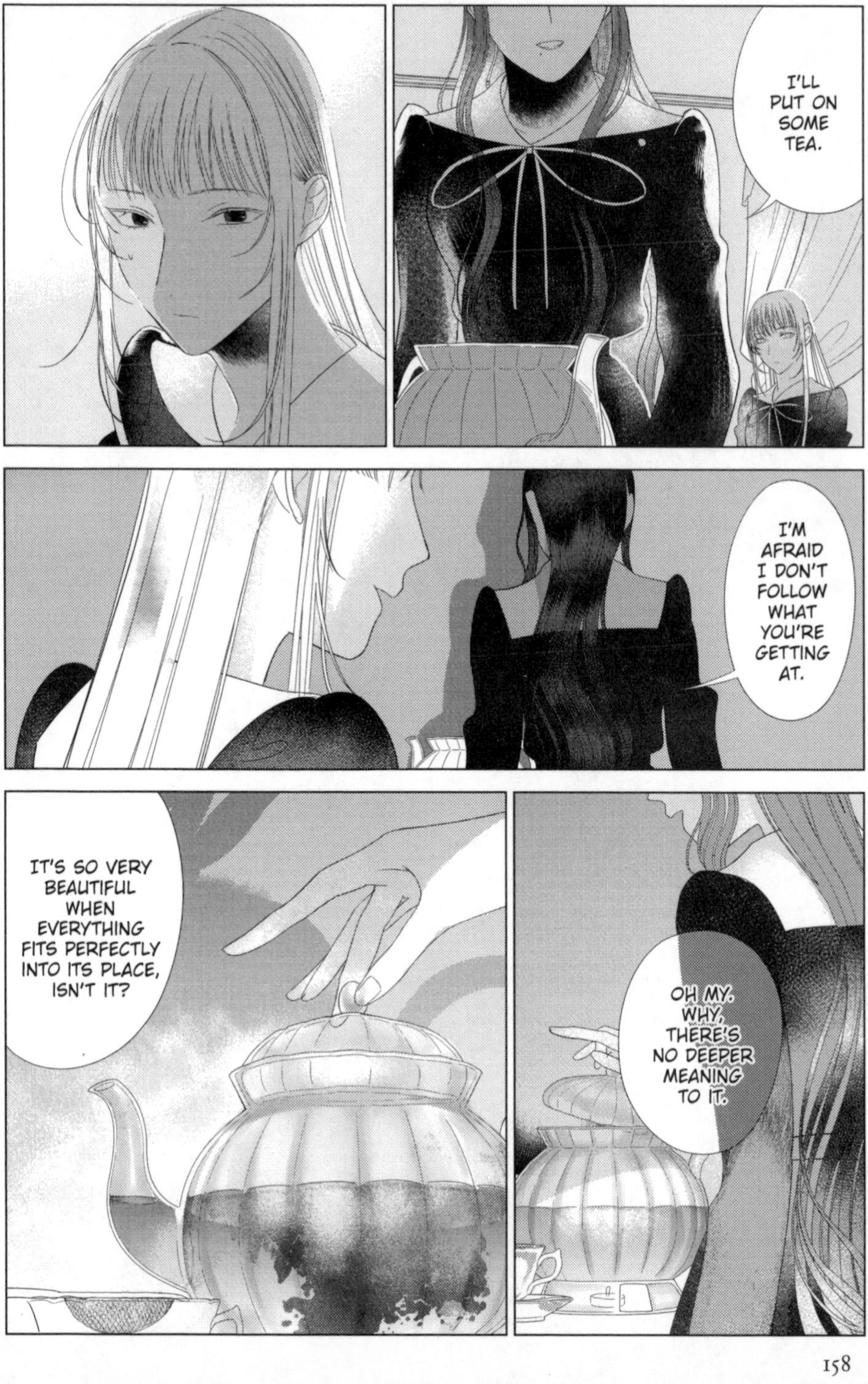
I'LL PUT ON SOME TEA.
I'M AFRAID I DON'T FOLLOW WHAT YOU'RE GETTING AT.
OH MY. WHY, THERE'S NO DEEPER MEANING TO IT.
IT'S SO VERY BEAUTIFUL WHEN EVERYTHING FITS PERFECTLY INTO ITS PLACE, ISN'T IT?

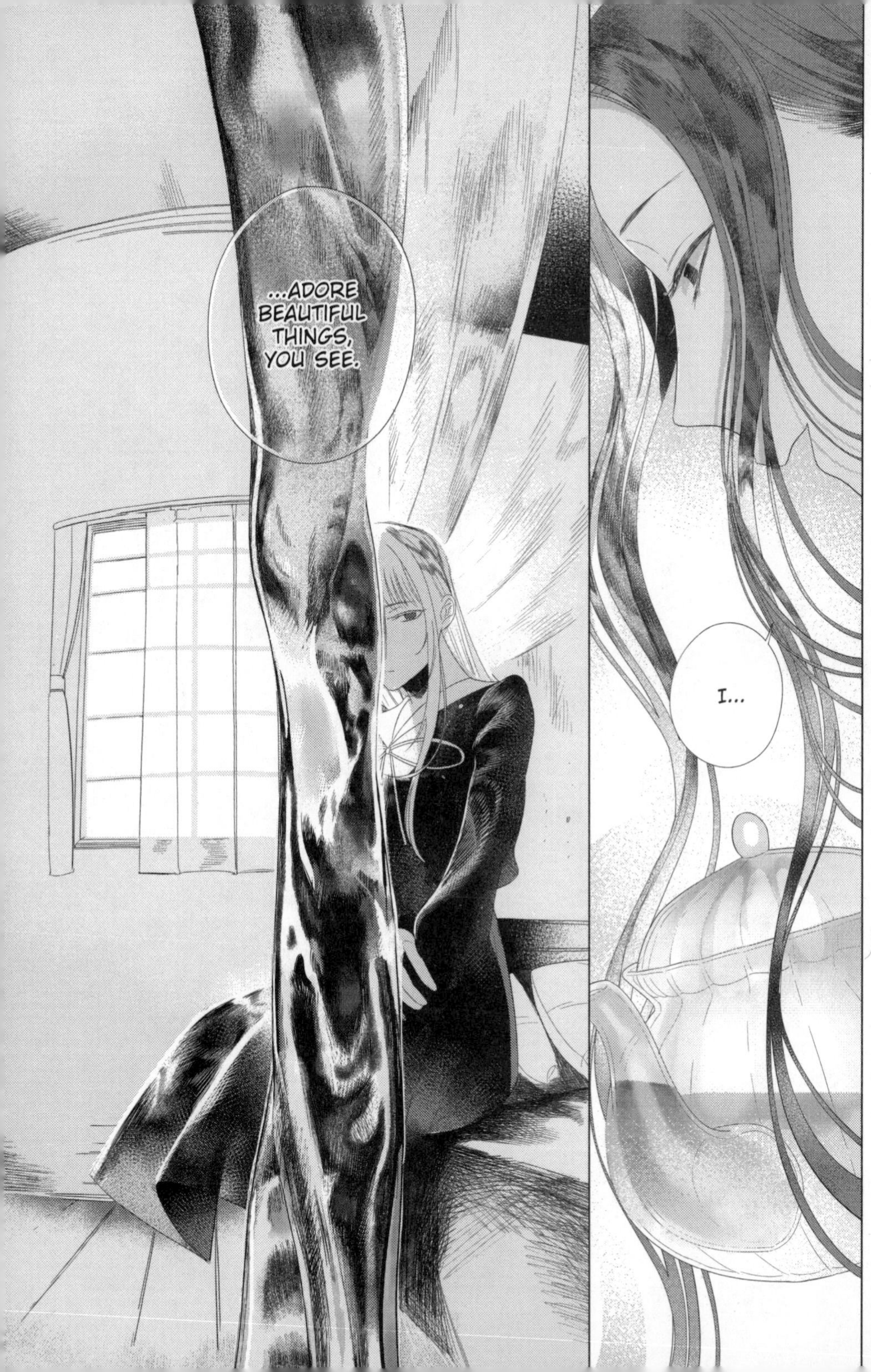
I...
...ADORE BEAUTIFUL THINGS, YOU SEE.

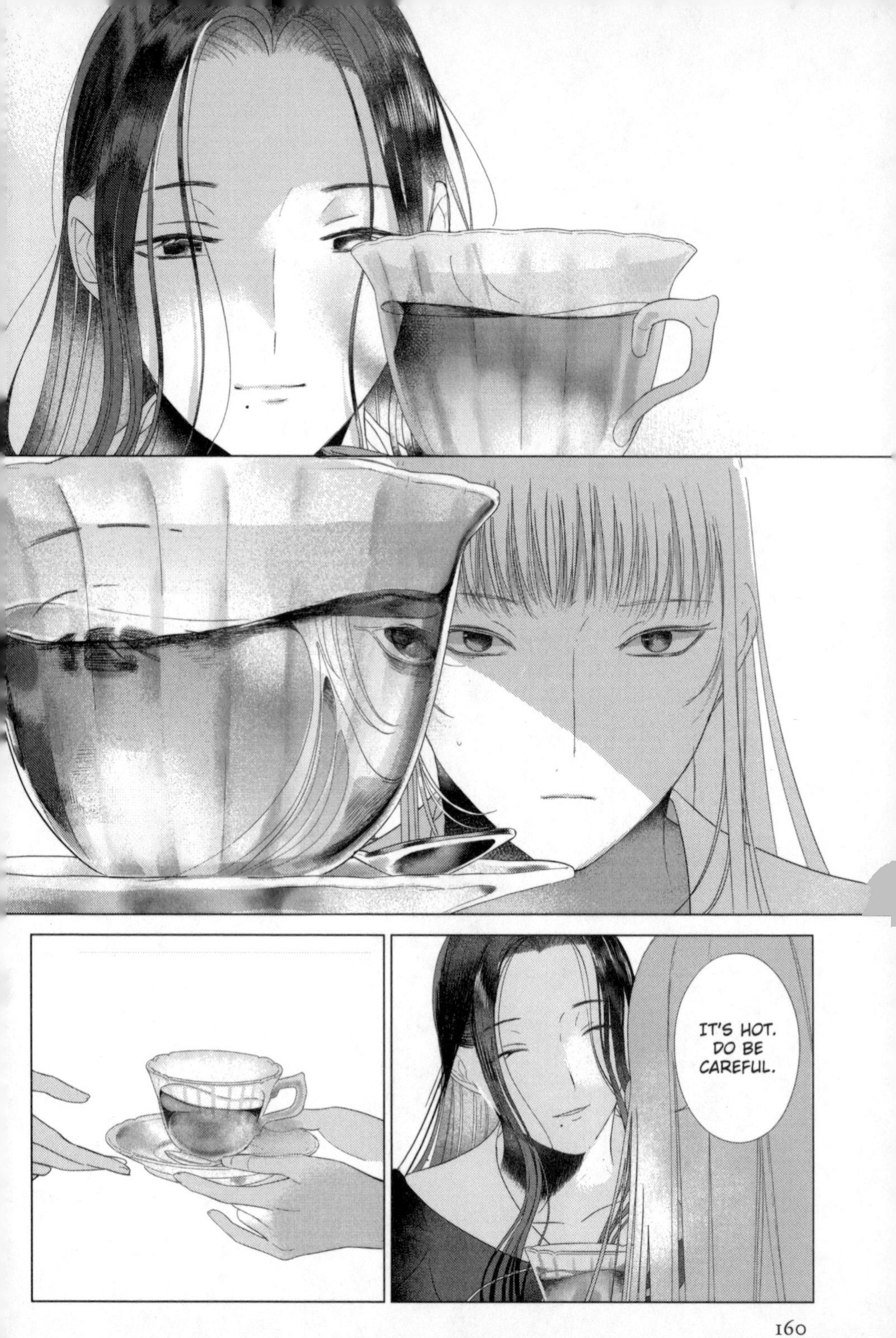
IT'S HOT. DO BE CAREFUL.

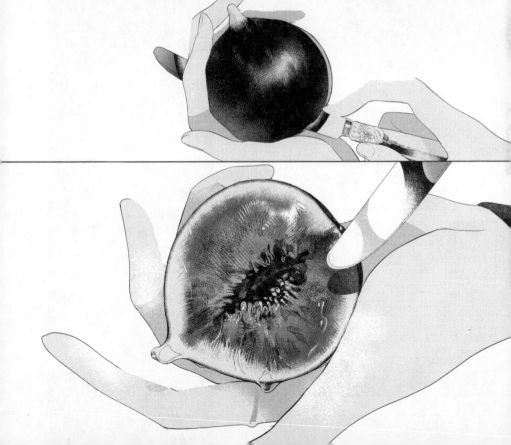

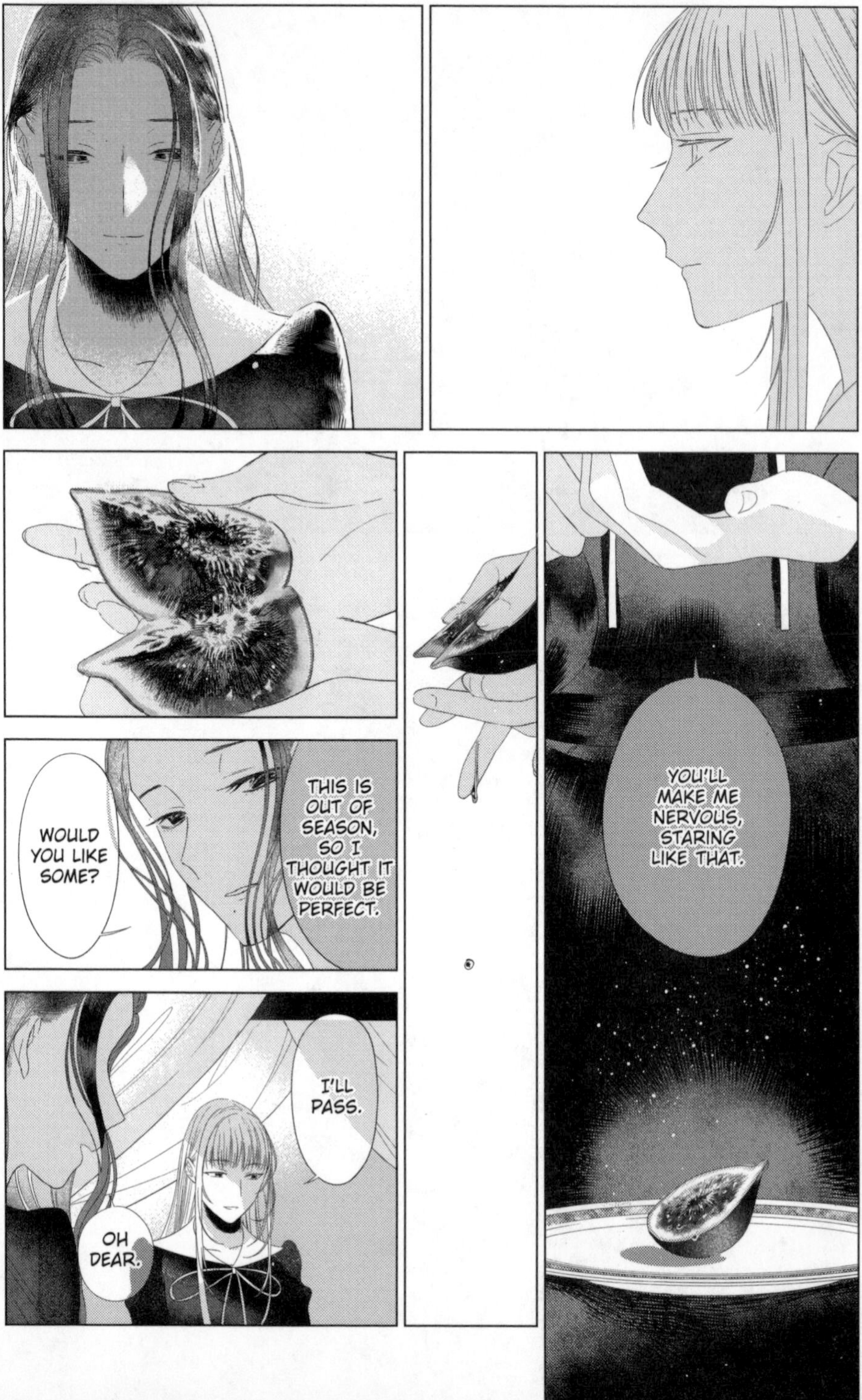
YOU'LL MAKE ME NERVOUS, STARING LIKE THAT.
THIS IS OUT OF SEASON, SO I THOUGHT IT WOULD BE PERFECT.
WOULD YOU LIKE SOME?
I'LL PASS.
OH DEAR.

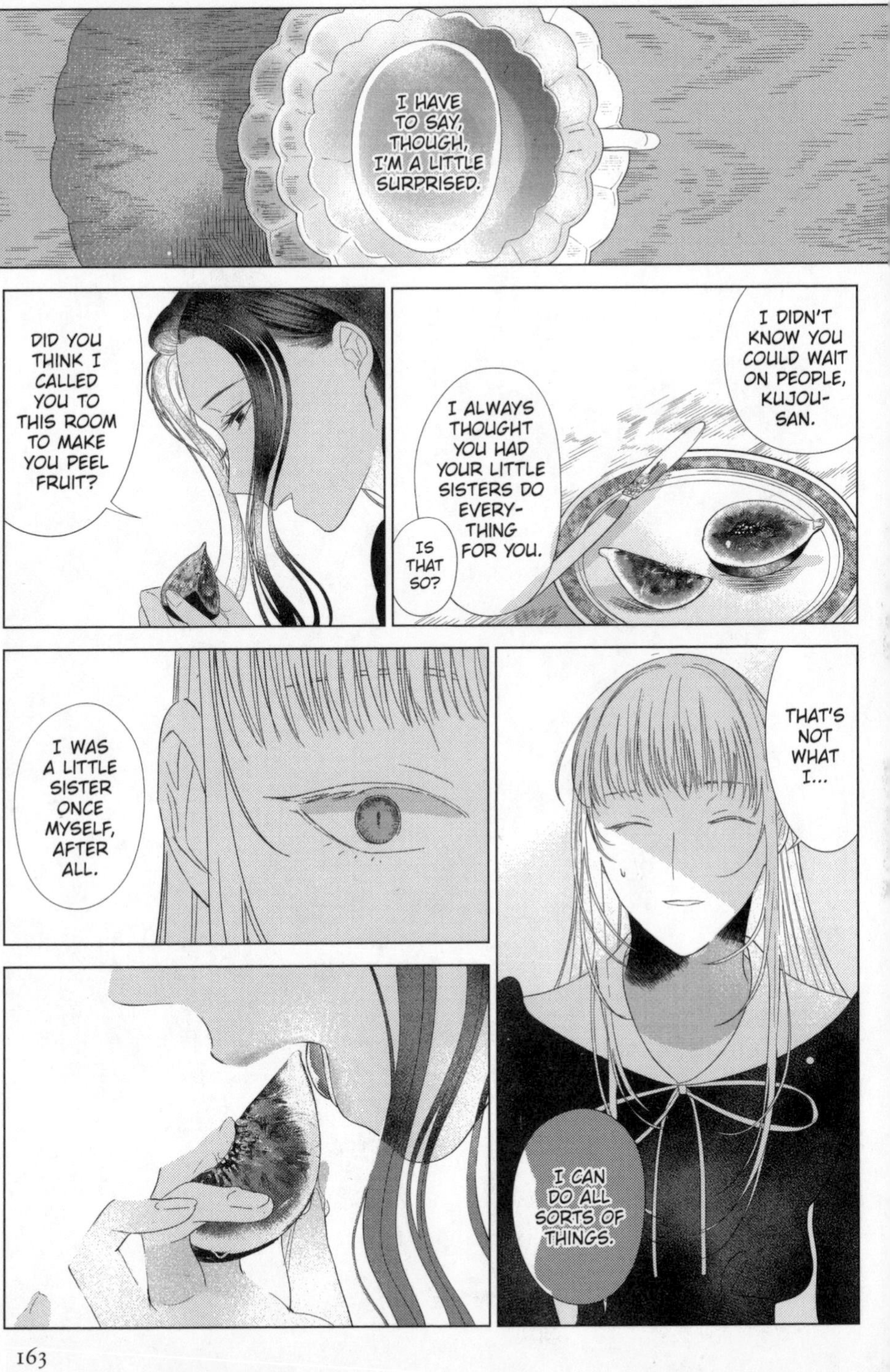
I HAVE TO SAY, THOUGH, I'M A LITTLE SURPRISED.
I DIDN'T KNOW YOU COULD WAIT ON PEOPLE, KUJOU-SAN.
I ALWAYS THOUGHT YOU HAD YOUR LITTLE SISTERS DO EVERY-THING FOR YOU.
IS THAT SO?
DID YOU THINK I CALLED YOU TO THIS ROOM TO MAKE YOU PEEL FRUIT?
THAT'S NOT WHAT I...
I WAS A LITTLE SISTER ONCE MYSELF, AFTER ALL.
I CAN DO ALL SORTS OF THINGS.

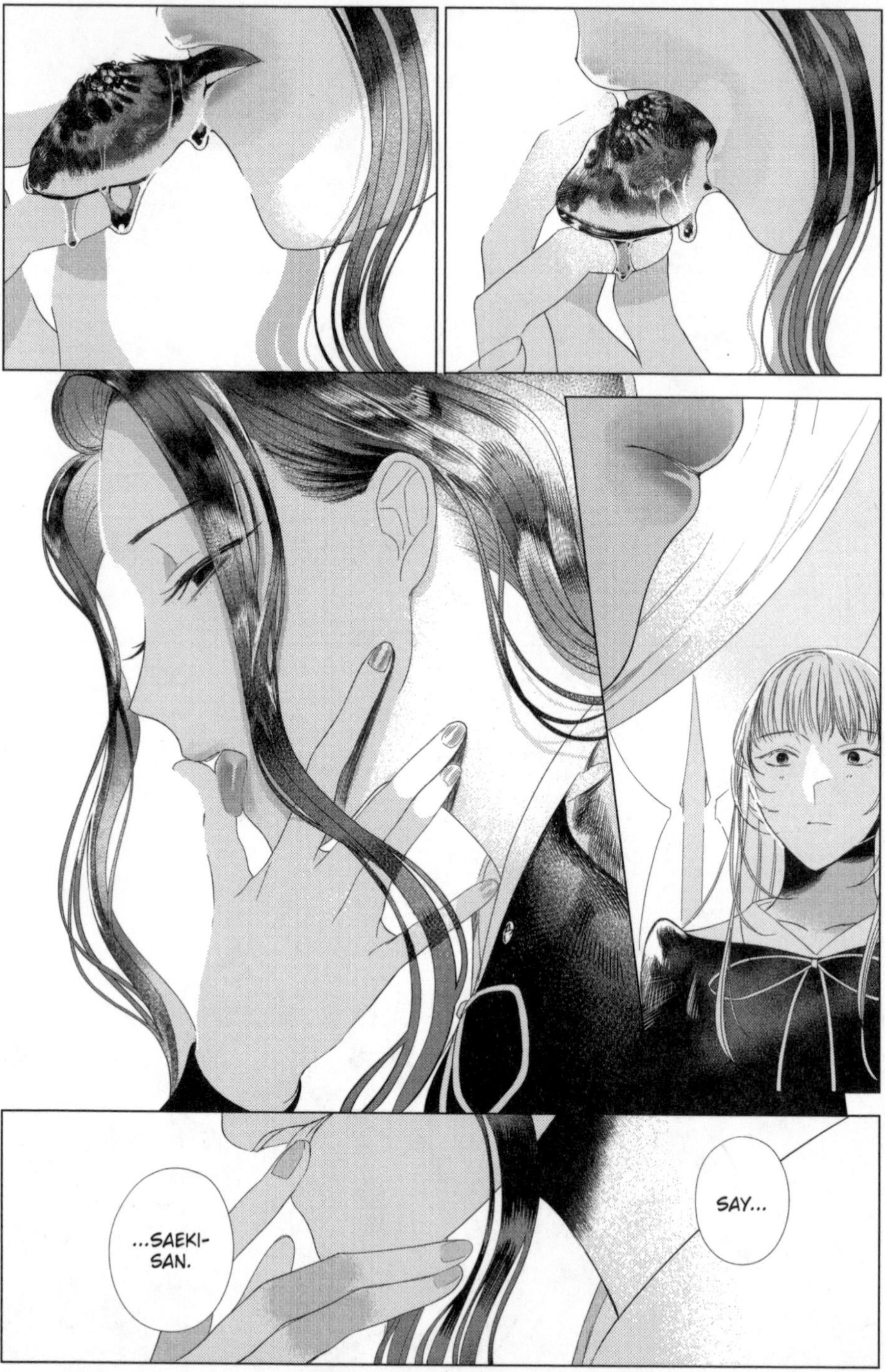
SAY...
...SAEKI-SAN.

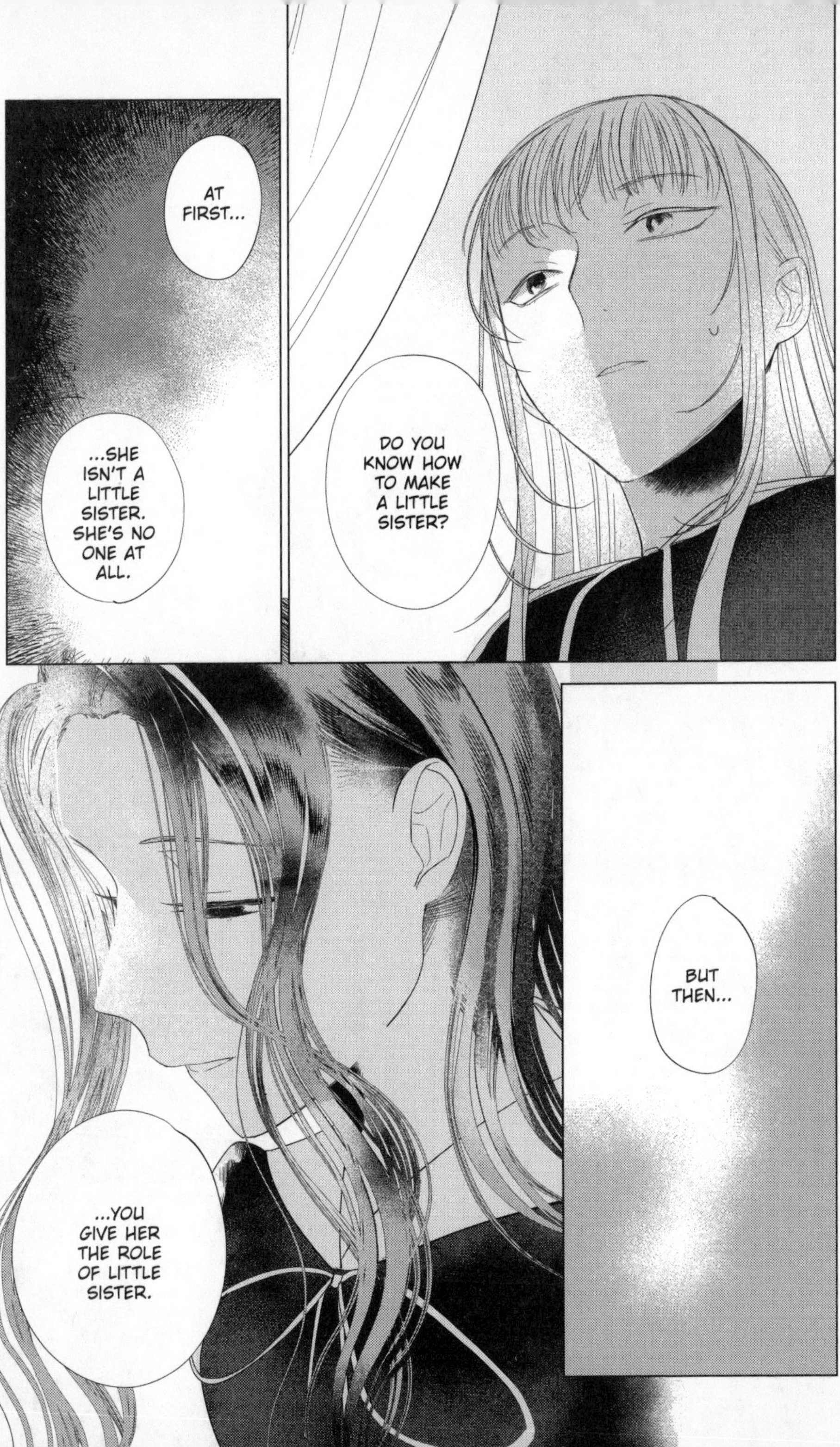
DO YOU KNOW HOW TO MAKE A LITTLE SISTER?
AT FIRST...
...SHE ISN'T A LITTLE SISTER. SHE'S NO ONE AT ALL.
BUT THEN...
...YOU GIVE HER THE ROLE OF LITTLE SISTER.

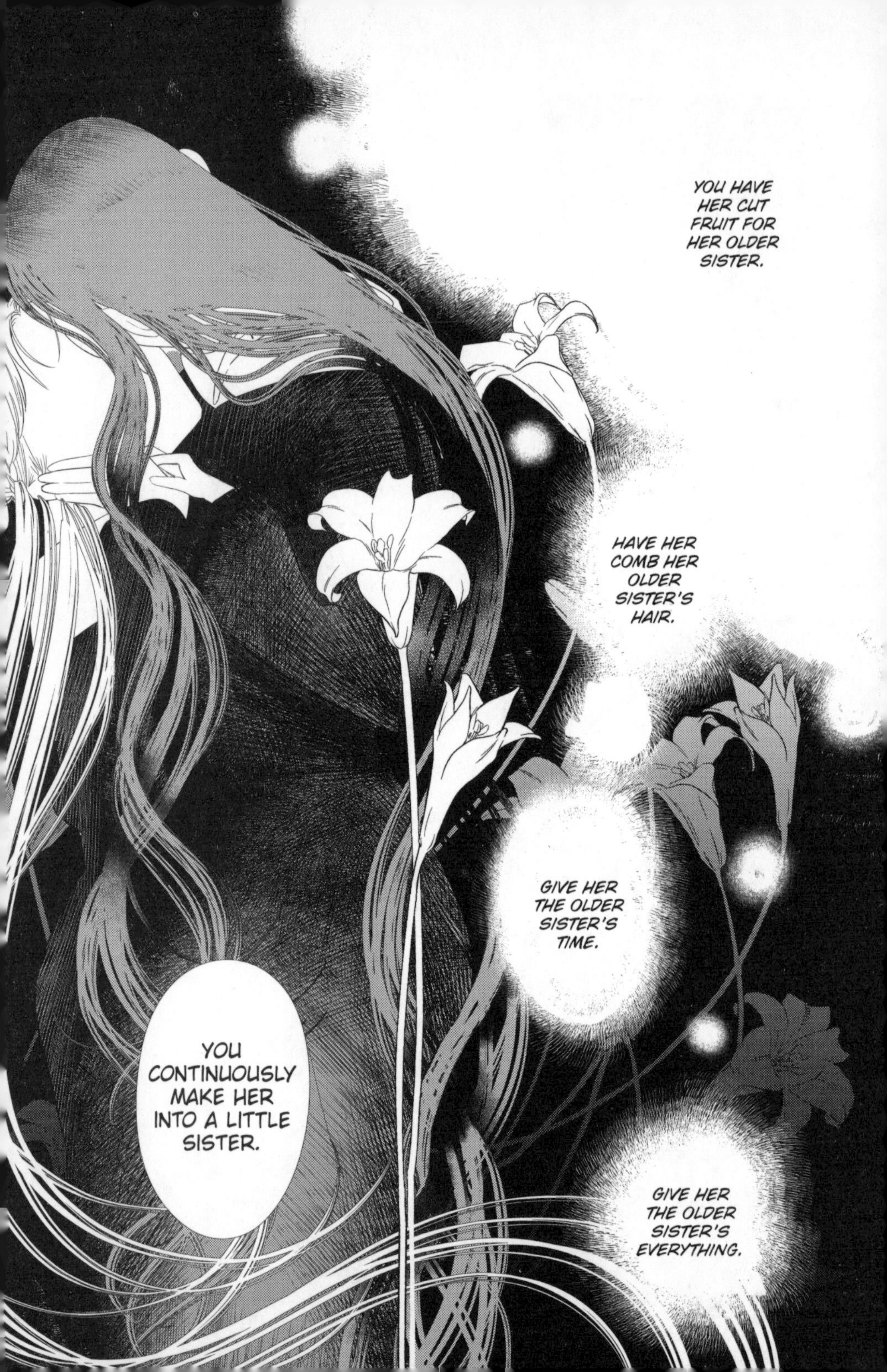
YOU HAVE HER CUT FRUIT FOR HER OLDER SISTER.
HAVE HER COMB HER OLDER SISTER'S HAIR.
GIVE HER THE OLDER SISTER'S TIME.
GIVE HER THE OLDER SISTER'S EVERYTHING.
YOU CONTINUOUSLY MAKE HER INTO A LITTLE SISTER.

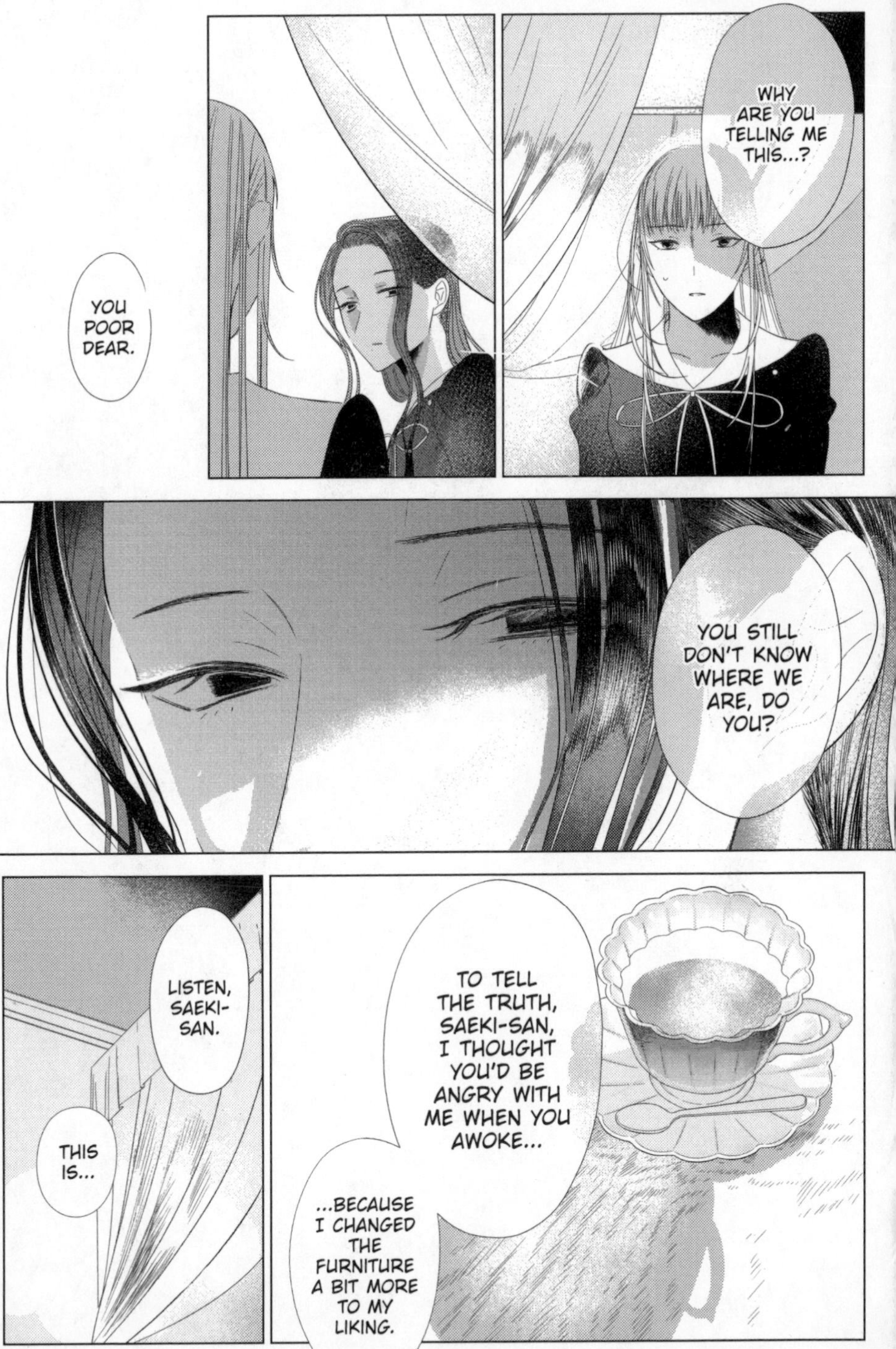
WHY ARE YOU TELLING ME THIS...?
YOU POOR DEAR.
YOU STILL DON'T KNOW WHERE WE ARE, DO YOU?
TO TELL THE TRUTH, SAEKI-SAN, I THOUGHT YOU'D BE ANGRY WITH ME WHEN YOU AWOKE...
...BECAUSE I CHANGED THE FURNITURE A BIT MORE TO MY LIKING.
LISTEN, SAEKI-SAN.
THIS IS...

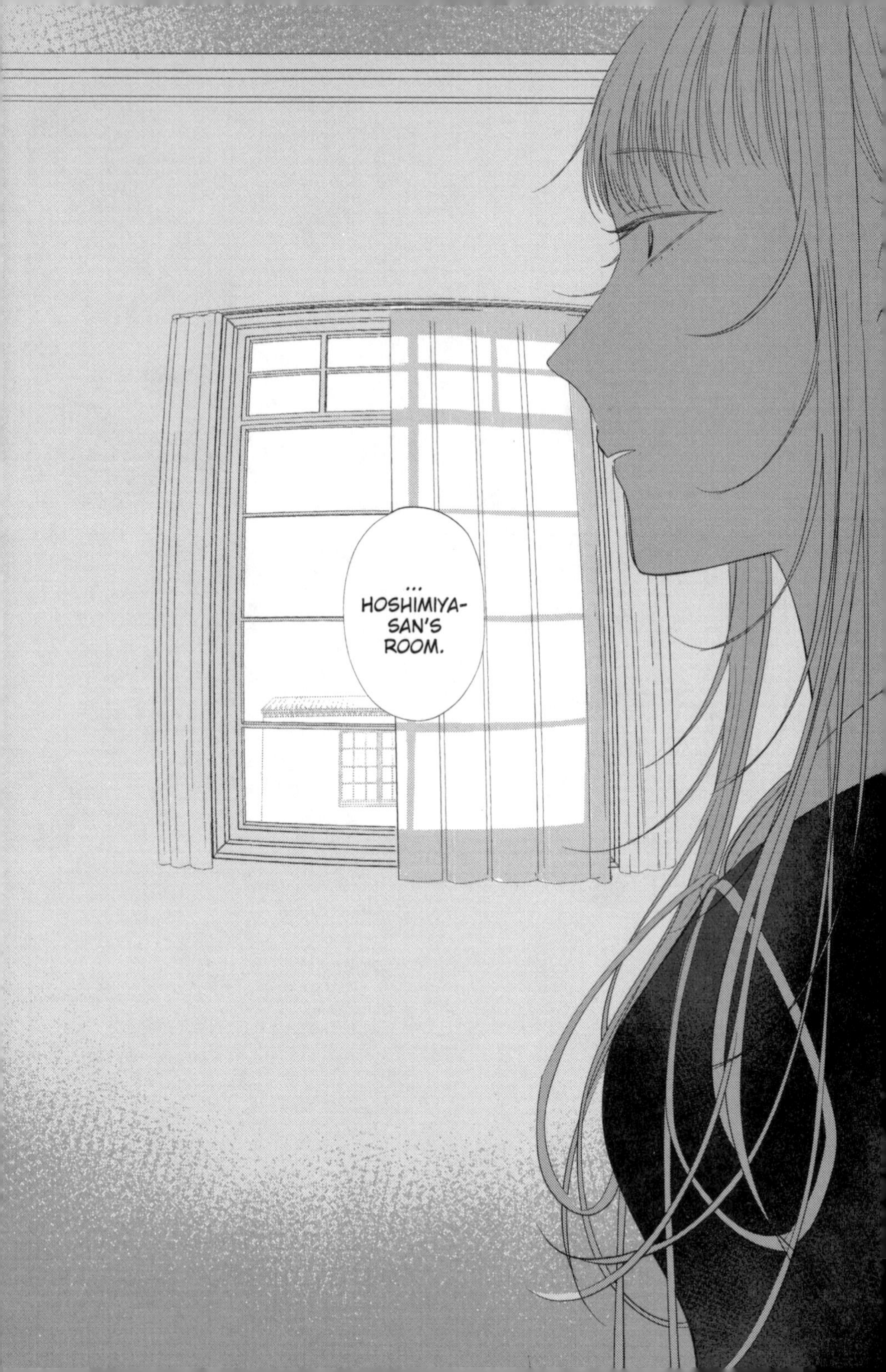
...HOSHIMIYA-SAN'S ROOM.

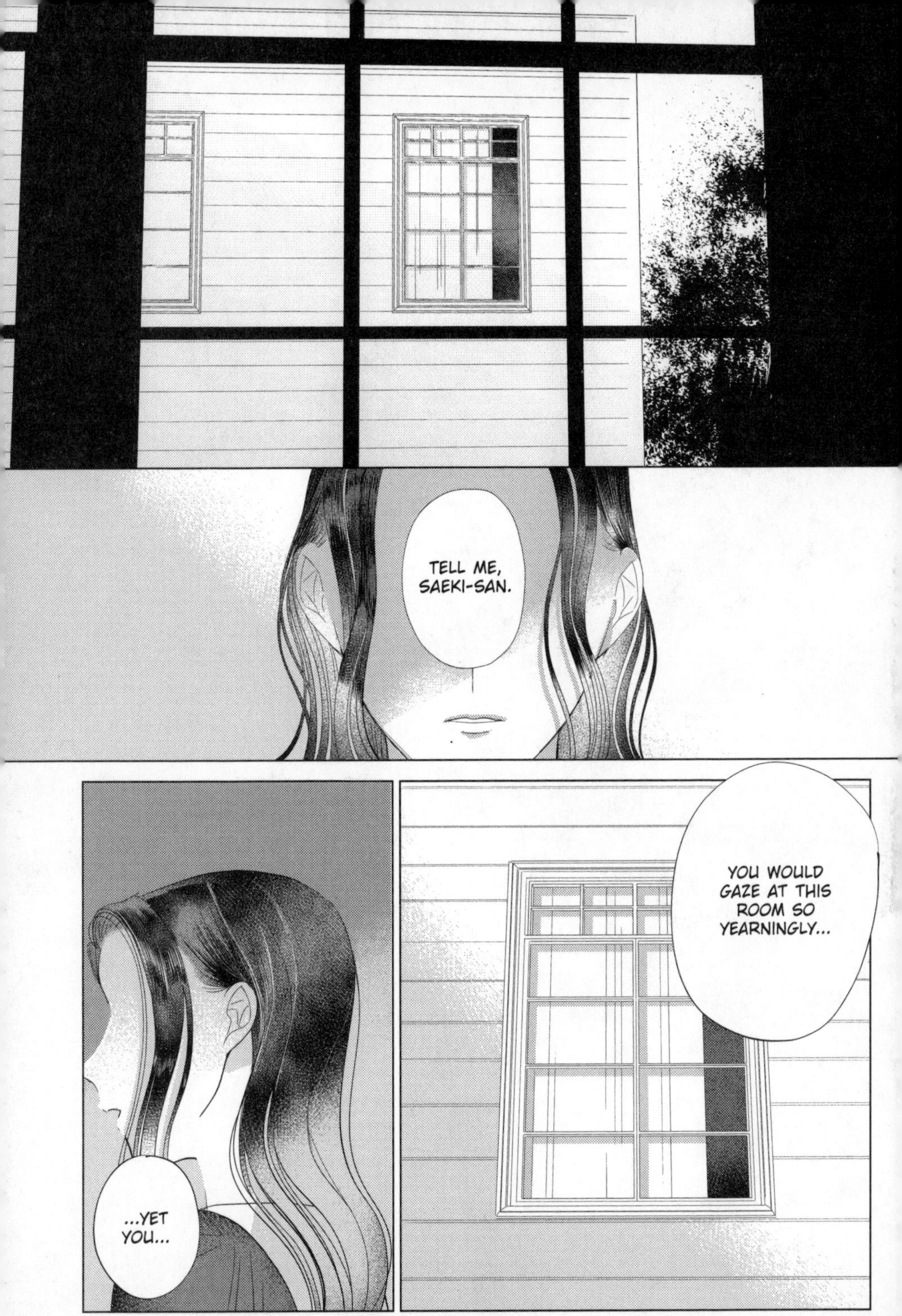
TELL ME, SAEKI-SAN.
YOU WOULD GAZE AT THIS ROOM SO YEARNINGLY...
...YET YOU...

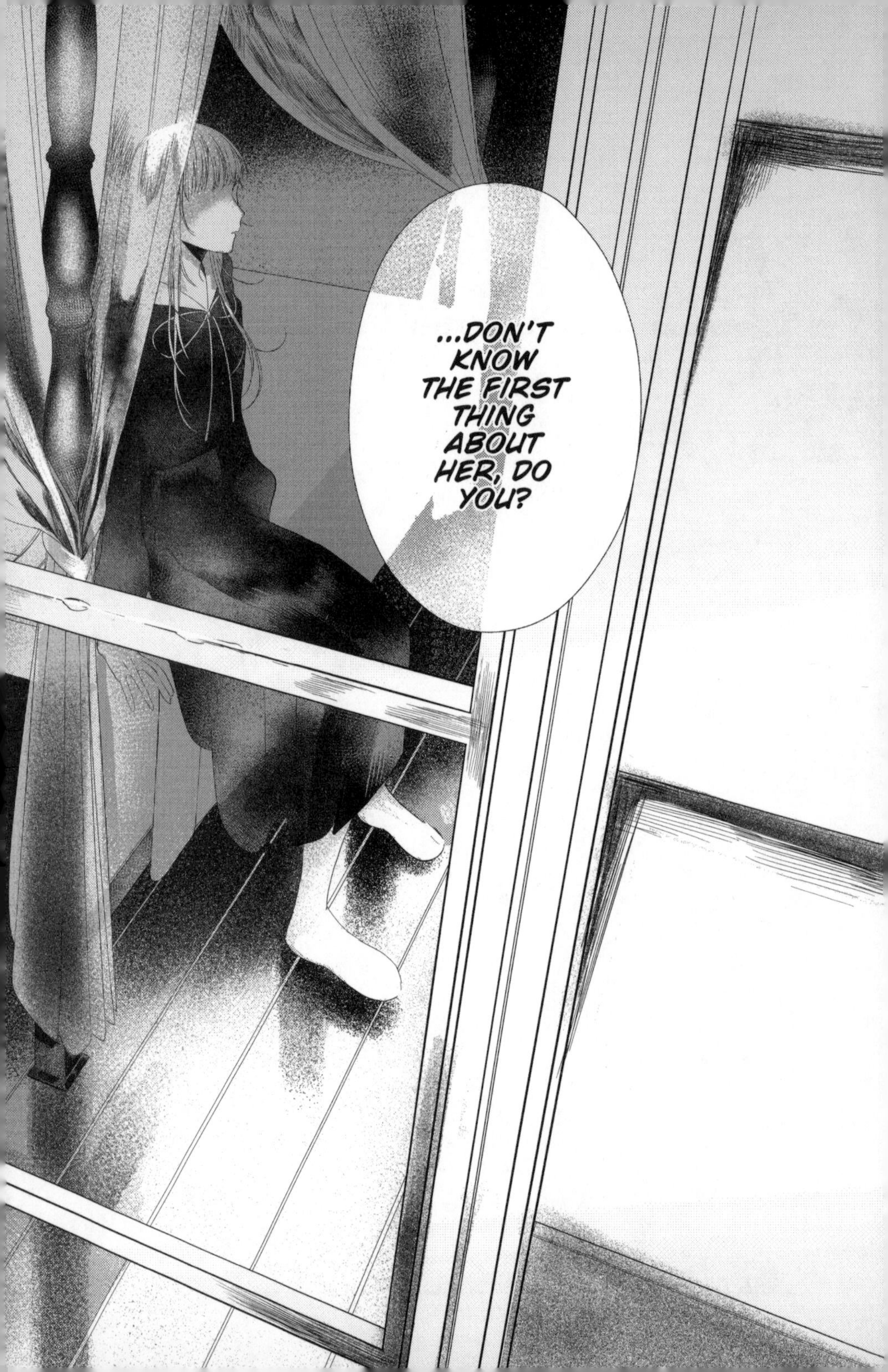
...DON'T KNOW THE FIRST THING ABOUT HER, DO YOU?

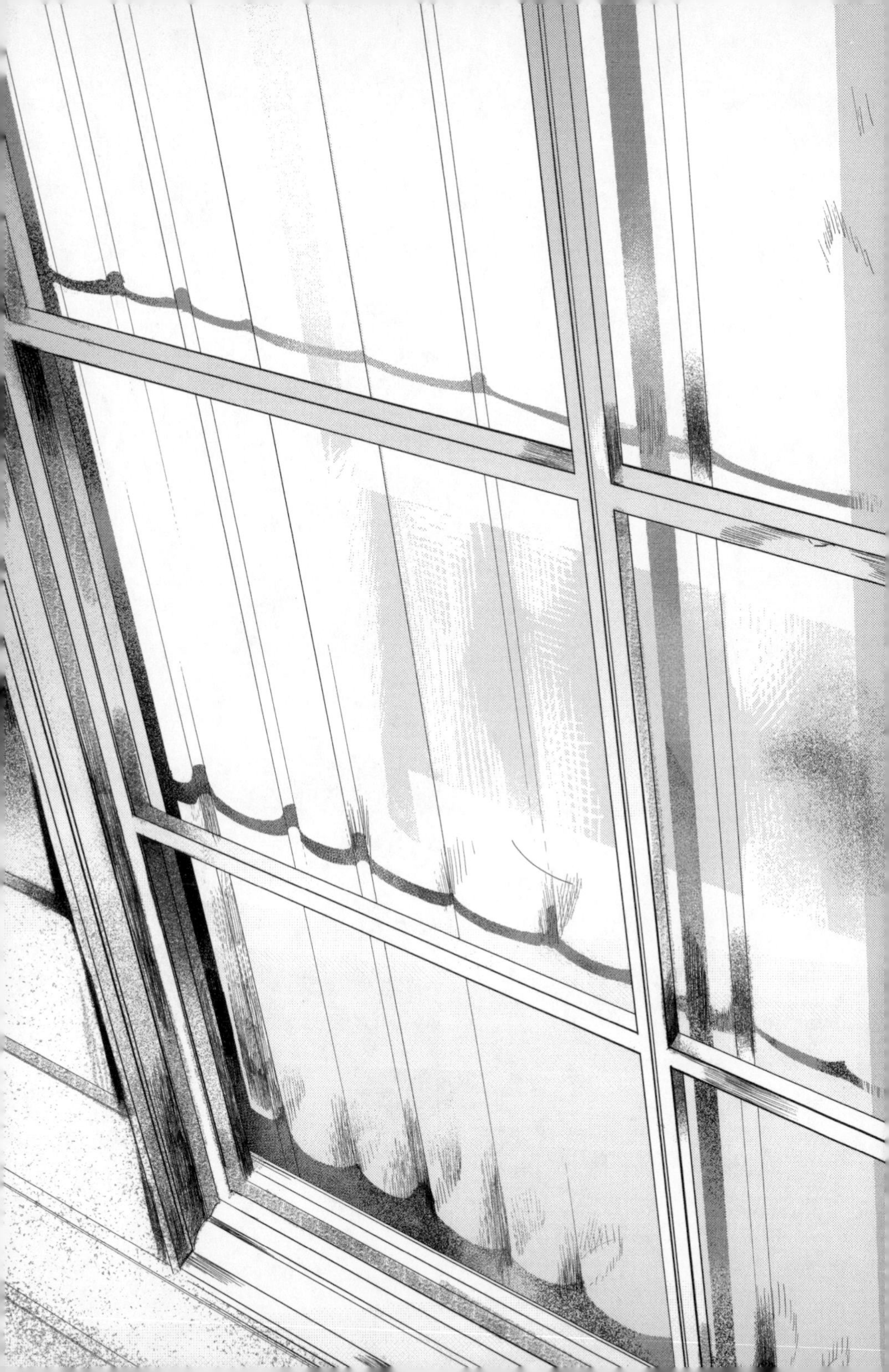

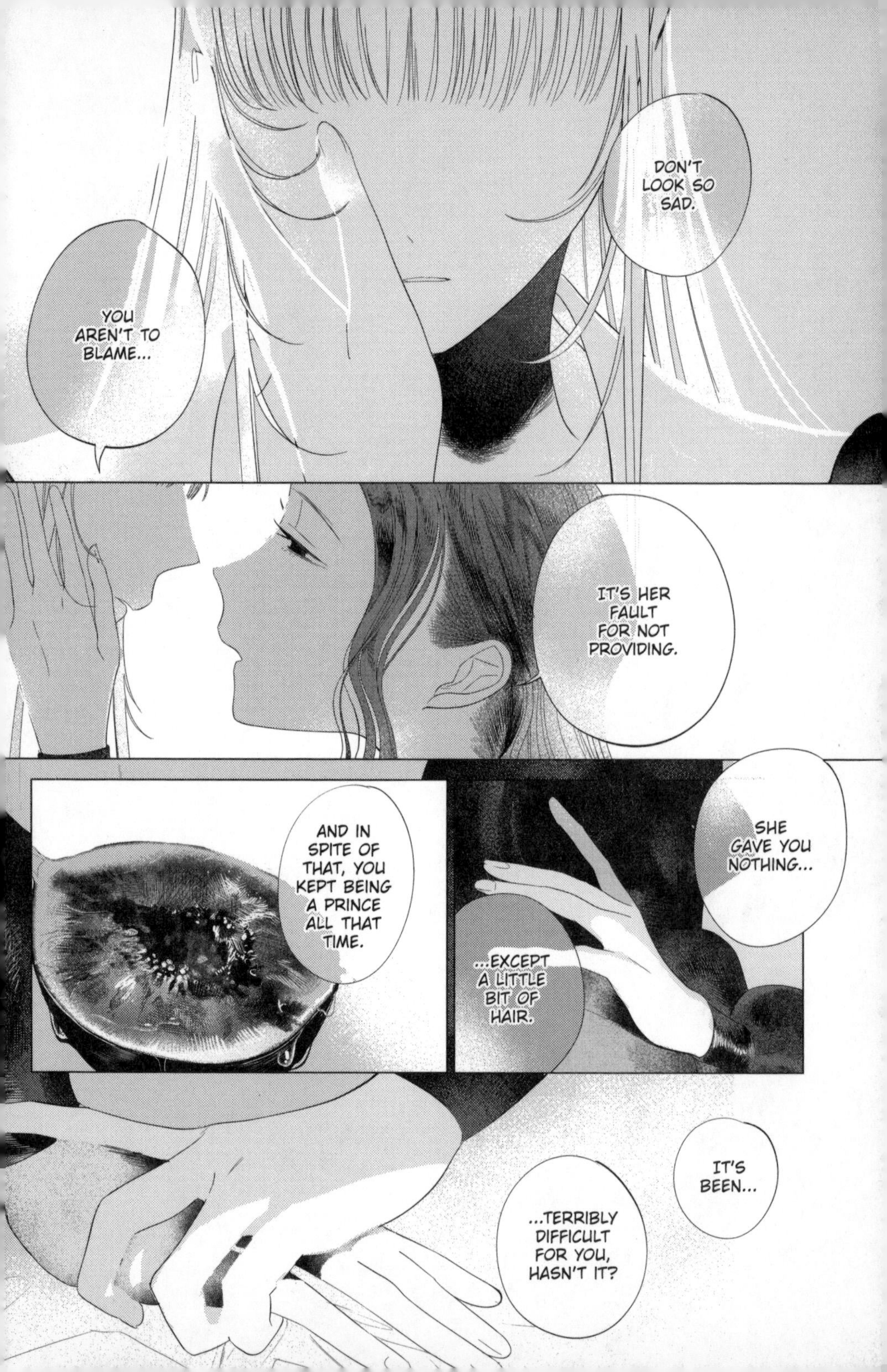
DON'T LOOK SO SAD.
YOU AREN'T TO BLAME...
IT'S HER FAULT FOR NOT PROVIDING.
SHE GAVE YOU NOTHING...
...EXCEPT A LITTLE BIT OF HAIR.
AND IN SPITE OF THAT, YOU KEPT BEING A PRINCE ALL THAT TIME.
IT'S BEEN...
...TERRIBLY DIFFICULT FOR YOU, HASN'T IT?

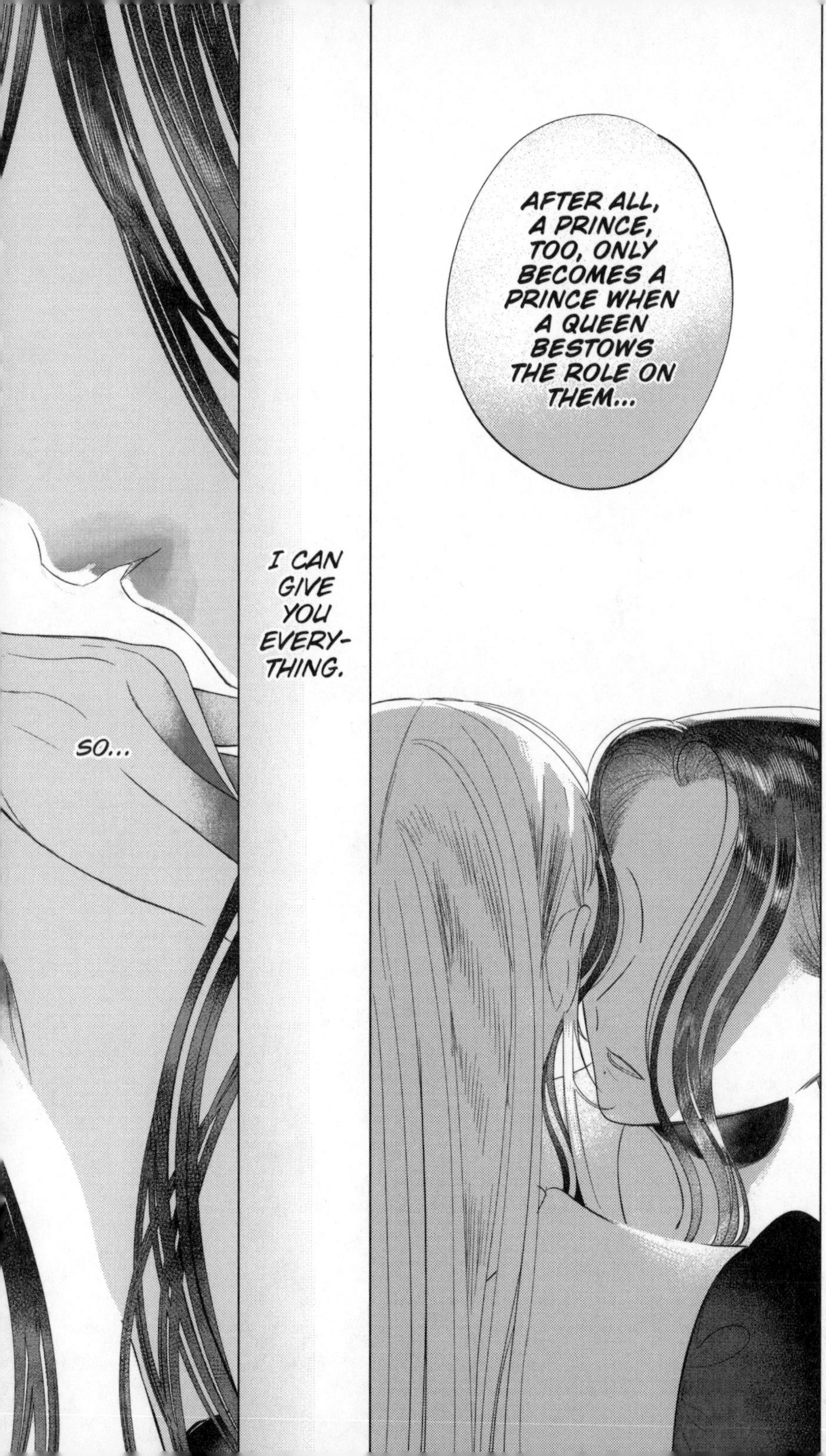
AFTER ALL, A PRINCE, TOO, ONLY BECOMES A PRINCE WHEN A QUEEN BESTOWS THE ROLE ON THEM...
I CAN GIVE YOU EVERY-THING.
SO...

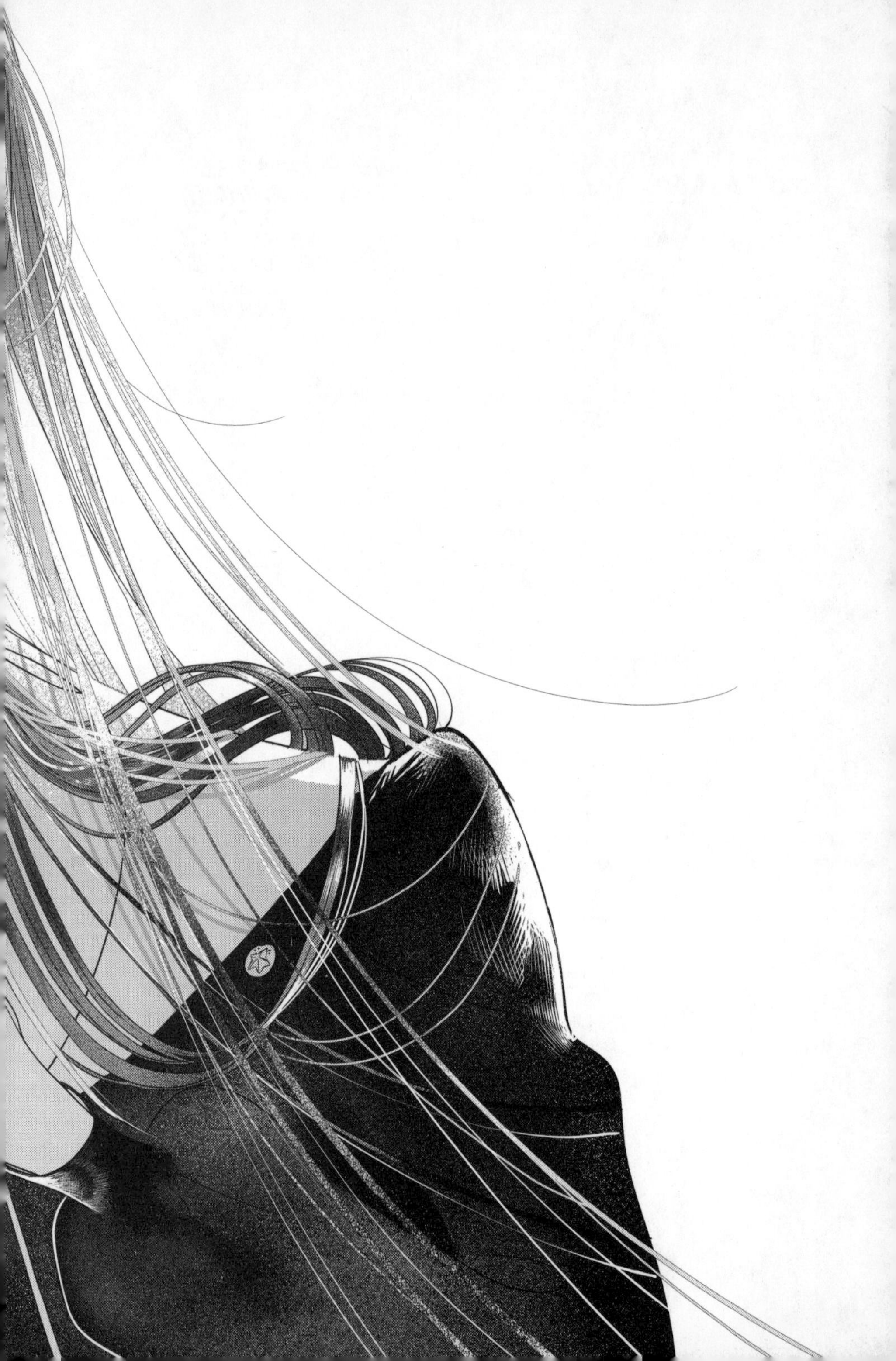

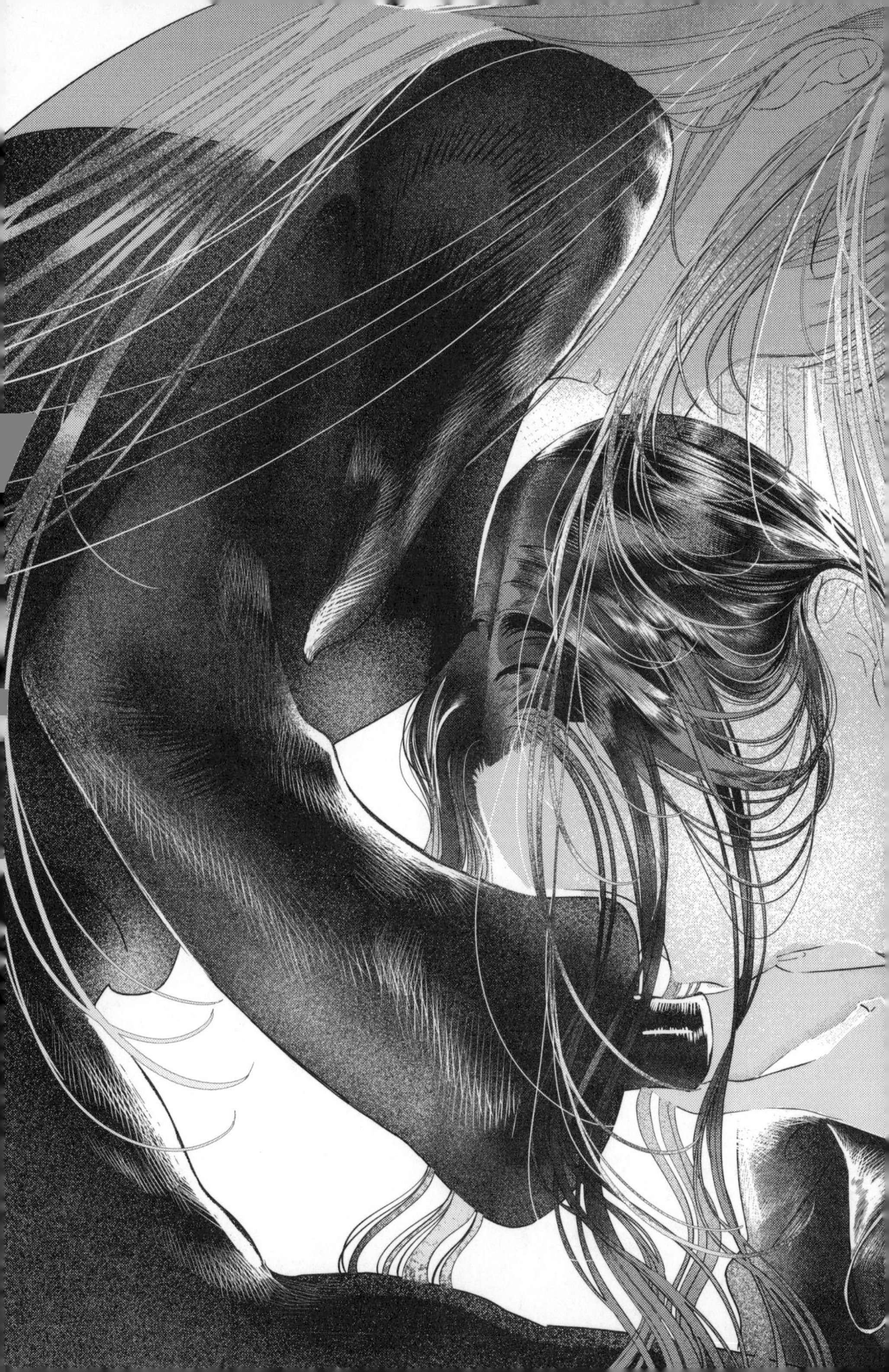

...*GIVE
ME YOUR
EVERYTHING.*

The thread of the girls' feelings is spun toward a holy night......

Youko starts moving for Hana—because she loves her. Giving up on it all and hiding her heart, Hana withdraws into her cocoon. Ayane Kujou guides the school toward perfection. Haruka Miyata is shaken by a nightmare and a nebulous unease.

Their desires entwine.

To be continued in Volume 5...

Cocoon 4 Entwined

Yuriko Hara

Translation: Amanda Haley · Lettering: Erin Hickman

This book is a work of fiction. Names, characters, places, and incidents are the product of
the author's imagination or are used fictitiously. Any resemblance to actual events, locales,
or persons, living or dead, is coincidental.

MAYU, MATOU Vol. 4
© Hara Yuriko 2021
First published in Japan in 2021 by KADOKAWA CORPORATION, Tokyo.
English translation rights arranged with KADOKAWA CORPORATION, Tokyo
through TUTTLE-MORI AGENCY, INC., Tokyo.

English translation © 2022 by Yen Press, LLC

Yen Press
150 West 30th Street, 19th Floor
New York, NY 10001

Visit us at yenpress.com · facebook.com/yenpress ·
twitter.com/yenpress · yenpress.tumblr.com · yenpress.com/instagram

First Yen Press Edition: January 2022

Yen Press is an imprint of Yen Press, LLC.
The Yen Press name and logo are trademarks of Yen Press, LLC.

The publisher is not responsible for websites (or their content) that
are not owned by the publisher.

Library of Congress Control Number: 2019938438

ISBNs: 978-1-9753-3973-9 (paperback)
978-1-9753-3974-6 (ebook)

10 9 8 7 6 5 4 3 2 1

WOR

Printed in the United States of America